UNVEILED

UNVEILED

Nuns Talking

———

MARY LOUDON

Chatto & Windus

LONDON

Published in 1992 by
Chatto & Windus Ltd
20 Vauxhall Bridge Road
London SW1V 2SA

A CIP catalogue record for this book is
available from the British Library:

ISBN 0 7011 3994 3

The line from 'Snow' by Louis MacNeice is from *The Collected Poems of Louis
MacNeice* and appears courtesy of Faber & Faber Ltd.

Phototypeset by Intype, London
Printed and bound in Great Britain by
Mackays of Chatham PLC, Chatham, Kent

For Jean and Irvine
- parents and friends -
with love

Acknowledgments

This book could not have been written without the considerable help and support of many people. Firstly, thanks must go to the ten people who so generously and courageously agreed to work with me, and whose stories make up the book. There were also many other communities and individuals who offered to be involved, and special thanks must go to the Community of Saint Mary The Virgin, Wantage, Sister Elizabeth of the Community of Saint Francis, Compton Durville, and Sister Alison Francis of the Community of Saint Clare, Freeland.

Thanks to my friend from CSMV, Wantage, who unwittingly set the ball rolling. Thanks to Mother Allyne of CSMV, Wantage, Emma Lindley, Simon Evans and Lesley Walmsley, all of whom believed in me and spurred me on from the beginning. Tony Parker provided great encouragement, friendship, and an assortment of jokes along the way. Many thanks also to Pat Franklin, Catherine Freeman and Annie Macdonald, with whom I have enjoyed both professional and personal friendships.

Thanks to my agent, Cat Ledger, and to my editor, Alison Samuel, who gave me both a free rein and superb editorial advice. Thanks to the Society of Authors, and to Education Services, Oxford, for their generous financial assistance, without which I would be bankrupt; special thanks to Mark Le Fanu and Owen Jones. Thanks to Dr Arnon Bentovim for his advice, and Teresa de Bertodano for hers. Thanks also to Julia Denzil for swift emergency assistance with some of the transcribing.

I was sustained by the strength and love of a great many people, but particularly by Dorcas Fiddian Green, Sian Edwards and Liz Peretz, who were there throughout.

Last, but not least, thanks to my parents, Jean and Irvine Loudon, for having encouraged me to carve my own path: without the love and support they have given me I might have done something far more sensible and infinitely less rewarding.

Contents

'World is crazier and more of it than we think.
Incorrigibly plural.'

LOUIS MACNEICE

Introduction

When I was eighteen, agnostic and thought I had all the answers I met an Anglican priest, twelve years my senior, and we fell in love. My family was amazed, my friends were shocked, and I was utterly horrified. We were happy, but the relationship was fraught from the beginning, partly because I found it difficult to accept what he had chosen to do with his life. After some months of attempts to explain, my boyfriend suggested that I talk to someone other than himself who might understand how I felt. I agreed, but was dismayed when he suggested a local Anglican nun. For a while I resisted, on the grounds that nuns were even more lunatic than priests and I didn't want to compound the problem, but eventually, more out of sheer curiosity than anything else, I gave in and made an appointment to see her.

Despite the fact that I had lived half a mile from it all my life, the convent was unknown territory. On arrival I was greeted by a nun clad in full habit, the *Daily Telegraph* crossword and acres of knitting. After establishing that I had reason for being there she showed me to a 'parlour', a room so chilly, and so high, that I felt as if I were at the bottom of a well. As I sat and tried to muster the enthusiasm I lacked for the whole affair, the door burst open and a strong young woman bounced towards me, hand outstretched. 'Hi!' she said. 'Mary! It's really great to meet you.'

Despite such an unlikely beginning, a strong friendship grew between this nun and myself. She was energetic, wise and enormous fun, someone with whom I was able to explore the faith I found so hard to accept, without being laughed at or criticised. I made all the usual complaints. I told her that I thought God was a figment of the optimistic imagination, that religious belief was a refusal to acknowledge self-responsibility, and that my boyfriend must be deluded. Sharing my doubts with someone whose own faith gave her the freedom to accept my lack of it gave me an alternative perspective on my own life, and although my increasing affection and respect for her made faith no easier to accept, it made it a good deal harder to dismiss.

I became fascinated by the notion of living a life of religious dedication. The fascination was entirely vicarious: I could identify with passion, belief and commitment, but not in that particular form. I couldn't imagine what had drawn my friend, a vibrant and intellectual woman, into a strict religious order, although it was obvious that such a radical choice made sense for her.

My friendship with her coincided with an extremely difficult period in my life. My relationship with my boyfriend demanded radical reappraisal of the religious beliefs, or rather lack of them, with which I'd grown up. As time went on, I found constant movement between university and vicarage, between my own agnosticism and desire for faith, less and less bearable, and in some confusion I went to talk to my nun friend.

Over tea together, I found myself asking her, amongst other things, why she had entered a religious community; when she told me, I was stunned. It suddenly occurred to me that her story could have a great impact on those who found the notion of entering a religious community as strange as I did myself, but of course there was no way of sharing it – except, I thought, by writing a book.

For a year I dismissed such a notion as madness.

At the moment there are around 12,000 Roman Catholic and 950 Anglican nuns in England and Wales. In fact, strictly speaking, many of them are not 'nuns' at all. Nuns are women living in enclosed communities, and those include the older orders like the Carmelites, the Benedictines, the Cistercians and the Carthusians. The women who live in open, or 'apostolic', communities (so-called because an 'apostle' is 'one who is sent out') are called 'Sisters'. Many women in religious communities try to get around this distinction by referring to themselves and one another as 'women religious' or just plain 'religious', although the word 'nun' is still used as a blanket term for both nuns and Sisters.

Gone are the days when religious communities went out looking for compliant teenage recruits: these days they rarely accept anyone under the age of twenty-three, and even then the training is lengthy and fastidious. The first six months or year of any religious training, or 'formation', is spent as a 'Postulant' – a word which means 'candidate'. During that time the would-be nun or

Sister will live as a member of the community, but she won't have to adhere to all the rules: she will still be able to wear her own clothes or spend her own money, for example. Many women still join religious communities as Postulants, but few of them stay for the next stage – entry into the Novitiate.

To become a Novice, a candidate makes her 'first vows' of poverty, celibacy and obedience. She does this during a service known as a 'Clothing', during which she receives her first habit, or, in communities which no longer wear habits, some other symbol of commitment, like a cross. The Novitiate training can last anything from two to five years, depending on the community and the circumstances of the individual. Although first vows are taken very seriously by religious communities, the Novitiate period is generally regarded as a time of exploration and probation, and not everyone who takes first vows automatically proceeds to profession.

'Profession' is the making of 'final', 'solemn' or 'life' vows. In many profession services a nun or Sister will receive a second habit, a ring, and a veil, although this varies greatly among communities. If she completes her training, a woman who enters a religious community will emerge as a fully-fledged member of it between three and six years later.

Everybody has an opinion about nuns, and it often has nothing to do with knowledge or experience of them as individuals. Nuns to most people mean Mother Teresa, *The Sound of Music*, or strippagrams at stag parties. Given the images that we are bombarded with – on television, in films, newspapers and schools – it is hardly surprising. Nuns are synonymous with guilt, girls' schools run by the fierce or repressed, and endless jokes about sex: either that, or they are patrons of the poor and sick who light up dark lives with their gleaming sense of purpose and, in films, with luminous Hollywood beauty.

Nuns also suffer from the popular supposition that they do not have the same needs and problems as everyone else, that they live lives of unshakeable faith, devoid of doubts, desires, and insecurities. Nuns, as far as most people are concerned, are either sub or super human.

Such images of nuns are as limited as our perception of the

people on to whom we project them. No stranger to such limited perceptions myself, I felt very strongly that they needed to be challenged. The most obvious way had already presented itself, although my intense dislike of theological books written only by and for those in the Church, made me want to keep the format as simple and accessible as possible. I decided to interview a number of Roman Catholic and Anglican nuns of varying backgrounds, ages, order and philosophies, and transcribe and edit the interviews into autobiographies in the conversational form.

The nuns I had already met were as interesting, as ordinary, as unique and as flawed as the rest of us, and their attitudes and concerns as contemporary as anyone else's. Although nuns are generally regarded a people who have found God, my experience of them was as people in constant search of God. I wanted to find out why their search took such a dedicated form, and what it was they were looking for.

I wrote to individuals and communities (the blanket term for religious orders, congregations, societies and institutes) all over the country explaining what I wanted to do, asking for help and expecting rejection. I sent around fifty letters and was turned down by only four communities or individuals. Despite the overwhelming choice, selection was fairly easy. I wanted to work with as wide a variety of people as possible, and decisions were made accordingly. No Novices were included, as it seemed unfair to commit someone to print at a stage of religious life when final decisions had not yet been made. No ex-nuns were chosen because I was interested in why people remain in religious life, and that obviously involved discussing the problems and pressures that force others to leave.

Before interviewing each contributor I went to meet her first, usually in her home, although one person had such a penchant for breakfasts that we had several of them in various London cafés and called it 'work', although it was nothing of the sort. In fact, food played a very important part in establishing relationships, as the first thing I shared with most of the contributors was lunch. Some of these were DIY affairs in flats, or sandwiches in the local pub, although many communities still have silent meals in large refectories, steeped in complex and initially baffling rituals.

After a day spent together I returned at a later date to interview each contributor over a period of one week. I was treated with courtesy and generosity by all the contributors and their communities. I was always shown the local area, taken around convents or houses, and introduced to neighbours. I was offered accommodation, invited to prayers and mass – even on a couple of political demonstrations – and one community asked me to lead a discussion group for them.

The work itself was informal, but demanding. The interviews were lengthy and detailed, and the pieces in the book account for only a quarter of the total recorded material. I covered the same areas with each person, but in varying ways; not unlike crossing a country several times over, but each time via different routes.

The structure of the interviews was simple. I began by asking each contributor questions about her early childhood and concluded with a look ahead to death. I never asked questions about the religious life in isolation, because that seemed to me to be the mistake that is always made: to see nuns only as nuns, and not as women who have been shaped by their families, friends, lovers, education, jobs and a host of other experiences. After all, the religious life only makes sense within the context of a person's whole life: in isolation it is meaningless.

I realised after a while that none of us had realised what we were taking on when we started work on *Unveiled*. While the interviews were interesting and often exciting, all the contributors said that they found the experience of talking so frankly about themselves fairly draining. Some people had not spoken about certain events in their lives for years – some not at all. As a result there were occasional outbursts of grief, despair or anger, which sometimes left me wondering if I had gone too far, and trying to remain objective when the work was so intimate was often very difficult.

Such problems illustrate clearly the need for a great deal of trust between the parties concerned when doing work of this kind. From the outset I promised the contributors right of veto over anything they said, showing them the transcripts and chapters before the publishers saw them, so that they could delete anything they felt uncomfortable about. 'You won't get the truth if you do that,' a friend said to me. 'I won't get anything at *all* if I cheat them,' I replied.

Whether or not I got 'the truth' is not something that concerns me, because I don't believe in such absolutes. I certainly got very frank answers to my questions, although some people were harder than others to pin down. Having said that, when I gave copies of the transcribed interviews to the contributors, very little was removed – usually just a name or a date here and there, so as to protect the identity of other people who'd been mentioned – and every word that I wanted to use in the final chapters was happily permitted.

Thus, the stories remained intact, although they are not complete and never could be: they are only snapshots in time in the written form. Writing, like the camera, captures only glimpses of a person, and fractured, subjective ones at that. While some documentary writers are quick to defend their positions of objectivity, I can't do that: to claim that this book is not painted in my colours would be dishonest, because it is. Although I have tried hard to retain the 'voice' of each individual by keeping the language, grammar and rhythm of each piece in its original, conversational form. The process of editing is highly personal, and the structure of each piece is itself a response to the subject.

Such responses were, to my relief, received with generosity and humour by each contributor. However, that is not to say it was all easy. It wasn't. Working very closely with ten different people, all of whom had very definite ideas about life – and that included this book – was a challenge. They were fiercely divided over the book's title (some told me it was 'wonderful' or 'inspired', others that it was 'sensational' or just 'bloody awful'). When I showed the cover design to the contributors, Barbara Anne and Eva Heymann objected so strongly to it, on the grounds that it was salacious and exploitative, that they very nearly withdrew their contributions from the book. Some thought this odd, but if, as a nun, you are sensitive to images of yourself and your Sisters, it's an understandable response.

The pieces in this book are not meant to be sociologically, theologically or historically definitive, nor do they give a detailed picture of daily life as it is lived by different communities. Although the vast majority of religious communities are founded on medieval monastic rules and practices, great changes have been brought about since the pronouncements of the Second Vatican Council, which was set up in Rome in 1963 to undertake the 'reform and promotion' of the Roman Catholic Church. These pronouncements had a major impact on both Roman Catholic and Anglican religious communities, and many of their founding rules were reinterpreted to accommodate an understanding of religious life that was more appropriate to the twentieth century than the thirteenth or fourteenth.

So, while some communities' days are still a strict timetable of prayers, meals and duties, others are like something from a magazine feature article, with people doing nine to five jobs or something different almost every day. Some people have paid jobs, some don't. Some wear habits, others wear ordinary clothes. Some live in huge convents with scores of others, some live alone or in shared flats or houses. Holidays vary. Some people go away once or twice a year, some once every five years and others never. Some nuns live lives of strict enclosure that apart from going to the doctor or dentist they never leave the convent, not even for a day; they never go home and they never visit friends or family, though friends and family may visit them. Some keep the names they were given as children, others take the names of male or female saints. There are lots of Teresas and Marys in religious communities, but I have also met nuns called Aelred, Cyril, Eustacia, Francis, Joseph and Kevin.

In the end there seemed no need to document the obvious differences in lifestyle because they are apparent in the pieces themselves. I have simply tried to offer glimpses of women living lives of religious commitment in spite of increasing social pressures to do otherwise. Despite their unusual lifestyles, the problems and challenges that nuns and Sisters face are common to all of us: love, pain, fulfilment, loss, achievement and failure – finding purpose in life that leads inevitably to death, and meaning in death itself.

When I was writing *Unveiled* some people asked me whether I'd thought about becoming a nun myself, to which the answer is no, because I can't imagine many things to which I am less inclined or suited. However, working with these women has radically altered my sense of perspective – and for that I will always be grateful. I have also had the privilege of their support and their trust: without it I would not have been able to write *Unveiled*, and I thank them wholeheartedly for making it possible.

I wrote *Unveiled* as an attempt to explore what motivates women who dedicate their lives to God. I was also keen to understand better the man I loved at the time, although the relationship ended five and a half years later: I felt confined by its boundaries, and took the coward's way out, falling in love with someone else before I would face the fact.

Nearly seven years after I met the two people who, quite separately and inadvertently, set me on such an unlikely path, I have learnt less about the God of scripture and theology than the struggle to live in truth and love. Although I feel unable for many reasons to subscribe to the established Church, my readiness for faith has increased: this is largely due to the experience of working with these women, an experience that has been challenging, moving, interesting and, above all, fun.

ANGELA THÉRÈSE

Carmelite Community, Darlington, County Durham
ROMAN CATHOLIC: ENCLOSED

Age: 39
Nationality: English
Age at entry to community: 29
Number of years in community: 10
Previous employment: Ballet dancer
(Royal Ballet/Northern Dance Theatre)
Undertaker's assistant
Dress: Habit

Angela is a short woman, with a round, open face, and a relaxed, slightly incurious manner. We were divided throughout the interviews by a large iron grille across what looked like an old-fashioned shop counter. The room in which we sat, and which we entered by separate doors from our respective sides of a dividing wall, had no windows and only one picture – an icon of the Holy Trinity.

The Carmelite order is the strictest of the female religious orders, and, contrary to popular belief, is not a silent one. The twenty-eight women who make up the Darlington Carmelite community rise at 5.15 am to begin a day which is divided into twenty-four separate parts. Eight of these are community prayers or mass, five of them periods of private prayer or 'spiritual reading', and, apart from two periods of 'recreation', the rest consist of domestic or other work. The community supports itself by printing religious texts and making vestments and communion wafers.

The nuns go barefoot, and although by the time I met Angela I was familiar with enclosed orders, I was taken aback by the austerity and discipline of the Carmelites. You can talk to the nuns quite openly, but only through grilles or small, sliding partitions, and you can never enter their part of the house. The L-shaped community chapel also has two parts; one for the community and one for visitors, and the division is marked by another grille.

9

However, physical barriers were the only kind I came across at Darlington. I'll never forget the warmth with which I was received there. I was given the run of the community's guest house, use of the community car, a fridge full of homegrown tomatoes and a wonderful – if faintly bizarre – welcome, as the nuns lined up behind the parlour grille to meet me in groups of twos and threes. Nor will I forget the bellowing laugh of the Glaswegian Prioress, her hands covered in pastry when we first met, or The Pretenders' heaviest rock number thumping out from behind a wall during working hours.

Angela Thérèse

I can't think why you want to talk to me. I was saying to one of the other Sisters only this morning: why does she want to talk to me? Oh goodness, do I have to wear a microphone? No, I'm kidding, it's okay, pass it through.

Tell you about my family? Well, I suppose it's a rather ordinary, middle-class family really, certainly not a churchy family, although since I've come to Carmel my parents have gone back to practising in the Church of England. I have two brothers, both married; neither of them are religious in any way, but they're quite happy with me being here. I don't think there's anything outstanding about my family at all, we're just very ordinary.

My father's an undertaker. He joined the firm at fourteen as an office boy, and worked his way up to being a branch manager, and retired just three years ago. My mother was always just a housewife, just stayed at home to look after the kids. They're a real Darby and Joan. Marvellous. I mean, even now, they're just heading for seventy and they still walk down the street hand in hand, it's rather sweet. I don't remember there ever being any real ups and downs between them.

My dad, he's the most easygoing, placid person you could possibly wish to meet. I mean, a silly example: we had a pretty bad car crash, I was driving, when I was aged seventeen, and the car was absolutely smashed to smithereens, a real mess. But he retrieved a primus stove from the back of the car, and when the ambulance arrived the three of us were sitting in deck-chairs by the road, having a cup of tea. You know, absolutely no fuss, no hassle. That's just him all over. I've never known him get in a panic.

My mother's rather the opposite: her side of the family are very highly strung and easily upset and oversensitive. I think when I was little I was inclined to be more like my mother, easily upset and probably pretty hard to get on with. I wasn't easygoing: my theatrical instincts came out very early. Even as a kid, once I'd

11

set my mind to do something it would be pretty hard to dissuade me from doing it.

I'm the youngest of the family. There are three years between myself and my brother Philip, and three years between him and Russell, but I think we were always pretty close. Weekends and things we spent together, rather than darting off doing our own thing. I was closer perhaps to my dad than to my mum, but I think one is always more close to one than the other. If he'd got a little job to do in the house or something, he'd ask me to do it with him rather than one of the boys, so we've always stuck to each other more.

We were lucky as kids because we lived very near Kensington Gardens, and so from a very young age we just used to go off on our own to the park, which is unusual in London, mostly kids can't do that. So we were very free as kids. We had a very easy time of it.

The three of us went to the Church of England primary school, because it was literally over the road from where we were. Then at eleven, I went to the Royal Ballet School, though not by my choice. I had a place at Fulham County Grammar School, but I'd been dancing from the age of four, and the teachers seemed to think that I had talent, so after a series of auditions I found myself with a place at the Royal Ballet School – a scholarship, actually.

There was no theatrical influence at all in the family, that's the strange thing. The only reason I was sent to ballet classes in the first place was because my mother felt I was very shy, which was this business of being a loner, I really preferred to be on my own. She thought that the ballet classes would bring me out, and that I'd meet youngsters of my own age, so that was the reason I was sent, it was nothing theatrical or musical or anything.

I was always a bit of a loner, even when I was at primary school. There were people who one got on with, but I wouldn't say there were any really close friends, and by the time I was seven or eight I was going twice or three times a week to evening dancing classes, so it had the opposite effect – it knocked out all my spare time. I did enjoy it, though, because I was doing tap and stage branch and all sorts of things as well as ballet. I enjoyed the exams and medals that I went in for, and I don't remember thinking I was missing out on anything.

What other things did I enjoy? Gosh, it's a long time since I've thought about all that. Well, animals were a great thing with me, I loved animals. I had guinea pigs and rabbits and goodness knows what in hutches. We had a flat roof, so my father turned that into a garden, and it was terrific. At one point I had an aviary with canaries too. But apart from the animals, I just liked being out of doors a lot; out on my bicycle, on my rollerskates and what have you, traipsing around Kensington.

The ballet was pretty heavy going. I was leaving home by half past six in the morning from the age of eleven, and I didn't get home in the evening until around six o'clock. I was having to travel every day from Kensington right out to Richmond Park, which is where the school is, and my basic education suffered. It was pretty poor, actually, for all of us there. Of my class of thirty-eight, in the end only three of us actually got in to the Royal Ballet Company, and those who didn't had to start all over again with college and all sorts because they hadn't the qualifications to do anything. All that training and then nothing at the end of it. It's terrifying. Awful.

At twelve, I was chosen out of the junior school to be in a performance at Covent Garden, and it was absolutely terrific. There was one girl and one boy chosen. That was at the time when Rudolph Nureyev had first come over to England, and we were actually on stage with him, so it was quite something. The other kids, needless to say, didn't like it. Terrific jealousy always. It was a very theatrical atmosphere, there was a lot of back-biting, because you knew that in the future you could be treading on your best friend to get on. It was pretty hard for children, but then there are always one or two that are outstanding, and it didn't bother me too much, because right from the beginning I got the first place every year, so I knew that I must be all right. I knew where I was going, kind of thing.

Funnily enough I wasn't competitive. If I hadn't come first, I don't think I'd have minded too much, but then I never fought for first place, it just happened. It wasn't as if it was my desire to go anyway. Mind you, I had a terrific sense of freedom when I was dancing. There's nothing more satisfying than bashing your way through a solo and getting to the end of it and knowing you've done it well, but I guess the whole thing really was to achieve. I've really gone from one end of the spectrum to the other on that one.

Do I ever dance now? No fear! Before I received the habit I danced a couple of times, just to give the community the pleasure of it, but then I've no desire any more, don't miss it at all, not a bit.

I did do other things too. When we got to the senior part of the school, then our evenings were free. We were all living in bedsits and flats in and around the school, and most evenings we met up at somebody or other's flat. I was known for parties, actually. We had a great big old coal cellar where the undertaker's was in Kensington Church Street, and most Saturday nights there was a party there, which was terrible because eventually the whole of London got to know about it. I can remember one night a busload of people coming from Richmond who'd heard there was a party on, and we'd never met them in our lives before. People would always pour in these doors and down into the cellars, and they were all strangers. But it was terrific; just booze and music and sitting around the place jawing, in amongst the coffins and stuff. That became quite an institution. There'd be a notice put up on the board at the rehearsal studios: 'Party on Saturday night'. You didn't even have to put where it was.

I suppose I was quite popular with the boys, actually, but I had a lot of close friends then. Though it was a funny situation, because even with Lois, who was my closest friend, you could one minute find yourselves dancing together and the next minute find she's treading on your toes to get the part that you'd coveted, or that you should have been getting. It was a difficult situation to have close friendships in because of this continual rivalry. Very difficult.

So there were plenty of boyfriends, but there was only one really serious one that I can think of. That lasted for about eighteen months or so. There was a small splinter group that used to go out touring schools and factories and places like that, called Ballet

For All. I was in that for about nine months, and he was actually Ballet Master. He was a good bit older than me, ten years. That lasted as long as I was with the group, and then of course when I went back to the mainstream of the company that was that. Probably, of all the relationships I've ever had it was the most important of the lot, but for it to last I would have had to have left the ballet company and have made some base in London for him to come back to. That would have been the only way, and I wasn't prepared to do that.

I think that was one of the sad things really. Relationships were always breaking up, with people off on tour. I think that's probably why a lot of theatrical marriages break up. . . Very sad. You know, human nature being what it is, too many temptations. Awful, but there you are.

More than anything I remember being permanently tired. Absolutely whacked. I was only resident at Covent Garden for a year, so I was on tour the rest of the time. You were thirteen weeks on tour, and each Sunday was spent travelling to the next city that you were dancing in, finding your digs, finding the theatre, and setting up your things in the dressing room – by which time Sunday was over, and you were back on the boards. By the end of thirteen weeks of that, you were bonkers.

You're on a perpetual diet. Your standard meal would have been steak and a green salad, and that's it. For years I never ate potatoes or chocolate or anything like that, simply never ate them. Now, if we get a bar of chocolate here, my eyes are hanging out like organ stops at the sight of it! We wanted to be normal, but we couldn't. I weighed six stone thirteen most of the time, and I'm five foot one and a quarter. I have a photograph, actually, which is quite a shocker. It's got a low front to it, the tu-tu, and it's nothing but bones, my chest is an absolute mass of bones all sticking out. Horrible. But then when you think that there's a chap trying to lift you above his head, you're going to find yourself on the floor if you weigh much more than that.

I left after six years. They were having a weeding-out process, and some of us had had enough; some people had weight problems. I remember one classic example, a friend of mine. After a certain amount of time in the Corps de Ballet you're moved up to what's called Coryphée. She was due to be moved up, and she simply said, 'Well it's time, isn't it?' And they said, 'If that's the way you feel about it, we'll terminate your contract now.' And that was it, she was out. That was the way they worked. Quite incredible. Appalling.

Anyway, the two of us had begun to put on weight. On tour I was at a real stretch the whole time, and then when you come to Covent Garden, you might be on once a fortnight, or once a week, if you're lucky. And because of that, I began to put on weight, quite drastically. Well, I say 'drastically', but this is the idiotic thing: I'd gone up to all of seven and a half stone! From six and a half! I mean, isn't it incredible? Anyway I went to dieticians and all sorts, and absolutely nothing was shifting it, and I knew that the only thing to do was to go back on tour, which they wouldn't have. So they terminated my contract. Despite the fact that I'd shone, yes. That's the awful thing, that you just don't know where you are from one minute to the next. Once you're out, you're out.

However, I had begun to be terrifically disillusioned with the whole set-up. I began to wonder if it wouldn't be better to get out now and establish some kind of life for myself, than to suddenly find myself at forty, unmarried and nowhere to go, kind of thing. So in a way I was almost thankful, actually, that it ended. But then I did go and audition for things afterwards, and that was when I joined Northern Dance Theatre. And I must admit, for the couple of years that I was with them I really did enjoy it, because it was a small group. When we were on tour, it was like a little family. There was no backbiting at all, the opposite if anything. I was Principal Dancer, but if somebody else was wanting to be pushed on for something, instead of trying to keep her out of the way, you'd go and help her to learn the part. It was a different atmosphere altogether.

My mum and dad were a terrific support. They followed me all around the country, watching my performances. They were very good, they would bring along bunches of flowers for every single principal dancer that would be on if they were coming to watch the performance. But it's funny, it was only about two years ago

I discovered through my eldest niece that my brothers at the time had really resented all this. She said that Russ had said that he and Phil were absolutely sick to death of all this dancing business, and that my parents were always ready to go and watch me and yet they wouldn't go to the school and watch their PE displays. I was quite unaware of all that. Certainly their annoyance didn't come across to me.

But then there were many times when I wished I had just gone to college or university and got a job in the ordinary way that my two brothers were doing. I don't regret any of it now, because looking back you see it's all in God's plan, that every single thing that has happened was planned in advance. But at the time, because I had no faith or any feeling of providence working in me, I quite often wished I'd just been like any other kid – had ordinary relationships, as much as anything.

And yet again, I became totally disillusioned with the whole set-up, so I walked out. I remember my grandmother was there when I came home. My mother was in a state, she thought it was terrible, my father just took it all placidly; and my grandmother, as soon as I walked through the door, said: 'This is the first sensible thing you've done in your life.' She was absolutely delighted that I was out of it all. It's a funny thing: I don't think my parents realised quite what a rat race it was.

So there I was, twenty-three, twenty-four, and my dancing career was already over. Relief! Well, then I worked with my dad at the undertakers. I did all the paperwork, and it was absolutely great. I remember one of the directors of the firm said, 'It won't last, you can't possibly work with your father: nobody could work with their father.' But we got on like a house on fire. There were three of us together, him, me, and one other elderly gentleman I'd known since I was knee high, and I stayed with them for three years.

During that time I was meeting people who were coping with death, and seeing their whole attitude to it, and this was the thing that brought me into the Catholic Church. There was one particular situation where a young girl of sixteen had drowned in the bath. She'd had one of these Ascot water heaters, and it had reversed itself and was pumping out carbon monoxide, and there was no ventilation in the bathroom. Her sister was on the telephone at the bottom of the stairs, and while she was shouting for help, the sister was on the phone to her boyfriend and kept shouting back up to her, 'Be quiet, I'm on the phone.' When she finally went up, she was dead. She'd drowned in the bath.

I just couldn't understand how the family could cope with all this, but to see them visiting this beautiful sixteen-year-old girl lying out in the chapel, it really was fantastic to see their faith, an absolute and utter conviction that she was in a better place, and what reason was there for being sad. It was incredible, and it was that sort of meeting that made me realise that that was what I wanted: whatever it was that they'd got. I wanted to know about it as well.

Being in that business, I got to know all the various churches, and I knew there was a Roman Catholic church in Kensington called Our Lady of Victories. I've no idea to this day really what drew me in there, but one afternoon I just wandered in, and the next thing I knew I was knocking at the presbytery door saying, 'I want to become a Catholic, what do I do?'

It takes a year of instruction, going weekly to the priest. When I told my family, they just said, 'All right, if that's what you want.' They were indifferent, really. I could have become an Armenian Orthodox and they probably wouldn't have thought anything more of it. At the end of the year, when I was received into the Church, I can remember saying to the priest – he came back to our house for a drink and whatnot – I can remember saying to him on the front steps, 'There's something more to come. I don't know what it is, but there's something more to come.' And he just looked at me knowingly and said, 'Well, we'll see.' I didn't know what he meant, but he too had realised that there was something more in it.

Then for a short while I wasn't working with my father, I was working with the Daughters of St Paul; they're a religious order, who have bookshops in various places. And the more I saw of them the more I realised that an active order was not what I wanted – I was obviously thinking along the lines of some kind of religious order by then, don't ask me why. It had to be all or nothing, but I don't know why, I suppose it's part of my make-up; like with the theatre, you know, I either had to do well or not bother. It was the same sort of feeling.

I became quite friendly with some of the priests at the Carmelite church in Kensington, and I said to one of them that I was going to go on retreat simply to try and find out what I was supposed to be doing with my life. I just said, I think I'll go to Carmel whatever, and he said, 'I'll go and make a phone call and I'll be back.' So he went and made a phone call and came back and said, 'You're going to Darlington Carmel for the weekend.' I said, 'Whatever do I want to go to Darlington for, it's in the back end of beyond.' There was Notting Hill Carmel, Golders Green Carmel, Quidenham in Norfolk, Ware, Chichester, and yet he was sending me here. Absolutely crazy. But anyway, I came.

Nobody could have been more amazed than I was. I remember the taxi driver saying to me as he brought me over the top of the hill, 'What on earth are you going there for?' and I thought, 'Yeah, what *am* I going there for?' But I came for a weekend and stayed outside, in the lodge where you're staying now, and when I arrived I came in here to meet Sister Margaret. It was really uncanny because there's nothing attractive about this parlour whatsoever, but I knew from the minute I came in that if anything was going to sort me out, it was going to be coming here. I had no idea what I was going to do with my life until I came here, and then it all just fell into place.

I stayed over the Friday night and all day Saturday, and during the course of the day I met all the Sisters; they all came into the parlour in groups of twos and threes, and that was really quite hair-raising, I must say. And then I thought I'd like to see what it was like inside, which is the next step – you don't just walk in the door and that's it. So about three weeks later, I came inside for the weekend. You know. Give it a go, kind of thing.

The strangest thing is there's nothing you can actually put your finger on and say, 'This is it'. Somebody says, 'How do you know you have a vocation?' and you just *know*. You can't put it into words. No way of describing what you feel. I remember my mother saying to me on my Solemn Profession Day, 'How did you feel?' Well, there simply aren't words for it. It's just total conviction that you've done the right thing, and you're in the right place. I just knew from when I entered that that was it.

I never really talked about it to my family, partly because I was the only one at that stage who was having contact with any kind of church, but also because I knew that although Dad would accept it, my mother had no idea of what contemplative life involved, and simply wouldn't understand why, if I was going to be a nun, I couldn't be a Sister of Mercy or whatever, and be outside where she could still get at me, and where I could come home for holidays and this sort of thing. But as I said, it was all or nothing. And with Carmel it certainly is all or nothing!

The lovely thing is that now my parents say the highlight of their year is their visits to Carmel. They love coming. They're actually coming tomorrow, so you can meet them. They have a dormobile van and they stay overnight in it, so I'll see them all tomorrow afternoon, and then they'll go shopping on Thursday morning when you and I are here, and I'll see them again before they toddle off home again in their van. They spend a day and a bit getting here, and a day and a bit getting back again, because they can just stop off anywhere, any campsite. That really is the highlight of their year, the visits here.

What attracted me to the life? What a question! Certainly the life of prayer attracted me, but also, knowing as much as I did of the world, the good and the bad, I felt that for me it would be far too much of a temptation still to be in that kind of milieu and trying to live the life of a nun. I have nothing but admiration for Sisters that are working in some situations. The temptations that are thrown at them day in day out, and yet they still remain true to their vows.

I had no previous notion of nuns at all. Very odd, isn't it? I think it was lucky that my first real contact with them was good. A lot of Catholics have memories of Sisters that taught them who were overstrict and all the rest of it: well, I never met any of that. Also the habit attracted me, I must admit that. I just thought, mmm, that's nice . . . Funny, isn't it? And that was something which worried me about some of the active orders – the fact that they're not in a habit. I suppose the witness value of it sort of hit me.

No, right, nobody *does* see me in it, do they? I suppose it is a bit of an irony! Except that my mother wears a picture of me around her neck in a locket, and at every possible moment she gets it out and says, 'This is my daughter.' A lot of people have that silly notion that nuns are just people who run away from the world because they can't cope with it. Well, they want to try and live the life: you might get away from certain aspects of the world, but there's one thing you don't get away from in here and that's yourself.

Mind you, I didn't think terribly deeply about anything for the first few months, until Clothing – which is the time when you are formally clothed in the habit – began to loom ahead. During that time, we had daily periods of instruction from a team of three different sisters; one doing scripture, one doing Carmelite spirituality, and the other doing theology and the daily humdrum goings on of Carmelite life, and I don't remember at any moment thinking to myself, oh good gracious, am I in the right place? I don't think I ever felt that.

But the first couple of months you're in such a whirl, you don't know where you are anyway! While in the old-fashioned Carmelite regime a Novice would never have had charge of an office on her own – she would have worked under an older Sister – that wasn't the way here. As soon as we entered, we were responsible for our own offices. I was doing all the typesetting for the booklets that we print from the minute that I walked in the door, *and* I was Choir Mistress. So the first couple of months I was in such a whirl, just trying to be in the right place at the right time, apart from anything else, that I went to bed in the evening absolutely exhausted. Never thought about anything.

Because coming here was quite a transition from the world I'd known, it's funny, but the obvious things, like not being able to go out, I never really found myself thinking about them. It didn't bother me. We'd go out to the dentist, the doctor, the hospital, anything like that. And even as a Postulant, before I received the habit, if I'd gone out, say, for the dentist, I always had a feeling of relief when I got back up to the top of the hill there and could see the convent. I never thought, oh, I'll stay out a bit longer. I honestly don't know that there's anybody else here that has ever felt that either. It's always been a feeling of relief that you're on your way *home*. And, you know, I think the thing that always hits me most of all when I go out, and I find it very sad, is how many unhappy-looking people there are around. You'll walk past a couple with a baby in a pram and they're arguing like mad and the baby's crying and I'm sure it's not just Darlington. That's what really hits me between the eyes. So I've no desire to be out there. No thank you very much.

I don't think any of the nitty-gritty things like food and hard beds – I don't think any of that really worried me, either. Our cells are very, very bare – stark. You've only got the bed. Bookshelf is an innovation: we never had bookshelves before. Table and chair, a wash-basin in the corner, a bare cross on the wall, and *a* picture. That's it. And I *loved* it. I'd never really felt that I was where I should have been before, and it took me an awful long time to get here! Twenty-nine seemed very old. Actually it doesn't really now when I look back on it.

In fact, when I look back over my life in the theatre and everything, I can see quite clearly the hand of providence in it all. I think there was just a terrific sense of trust that there was somebody that had everything in hand. Even when I felt things were in total muddle and chaos, it was marvellous to be able to look back and realise that it all happened for a reason, and that things were leading the way they were because everything was in His hands. And because I've always felt that He knows what I want, I've not really had anything to tell Him. He knows how I feel and He knows why, so He'll sort it out.

What do *I* contribute? Well, I hope that He's able to do what He wants with me, that I can be completely open to His will in my life. That's the whole thing, isn't it? To be here in Carmel is to be completely open to what He asks of you, and not trying to manipulate things to how you would like them to be. It sounds very easy, I know, but it ain't. Even silly little things like when the bell rings and you're in the middle of doing something that you are enjoying, you respond to the bell because it's the Lord calling you to the choir. And that's not always easy. You may want to continue what you're doing, and you can't. I think those things in the early days are the hardest to come to grips with: the fact that one's time is not one's own. In fact, the day isn't one's own, from beginning to end. We've got an arrangement here where at recreation time you're free to do what you want for half an hour, but that half hour is the only time you can really call your own.

But even then, you see, most of us have regular meetings. For instance, on a Thursday night I meet the little Novice and am teaching her to play the recorder, so we play the recorder together. Well, come one Thursday night and I don't feel like it, I can't say, 'Don't bother coming tonight,' because it's an arrangement we've made. And those kind of things can really get you down, not the bigger issues like food and hours and getting up early and all that, but the interpersonal things.

Yet the strange thing is, I never felt at any time, uh oh, no, I'm not going to do this, which some of them here have felt. I was one of the first three to enter since Vatican II; they hadn't had any for a long time. Three of us entered together and were the so-called 'new generation'; the way of bringing Novices up was very different from the way it had been. You have several months as what's called a Postulant, then two years as a Novice, then you make your Temporary, or First, Vows. Another three years after that you make your Solemn, or Final, Vows. But anywhere along the line, if necessary, Postulancy and the Novitiate can be extended. So it's quite a long business; four to five years before you receive a black veil, the sign of permanent commitment.

Anyway, when we arrived, they changed everything. The form was still the same, but all the old customs had been thrown out of the window, and we were really free; we weren't tied down to the regular hours and we weren't tied down to the Great Silence (the silence after the last bell goes at night until after prayers the next morning). So there wasn't such an immediate initiation into the religious life. We had entered, yes, but we were still pretty much living our own life. Still drinking our whisky, yes . . . Hang on, how did you know about that? I bet Sister Margaret told you, didn't she!

Oh gosh! Well, I'll explain. My parents had just been to Scotland and they brought me a bottle of Glenfiddich, right? So I put it out on display, which is what we do here, and Sister Margaret said: 'No, don't put that out! Put it upstairs!' So I put it upstairs and we Postulants proceeded to drink it between us. She doesn't drink, unfortunately, Sister Margaret, so she didn't have any, but she's good fun, realistic with Postulants.

Anyway, when we were actually clothed as Novices, after six months, then we had to knuckle down and get on with it, which is the best way; it gives you six months to find your way. Some of the things we got up to before we were made Novices were really quite hair-raising, but they didn't judge us, which says a lot for the community here actually. And when we chose to stay we chose freely, despite the fact that all those things – like whisky – were going to be put aside as soon as we donned the habit.

For me the silence and the solitude was such a relief. I think the silence can be quite frightening at first, for some, but it never affected me that way. I love it. I've always loved the Divine Office, too, which is just as well seeing as we say it seven times a day. I suppose that's the loner coming out in me again, liking the silence and the solitude, and being alone with the Lord. That doesn't mean to say I don't enjoy being in community too, because I do, but solitude suits me: I feel, when I come out of it again, much more whole, somehow it has a very healing effect. If you've had some kind of disagreement with somebody – which can happen, because we've got quite a pressure of work here – you can go into prayer time and offer the whole thing to the Lord, and when you come out at the end the thing is usually resolved. You know, it's fantastic the way it can heal rifts between people, and rifts that are inside yourself as well.

We're also allowed five hermit days a year. A hermit day means you have the day completely away from the community. You only come to mass and meals. Apart from that you're completely apart, and nobody would speak to you even. I really think I could live that way all the time. For that reason, I love feast days and Sundays because they're always that bit quieter. The loveliest time of the day here is between half past eight in the evening, the end of the Office of Readings (which is when the Great Silence bell rings), right through until after Lauds at six thirty in the morning. The silence is beautiful, it really is. Obviously if there's an emergency of some kind, one would speak. Oh, we also have a Recollection Day every month, which is like a community hermit day. Everybody looks forward to those days, without exception.

As well as the silence, I liked being in one place too, when I came here, which is surprising when you think how I've gadded about all over the continent. But it's strange, I can look back on that quite happily and not yearn for any of it. We had a super time in Monte Carlo the last tour I did with the Royal Ballet, but I wouldn't want to be there now. I suppose it can't have mattered that much, can it? Yet you know the odd thing was, they kept on about me being just like Lynn Seymour. . . I'm out of contact with everybody now, though. They actually put in the *Dancing Times* a little extract to say where I was. But I think people think they can't write, you see.

I never told anyone I was coming. I just slid in without telling anybody what was going on. My parents didn't tell the rest of the family, even. They'd say 'She just isn't around.' My father was very good. He said, 'At the moment, she's in so and so, but we don't know what's going to happen, whether she's staying or not.' I didn't want to face a whole lot of fond farewells. The thought of all that was just awful. A friend of mine at the Carmelite church in Kensington wanted to throw a party for me the night before I left, and I said absolutely not, on no account. I couldn't have coped with all that. Once I'd determined I was coming and I'd been received, that was it. Just leave it and go.

It's funny, you know, my mother reminded me, I think it was last time she was here, about Lynn Seymour. I'd forgotten all about it. Kenneth MacMillan – a lot of his works were done for Lynn. Even his Romeo and Juliet, although Fonteyn and Nureyev danced the first performance, it was actually written for Lynn and Christopher Gable. Those mid-seventies dancers, oh, they were great. Sibley and Dowell, Merle Park. And my great friend Georgina Parkinson, she was of that era, too. Oh gosh! Memory Lane! But you know I don't miss it. Because towards the end, as I say,

I was so disillusioned with the whole thing that when I left it was as if a burden had dropped off me.

So where were we yesterday? Oh, yes. Being here. Well, I really do feel that everything that has happened in my life has all led to my coming here. Certainly I believe in God's plan. He has one for all of us, but we never actually see the thing; that's what's so difficult, isn't it? I do feel it's pre-determined, and that's not just a way of brushing off one's failures and trying to make light of them. Also, we know for sure that out of any kind of difficult or evil situation, He can bring good. I suppose in the same way one would say one learns by one's mistakes; it's the same sort of thing. I'm quite convinced.

Actually, that's why I'm so detached from persons and things, because if you really do believe that He has everything in hand, what is there to worry about? One can, in Carmel, become very centred either on material things or quite often you'll see relationships that are perhaps too strong. When you see somebody who is dependent on somebody else, well, I mean, that can't *be* in our life, it really can't. It can lead to divisions in the community, and if you find a community holiday coming up, and you only want to be meeting one person, then something's going awry; if you can't freely bring a third person in to join you, something's wrong. Becoming too close in our life; it can be dangerous.

Everybody is going to relate with some people better than others, though. In days gone by it was absolute anathema to have any kind of one to one relationships. It simply wasn't allowed, and that was all there was to it. You never met one to one with any other Sister. But then you're giving up the one type of relationship for something better; which is the same as you would say of giving up marriage and family and all the rest of that. Giving up the one human love for something which we know is better, and deeper and stronger, and totally reliable.

It's not comparable to human love, because there is that basic, total trust in it which you can never have with another human being. Even one's parents could let one down from time to time, whereas the Lord never does that. He may not sort things out the way you would perhaps like, but if you have complete trust and complete surrender then even if things are going awry, it's all okay. From the point of view of the risk of being hurt, obviously there isn't the same sort with God that there is with a human being, but it can be a pretty risky business putting yourself in the Lord's hands. He does turn you inside out and upside down, and stand you on your head.

I'll give you an example: I was away from this community for ten months, helping another Carmel, which was short in numbers and very elderly. And there's no doubt it totally changed me – for the better, thanks be to God. It really was ten months of living the Lord's passion with him; it was *hell*. This Carmel hadn't updated itself, and they simply weren't living the life truly, and for me to stay faithful and to keep my discipline of prayer and the essentials of our life in the midst of all that was pretty terrible. It made me mature, that's for sure, and I think it's made me much more understanding of other people and their problems and limitations and weaknesses, but if I'd stayed any longer I think I would have had a breakdown. He had all that in hand, too, but it was pretty risky to put oneself in that kind of situation.

Why? Well, they just weren't living the life.

No, they weren't doing that, though there did used to be that in Carmels a *very* long time ago. Flagellation. Every Friday. Everybody would go into choir, the lights were put out, and they whacked themselves. A lot of the Sisters who are present in this community now have experienced that – the older Sisters. *Isn't* it extraordinary! Once a week! And *what* has that to do with religious life? Now, I couldn't say for sure whether there are still communities that do it, but as little as ten years ago I know there was a Carmel doing it, because a Sister went from here to help, and discovered that they were. But you have to be careful what you say, you see, because all these weird things are what still turn up in books because they're interesting – and they're not the truth, not any more.

There are thirty Carmels in Great Britain, which I think is too many. We've got to amalgamate or close some, and then we've got to really re-evaluate things, which we've done here, and it's why the young ones are coming. I suppose we're experiencing something different from most communities here, because we're over-full. We've just had one more Postulant, we've got another one coming in December, and we're six too many already. But the communities that haven't updated and renewed themselves are not getting the vocations, because there's nothing to attract a young person to our way of life. You can't be throwing out the window things that are part of our tradition simply to please the young ones coming in, but you have got to make it acceptable to somebody of our day and age, so I think by the time we've gone through that, we'll be seeing a re-emergence of monastic life.

I know people feel that nuns should be out doing something about the state of the world and all the rest of that, but we *know* that prayer is the answer to it all. A certain amount of the daily news comes in to us. The Sacristan, Mary, gets the paper, and she cuts out the various headlines for us. We don't want to know about all the latest rapes and things, thanks very much, but the wars and all the rest of it, we know about them. So that's all held in our hearts during prayer time. We're aware of the whole world situation, so I don't feel the need to justify why I'm here.

I mean I think I'm doing the best I can do by being here and praying for the world. But we do get people coming in here bombarding us with those sorts of questions, about what good are we doing, and then it's back to the thing of trying to put a vocation into words, and you can't do it. I just have an utter conviction, an absolute faith and trust in God that I am in the right place, and that my life of prayer is certainly efficacious in the life of the Church, and there's nothing more one can say. You can get terribly tangled up in arguments, but in the end what can you say? Very rarely does one actually *see* an answer to prayer, but two or three times somebody has asked me to pray for a specific reason, and I have seen the thing fulfilled. So there's no question that the answer to all problems is a prayer relationship.

The faith is there for me, and I pray for the gift of faith for the sceptics. And first of all, I'm here for *God*. I mean, it can be that one enters for selfish motives, but I think one sees very quickly that if that's why you've entered then you're in the wrong place. You wouldn't last very long if you had entered for the wrong motives, because the life is too hard. It's harder now than it was in days gone by, because now we have to earn our living, which we didn't before, because we lived on gifts of alms from people, and Sisters brought whacking great dowries with them. That's mostly gone by now, so if you entered with the wrong motives, you simply wouldn't last.

Both of my brothers claim to be agnostic. I don't think they are. I think that's part of their reaction to me. I think if they really thought about it they'd see that they're a couple of idiots! They're so tied up in their own lives they haven't got time for anything else. Which brings me back to why we're here, because I feel that it's only through the power of prayer and the sort of life that the contemplative communities are leading, that somehow or other we're going to pray the world back into being God-centred. You see people hungering for prayer, and they're going for gurus and heading out for the Middle East, not looking at their own churches . . .

Yes, that's fine if you want to stop there. Same time tomorrow? Fine. Oh, do go and say hello to my parents. They'd love to meet you. Where are they parked exactly?

So. What's this afternoon then?

How do I see God? That's a tough one. I don't personify God, not really. I have no visions of an elderly gentleman with a white beard and all that business. Again, I think it's my upbringing. As a child I wasn't taught any of those things which most kids are. Nor do I have that fear that a lot of children have been brought up with: 'Be careful, because God is watching you' – thanks be to God.

I see God more as a presence, both within us and without, because He's everywhere all of the time, and within us as well. That's a very Carmelite thing – the practice of the presence of God. We call it the Divine Indwelling, the idea that He's with us everywhere all of the time. He's with us amongst the pots and pans as much as He is when we're in the choir on our knees.

'Him'? Well, I just don't think of it the other way. I'm afraid I'm one of these people that gets irritated by this sexist language business. They keep changing the intercessions at the Office; every time it says 'men', they say 'men and women'; every time they say 'brothers', they add 'sisters'. I'm more irritated by them trying to remember to do that than just leaving it as it is. I mean I don't really think of him as male, female or anything.

Well, that's quite a question, isn't it? 'Is it important to me that I'm a woman?' In what way? I'm still a woman, that doesn't go, no, you don't lose your identity. As I said yesterday, I feel more fully myself here than I ever felt anywhere else, and that includes sexually, and that's not a cop-out from all that went before, that's just the way of things. But I suppose it is quite surprising, so I can see what you're driving at: with all of us in our habits you could lose your identity. Certainly in times past you could have, though I don't think you would today. Here we can just be ourselves. You're not expected to fit into a mould and all be the same, which in the old days was the ideal. That sort of thing is absolutely out-dated now.

There's pettiness. It's inevitable. You get bouts of it, and then it all blows over. Quite often you'll have what we call 'grumbles' at recreation. Sister Margaret usually starts off and says, 'I've got a grumble – you're making too much noise in the refectory,' and that's it, everybody's off then. They're all grumbling. 'I've got a grumble, I've got a grumble.' It's only a way of letting off steam. Healthy really.

But it isn't always so civilised. Sometimes when you've been corrected you think, oh, blow this. It's an unusual thing if there's an outburst, and usually there's a pretty good reason behind it – but it happens. And I suppose you cope when things are difficult by making an effort to do the opposite thing you feel like doing. I mean, there is one individual in the community who I really do find extremely difficult to get on with, and my natural instinct even if she's going up the stairs is to think, 'I'm going the other way'; but once you've stopped yourself doing that, and done the opposite, it's surprising how one can cope. It really does work if you just stop long enough to say to the Lord, 'Look, I can't cope with this, you're going to have to do it for me.' But obviously there are people for all of us who just get under our skin.

That is why the recreation hours are so important, because that's the time when you can be free for a while and you should be able to go back to your work or your silence feeling refreshed and ready for it. Some communities, because of the pressure of work, have dropped the mid-day hour of recreation and work on through it, or else they'll do the peeling of vegetables or something at the beginning of it. But we opted here definitely not to do that.

I play my guitar at recreation time and that, for me, is one of my greatest outlets. I find it really relaxing. Some people will go out gardening at that time. There are Scrabble players galore in here too. I play once a week with Sister Margaret and it's the most hilarious half hour that we have, the pair of us roar with laughter. She's a terror for trying to put in words that don't exist and then she says, 'I can have that, can't I?' So I in all my innocence say yes and then discover later there's no such word.

We have music too. We acquired a decent record player through a Postulant. She left, but she left the record player behind, which was quite nice. There was an old-fashioned portable thing which they'd had for years, but that's finally bit the dust. We have music in the refectory if it's a big feast like Saint Teresa's, but normally somebody reads in the refectory during dinner and supper; we have some scripture and then something from whatever book we've chosen to read at that time. But on a special day we would have some kind of music to make that bit of difference. Which is nice. I did miss listening to music when I first came here.

I suppose those sorts of limitations are part of the poverty thing. Certainly poverty has never meant to me a matter of not possessing things, that's not what it's all about. It's about poverty of spirit too, though our thing as Carmelites is austerity, which means that everything's very simple in the house and there's an absence of anything that would be considered luxurious, so we have basic necessities. As somebody pointed out to a Sister the other day, who was in here with her family, you've got a light shade on your light over there but we haven't got one over here.

We have no curtains, no carpets, wooden shutters on the windows that need them. Walls are just emulsioned. Some of us have got pictures in our cells – Saint Teresa, John of the Cross, Our Lady of Mount Carmel – but they're only sepia things, they're not coloured and they're not in frames. For a feast day we would bring flowers into the house, but normally there would be no decoration. Our beds are just a basic wooden frame with a coconut hair mattress. They're hard but they're very healthy. Certainly straw-filled palliasses went out with the ark. When I came here we still had an enamel jug and basin, and you washed kneeling on the floor. We wouldn't have *dreamt* of having hot and cold water in the cells! Good gracious! But when the plumber came to put them in the infirmary and said, 'Why haven't you got them everywhere else?' Within weeks there we were with hot and cold water. In the 1990s, a community of twenty-eight people trying to get into three baths is ridiculous!

Food is very basic. Breakfast's simply bread and marg or cereal. Butter only comes out on feast days. And there's tea and coffee. Lunch would be soup, or if it's very hot we would have a drink of some kind, orangeade or something. Today's Wednesday, it happens to be a feast day, so it would be fried fish, or boiled eggs for those of us who can't eat fish, and marrow and plain boiled potatoes, and stewed fruit and milk pudding of some kind. Supper amounts to soup, boiled egg or cheese, or porridge if you don't take the soup. There's always tea. Oh, and there's also fruit and jam.

There's no reason why anybody should go hungry. What's the good in it? You simply can't be working the hours that we are on an empty stomach unless you want to break people's health, which has happened in the past. There are Sisters with ulcers and all sorts, which go back to the days of the Black Fast. There was a time when Lent was a Black Fast, which meant that there were no dairy foods of any kind. But thanks be to God, all those things have stopped now.

Do you know, it's quite amazing having to think about all these things again. But I don't feel that they are negative, which certainly most people outside the walls do. It's the total gift of oneself to the Lord that counts, and the giving up of these things for something better, something that's utterly fulfilling. The Lord can fulfil us in a way that nothing else can. And in a way that no human can ever do.

I suppose the two sorts of fulfilment are not incompatible. One can say quite happily that married couples can be just as holy and just as devout as us in here. Certainly there are lay people who are astoundingly good and holy, probably better than a lot of us in here. And even in here, although the actual vows haven't changed, the emphasis has. Whereas before one emphasised all the things you were giving up, now you're emphasising the positive side, what you're gaining. Because of course one's giving up a great deal by giving up, say, sexuality, but you're doing it freely. If you don't want to do it then you don't come here.

And we've always got one another for support, you know. We're a family, and if you're having a bad day, actually knowing the community are around is an incredible support, knowing that they're there and that they love you even if you've caused some kind of uproar in the house!

Not everyone feels like that, though. A Postulant here – who needless to say didn't survive – she'd say to me every evening. 'Oh God, I'd give anything to be just sitting here with John with his arms around me and a gin and tonic in my hand.' And I'd think; well, *you're* not going to last long chum! Things can be difficult in the beginning, obviously. But the only longing I have – it comes quite regularly, but I never think anything about it – would be to walk on the beach by the sea. So I simply do it in my mind instead. It's only a moment of temptation, anyway; it passes pretty quickly.

No, not kids. I would be terrified of bringing kids up in today's world, I really would. I doubt that, even if I'd stayed outside, I would have had a family or got married. It's quite doubtful actually. Quite doubtful.

Anyway, these days if you have any doubts before you come in, you can go through all that process beforehand. I think in the past, certainly there were more mistakes made, but I still think that making a permanent commitment is important, because of the instability of our times. The Novitiate training has changed recently to two years because young people coming in are less stable and less ready to make full commitment, and although we call it Temporary Vows after the two years, the idea is that once you've made them, you stay; they're not temporary in the sense that you can make them and then six weeks later decide to push off. But then even if someone does push off, I've never heard of an instance where there wasn't good reason for their doing it.

After all, they say that it takes ten years even to settle in the contemplative life. Ten years to really know.

And you know, thinking over what you said yesterday, it is important to me that I am a woman, and I don't feel it diminished by being here and being in my habit. I can take just as much pride in myself, just as much pride in this being clean and tidy and pressed. I do think the habit's important – as an act of witness. The house is a witness too, and so are the walls. Mind you, the building is a bit of a pain because it's listed, and it means having to do things we might not otherwise do – like having the whole roof renewed. That's why there are houses all around us, we had to sell all the fields to pay for the roof. But the house is important; it's a witness to our life of dedication, it's our uniform, like the habit. I've seen a situation where a community had thrown off the habit, after Vatican II came in, and a lot of members of the public who had known them previously – they were really quite shocked. They sort of lost their respect for them.

People do like to stick nuns up on a pedestal, certainly. There is that in it, yes. But you see even if we're out to the dentist or whatever and it's only a matter of being out for an hour or so, the amount of people that will stop to ask you for prayers or even just to say good morning to you, because you're in a habit, is quite amazing. People will always come and talk to you. Always. I can't say I've ever encountered anything really bad but then we're not out much.

Do you think some people get upset by us? That's interesting. I wonder if it's to do with the sort of attitude that came across in the past; that kind of superior attitude some orders had. Perhaps we're a threat, to men particularly, because we've rejected the whole male thing and said, 'We've got something better.' I really don't know. I'll have to ask some males that I know what they feel! Nobody gets worked up about monks. Funny, isn't it? People generally have respect for monks rather than think they're a funny lot of weirdos. Isn't that odd? And yet when you consider the Carthusian way of life, that's a jolly sight weirder than our life here!

The thing I thought was really dreadful when I first came here was the vow of obedience. I had the notion of it simply being that I had to do what Sister Margaret told me all the time. And of course that's not it at all. Sure, there's that angle in it, but that's not obedience. Obedience is if one knows that one should be in a certain place at a certain time right through the day, which is why it is freeing rather than something which ties you up in knots. In days gone by, it was blind obedience, in the sense that even if the Prioress gave you three or four conflicting jobs to do you wouldn't have questioned it; you would have said 'Yes, Mother.' So there's much more of a personal responsibility angle that wasn't there before. And we have dropped the term 'Mother' now, incidentally.

When there was a community vote round about 1984, 1985, we voted to drop 'Mother' but to keep the title 'Sister' (though we find ourselves just calling each other by our Christian names because it seems the more natural thing to do), but some people feel that even in dropping the title 'Sister' amongst ourselves it's becoming 'worldly'.

'Worldly'? Well, I think in any community you could find yourself being infiltrated by things that really aren't part of our life, TV for one thing, which we don't have. We do have videos on if somebody has a golden jubilee or something like that, but again it would have to be something that was, you know, *suitable*. It's like I was saying before, we have to know about the state of the world, but not every last gory detail. For one reason, if you're forever reading about all these awful child abuse things and rapes and all the rest of it, it is going to affect you and cause you problems physically. So the videos have to be suitable, and as far as novels and free-time books are concerned, while we've got a lot of thrillers and things like that, we've got nothing that's particularly sexual, because that's going to conjure up all sorts of images and things that aren't terribly helpful to anyone.

After all, we *know* those things are going on, so it's just not particularly helpful to our lifestyle to know all the details. And we do have the Catholic papers. I think one absorbs enough from the daily newspapers and little snippets that get passed in. We're out of touch, but I do feel that in our situation you can draw so much in that in the end our life is questionable. Why bother being in here with the TV and radio and the papers and all the comforts that you can have when you might just as well be out there?

It really does become a farce if we have everything that we could want. Even if you're going for what we call a 'permission' for something, you do think twice about whether you need the thing or not. Not the obvious ordinary everyday things like a refill for your biro (though in days gone by you didn't even have a biro, you had a pencil and it was about so big), no, it's other things. Something came up recently; it was postage. When the postage went up again we agreed as a community not to write any first class letters. Yet we freely go to a cupboard where the stamps are kept, and there are folks who haven't got a stamp to put on a letter, so it's a bit of a farce for us to be freely taking stamps. One has to question even these small things.

You were asking me if I ever felt cut off or hemmed in. Well, for instance, at recreation last night Sister Margaret told them about you being here, so we got quite a lot of outside feedback that way. If Sisters have had a parlour visit, they always share it at recreation.

It's not something that I think about, but a friend of mine said to me in a letter exactly what you've said. He said: 'I don't know how you cope. I couldn't exist unless I had all these friends and all this traipsing around. I could never consider staying in the same building for the rest of my life.' And yet I don't really think about it. We sometimes joke amongst ourselves about going away on holiday but it's only said in fun.

Anyway, we do have holidays. Apart from Easter, which is obviously the most important feast of all, we have one other big feast in the year that's important and that's our community feast. Three days in August – the date of St Teresa's Reform of Carmel. Christmas too, of course. Christmas is great. We have three days' holiday. No work obviously. In the evening we either have a concert to entertain each other, or we do a Christmas play, some kind of nativity-based thing.

Over those kind of holidays when there's no work, we're free to meet each other during the daytime. We also meet as a group, and the inevitable Scrabble boards come out. On those days we also put the tables together in the refectory. They're usually on either side in lines and we move them into the middle – you can see in the pamphlet photo how it normally is. We're normally in silence apart from the reader up in the pulpit, but at Christmas we allow speaking at mealtimes, so we're chatting to each other across the tables, which is nice.

No, no presents. We have what we call a Christmas Shop. During the year, Sister Margaret collects all sorts of things that come in, and it's up to her to decide if you can keep it. Which is fair enough, as we've renounced all earthly goods. So at Christmas we all charge around with paper money buying things. It's quite funny to watch actually, quite a scream! But mostly people are getting things to give away to their family, we're not buying things for ourselves.

You do get into a rut with your routine, and it's very important not to, you can stagnate very easily. So holidays are very welcome but we can't be out of gear for too long. We're very reliant on structure, maybe too reliant. But I think the fact that none of us here want to go away is a good sign. If we were wanting to spend time away then it's maybe a sign that you're in the wrong community, that you're not fitting in in some way.

We do go out to vote. We feel that's important. The local people are very good; they ferry us down in cars to the local polling station. And those who can't go out do it by post. But I don't think we would ever go on a protest, because we can do more by living our life of prayer inside than anything we can do outside. I know one or two communities who probably would. Certainly we would write off letters of protest, and we have done in the past, but I don't think we'd go and wave banners. That would be against the hidden and silent witness of our life.

Why the bars? Those we agreed to keep purely as a witness to our enclosed life – for people who come to the parlour I mean. Otherwise what is there? Some of the Carmels have either removed the bars or else they've got them so that they open, but so far we've agreed to keep them. They don't bother me in the least; I don't even notice them. No, the only thing that bothers you is your eyes after a while when you're talking through them. When I go away from here I'll see lines for a while.

It would bother me if they weren't there because I appreciate their witness value. Somebody once said, 'It's so nobody can get hold of you and give you a hug and a kiss.' Well, I can assure you, you can manage that even with the bars. That's not the reason for it. We're not trying to keep the big bad world out.

There's another thing that people in days gone by would latch onto. You see these holes? There was another set of bars here, a second set, and a black curtain. If you'd been talking to me then, you wouldn't have seen me. The black curtain would have been down and there would have been a Sister sitting in the corner listening in. The only time you would have had the curtains drawn would have been for parents, not even for aunts and uncles or brothers and sisters, and you'd still have a Sister sitting in. That was the way things were.

If the doctor was coming in, then the Sister at the door would have had the veil over her face so you wouldn't see it. The Infirmarian would have had a veil over her face too, and the Sister at the door would go ahead ringing a bell to warn the other Sisters there was someone coming in. When I entered, the Great Veils, as they were called, had gone. But we had a bedridden sister then, whom I was partly nursing, and even then, when the Confessor came in to see her, the Portress went ahead ringing the bell. Those kinds of things, they really are mind-boggling. Can you imagine how my parents must have reacted to a thing like that! Not being Catholic to begin with, not understanding anything about the contemplative life, and then on their first visit to be faced with that!

But these things have never really bothered me. I suppose because your intention when you enter is to stay, you accept things that would otherwise be questionable.

The priesthood? No! Absolutely not! Absolutely not, no; anathema to me. It just seems totally wrong. The whole concept seems weird to me, the woman priesthood, I mean. I can't explain why, but I'll give you an example instead.

We have an ecumenical service here every year, and a couple of years back there was a lady Methodist minister. She was an absolutely lovely person and she was great in the parlour and all that, but when I saw her trudging into the sanctuary, well I'm afraid most of us – I can't explain it, but it just does something to me, it's just weird. It's a butch image almost, with a dog collar and everything. It just has a strange effect on me. Ugh. No thanks.

I don't know why; I suppose it's just because as a woman I find it more offensive seeing a woman playing a butch part. Yes, well, all right, maybe it's not butch, but it's offputting. How? Gosh, this is getting deep, isn't it! Well, if one goes back to scripture and all the theories people are putting forward . . . I'm not saying that it *won't* come because I think it *will* come, in which case then one accepts it. But it just seems wrong to me.

It's just that the whole thing's going to snowball in the end because if you get women priests, then you're going to get married women priests, and the motherhood thing comes in then and it gets complicated. I can't see how a woman can be a parish priest and a mother, when you consider how busy parish priests are, from the practical point of view. But I suppose I'm thinking of the old-fashioned way of the mother being the housewife, and that's changing anyway, isn't it.

I think the image that we've rather had thrown at us of women priests, and which I find offensive, are of all these Americans. There was a ghastly image: a Negress, half a dozen times divorced or whatever, and there she was, the first Bishop – or something daft – in America. And the whole thing kind of upset me, just her whole image. Thrusting herself forward. 'Anything you can do, I can do better,' sort of thing.

When men behave like that? Well, one sort of accepts it. It's different isn't it?

What do I think about death?

Well, when I came here, I suppose I had a different attitude to death from working with Dad in the undertaker's. It was something that never really bothered me much. As children we used to play in and out amongst the coffins and the chapels and all that, and it didn't mean anything, it was just something you accepted. Certainly my personal attitude towards it has changed though, since I've been in here. Sometimes I think it'd be lovely not to wake up in the morning, I can think of nothing nicer. We've got a standing joke in here about that, actually, and the old ones are forever saying, 'I can't wait to go.'

I don't relish the thought of dying in absolute agony of cancer, nobody wants to die in agony, but then that shouldn't happen anyway nowadays, not with all the drugs that are available. In the last century Sisters were refused painkillers. The idea was that you suffered like the Lord suffered and that was it. A mistaken view.

When someone dies here the attitude is one of rejoicing: we have an extra recreation day. Yes, really! There've been five old ones go since I've been here, and they've been really beautiful moments, with the whole community gathered around the person that's dying and the priest there as well. It really is lovely, and I don't think I've ever seen anybody shed a tear. They're all thinking, lucky thing!

It's something I find hard to get across to my mother, because although she's now a fairly devout churchgoer, actual death and the afterlife is something she simply cannot grasp. It really frightens her. But then that depends what one's concept of heaven is. People have so many airy-fairy ideas but it's a mystery isn't it. I'm not like my grandmother who was quite sure she was going up to mansions and pavements of gold and all that sort of thing.

The only thing I think about heaven is that it might be exactly as we are now except that everything's perfect. All the nitty-gritty and moans and grumbles of life are gone, but we're as we are now. I find it difficult to grasp that we're all spirits sitting round playing harps and this kind of thing. . .

Gosh, this is quite tiring, isn't it. Do you know, I hardly slept last night? My head was buzzing. I got to bed wondering what on earth I've said! *Am* I going to shock the community next time they talk about women priests. I'm going to say 'What *are* you all complaining about?' You know, I said to my great pal Sister Jacinta, 'Is it important to you that you're a woman?' and she looked at me and went 'What?!' She thought I'd flipped! So I thought, oh good, I'm not the only one that had problems with that one! Which reminds me. She didn't give me an answer, so I must find out what the answer is.

Oh my goodness, is that it? Oh well, it wasn't so bad after all. I still can't imagine why you're interested in me, though. Funny isn't it?

EVA HEYMANN

Holy Child Jesus Convent, Oxford Circus, London
ROMAN CATHOLIC: APOSTOLIC

Age: 63
Nationality: British (German by birth)
Age at entry to community: 30
Number of years in community: 33
Previous employment: Teacher/Psychiatric Social Worker/
Family Therapist
Current employment: Volunteer Counsellor working with those
affected by AIDS and HIV
Dress: Ordinary

A slim, brown-haired woman, Eva dresses in plain skirts and blouses, often with a patterned scarf at the neck. Despite her unassuming appearance, she can be intimidating, and has a self-confessed tendency to stubbornness. I got the distinct impression that Eva wouldn't suffer fools at all, let alone gladly, yet the flipside of her occasional abrasiveness is an acute sensitivity. When I was half-way through writing this book I went through a period of almost wishing I'd never started it, and Eva would ring me frequently to say: 'What you're doing is really important and don't you forget it. Got that?'

We talked together at the large convent she shares with nine others in the heart of central London. The building is very long and narrow, and for the most part only one room thick. Although the congregation was originally founded as a teaching one, the Sisters now do a variety of paid and unpaid jobs, and Eva works as a volunteer counsellor for the Terrence Higgins Trust.

Eva and I talked in a small, sloping-ceilinged, attic room in the convent, which she has been given for the purpose of confidential home counselling. She and I spoke there too, so we had the luxury of total peace – something which is surprisingly rare in convents. There were postcards of flowers and landscapes on the wall, William

Morris curtains at the window – which, Eva was eager to point out, she had chosen herself – and a folded camp bed in the corner. The atmosphere was cosy and informal.

At the beginning of each session Eva would produce mint or camomile tea and quantities of biscuits. The first time I visited her, she also produced eagle-embossed paper napkins from the White House in Washington, but was unable to account for their presence in the convent.

Eva Heymann

I have very mixed feelings about my childhood. I would say that the first eleven years of my life were not particularly happy ones, though they had their high spots. I was born in Breslau, Germany, which is actually now Poland. I come from a German-Jewish family, upper middle class. We had a domestic staff – chauffeur, cook, that kind of paraphernalia. My father was an architect and a chartered engineer. I had a brother who was eight years older than I am, and a sister who is four and a half years older. She lives with my mother now in Hertfordshire.

My father was the director of the East German Electricity Works, which was Civil Servant status. He was very much a Kaiser's man: he loved culture, music and the arts, and he thought that nothing could destroy those good things. My mother had trained to be a concert pianist and didn't finish her final training when she got married, but she kept up her music as such. In 1933, when Hitler came to power, my father was among the first group of people pensioned off by the government because he was a Jew. They worked their way down the professional scales and Civil Service people were taken off very early on.

My mother and father's marriage was very fraught and I was always aware of quarrels. My father was a brilliant man, but like many brilliant people found it very hard to live together with others, so he was a very Victorian kind of father; children had to be seen and not heard. He was also a very violent man. He was very violent with my brother who I think in present-day terminology was a battered child, because he was not as brilliant as my father had hoped he would be. He was a slow learner, and was beaten very often for not being able to achieve. My father also lashed out at me physically, and while on one hand I was quite frightened of him, on the other I was the one who was able to stand up to him.

I have one memory particularly of when I was about five – I've forgotten what I'd actually done – and he was saying to me, 'What have you got to say for yourself?' I remember this tall figure towering over me and I felt very small. I thought for a moment, and apparently I said, 'My thoughts are my own and I keep them to myself.' He was so shattered by a five year old confronting him with that, that that was the end of the episode. That went down in family history. Somebody was actually saying to him, 'You can't rule me, because there's a part of me that you can't get into.' It gave me an enormous sense of power, knowing that I'd said that, and finding that these big grown-up people can't actually get inside me. I think in later years that stood me in very good stead on many occasions.

I remember a lot of shouting and arguments between my parents, and feeling quite frightened by that. I also remember very much wanting to take sides, in the way that children do, wanting to make sure that one of them was for me, and playing that in quite a consciously manipulative way. I remember, when my mother was away, saying to my father how wonderful it was to be with him, just the two of us, and yet hating him. I had that sense of hating him right the way through my childhood.

He had other women, and in that strange way in which middle class culture works that was accepted. We used to go away for six weeks' holiday to the Baltic coast every year. We had a house there, and my nanny/cook came with us. After a certain period, a train from Heligoland would come; the fathers would come back to see their wives and children, and the train was called 'the Bulls' Train.' There were mistresses around, and I think women had no other way but to accept it. Women had no rights. For women to actually leave their husbands would have been impossible because they had no financial, no other supports. They couldn't go out to work in the way that women can now, and with three children to support that would have been very difficult for my mother.

Another extraordinary thing is that although we had enough money, my father was extremely tight with it, though he would always pay for my mother to have good music lessons, and for my sister and me to have music lessons, I think that was a kind of feather in his cap. He had gifted children and a gifted wife, and socially that was very acceptable. It was the done thing for women to be artistic in that way; that was the role of women.

I think in terms of the social life we lived it was very structured.

There were certain people who left their cards, and those were the people that my mother would socialise with, and we would socialise with their children, and not with other children. It was very carefully structured as to who would forward my father's career, or uphold the status that he had, and there was enormous snobbery in that.

When I was eight we left Breslau and came to Freiburg. My father bought some land on which to build a family house. He hoped that the three of us would get married and have houses on the land – a sort of manorial estate. In 1936 that was a crazy way of thinking because all the writing was on the wall, but he could never believe that in the Germany he loved anything so drastic could happen, he lived in cuckoo land. As things turned out it was good to have the land because when Jews were forbidden to go into shops to buy food, we were self-contained.

I went to the village school in a very Catholic area in the Black Forest on the outskirts of Freiburg, and I had a very happy time at that school. But from a very early age I felt a failure and that I could never win my parents' approval in the way that my sister Lotte did, with the result that I felt I was the *bête noire*. I was the person who was always on the wrong side, and the rebel. I think looking back on it that was my sense of survival. I was the naughty one. I was the one who got into scrapes. I did all kinds of deceitful things, like changing the marks in my report book, changing fours into ones. I lied a tremendous amount, and later on also stole quite a lot. I remember a tremendous fuss once because I'd gone into the larder and eaten a piece of meat which was put by for my father, and totally denied I'd done it. For three weeks I was in a kind of land on my own, and each night my sister was sent in to my room to ask whether I'd done it. I think that kind of situation was part and parcel of my relationship with the family and my parents at that time.

My mother led her own life very much. She had her circle of friends with all the afternoon coffee parties and going to the opera and concert in the evening. For me, Elise, the cook/nanny, was always the person who was there for me. I really adored her, and she adored me. She was the person to whom I was sent, when I was sent away from the dinner table because I wasn't eating. Well, that became kind of a game. My mother would be the person who'd be the disciplinarian and Elise would be the person who'd cuddle me, but very much more on my terms than when my mother showed me affection.

I always felt, even from a very early age, that I ought to love my mother more, and didn't. That became very poignant at the time when I was actually leaving Germany when I was eleven. She was in hospital having a hysterectomy, and my sister, who was supposed to come with me, stayed behind to look after her. I had been visiting her in hospital for a couple of weeks and always passed by a chocolate shop, and in the window was a little gold watch made out of chocolate, and I had my eye on this, but I hadn't got enough pocket money to buy it until the very end. Then came the awful moment when I had to decide whether to keep that chocolate watch and take it with me or give it to my mother. I gave it to her and she was delighted. She was very touched by it. I then found myself crying when I said goodbye to her and I knew, but she didn't, that I was crying because I'd left my watch behind. That was something that stayed with me as a kind of guilt for many many years afterwards – that I would not have cried to say goodbye to my mother but I did cry to say goodbye to the chocolate gold watch, and I think that kind of thing says something about where I stood with my mother then.

So I lived very much in my imagination. When I was bad I was often sent up to my room to go to bed, and I would tell myself stories, endless stories. I found fantasy a sort of escape route. I also remember having at any house that we lived in, a favourite tree that I would climb and sit in. It was a kind of oasis where I could get away from it all, and there again I would fantasise quite a lot. In Freiburg quite close to our house was a field covered with wild snapdragons. I remember sitting in that field talking to the flowers and making them talk back to me.

Apart from that I was a tomboy and I remember most of my companions were boys. I felt very honoured because I was part of the boys' gang in the village, and that felt good. I never found it difficult to make friends, and to fall out with them and fall in again. I've always been blessed with a lot of friends, and there's always been, at any stage in my life – and I go back to six years old when I had my first boyfriend – a very close relationship with somebody, and considerable trauma when for one reason or another that had to break up. I remember being very upset when that first boyfriend – Christopher – couldn't be asked to my birthday party because by that time it was already dangerous for non-Jewish people to be socialising with Jewish people. I was also sent home from school, because somebody had objected to me being in the school choir preparing for Corpus Christi. My mother put me on her knee and said, 'Well, it's because you're Jewish', and I said 'What on earth has that got to do with it?' And then very shortly after that I was not able to go to school at all.

We were not practising Jews, though I had quite an experience of it. My mother's sister married a devout Jew and I often used to spend Easter there and Passover, so I do remember Jewish ceremonies and was very impressed with them. I suppose as a child it was almost a kind of magic ritual, though I think possibly more than that. I think children have the capacity for the spiritual and a sense of wonder and mystery.

The bit that I didn't like about God was that He was a father, but I was also fascinated by the idea that there might be a father different to my father. There was a certain amount of fear in this God who could be like my father, who would check up on me and punish me and expect me to be perfect when I couldn't be. My father once said when we asked him what did he want for his birthday, 'I just want an assurance that you're going to be good for a year, and if you can't give me that don't worry about the present.' That kind of Victorian and neurotic attitude to children made the idea of God the Father not terribly attractive, though there was an occasion when I experienced Christianity as meaningful and protective towards me.

My sister and I were called out of school, out of an orchestra practice, and told by a teacher to go home a different way to the way we would normally go. That way we didn't see the cattle trucks of Jews – hundreds of them – that were being whipped and jeered through the main streets of Freiburg, into the synagogue where they were burnt. For that woman to take the risk of sending two Jewish girls home safely – that could have cost her her life at that stage . . . There was also another teacher who used to greet me with the greeting *'Grüss Gott'* (which is 'God be with you'). And I remember her saying that she would no longer be able to say it to me because she would have to give the Hitler salute, but that it would be a secret between us, that she would raise her hand in the Hitler salute and yet in her heart she would say *'Grüss Gott'*. And that impressed me enormously as a child, because this God element was something to do with what goes on in your heart. The thought that God could be somewhere in there was fascinating.

Apart from that brief period at secondary school, that was the end of school for me. I enjoyed school, even though I didn't do well, and I enjoyed being there with my friends, but now I lost the opportunity of playing with people. In the last six months of that year I began to feel very isolated because one by one my friends were all withdrawn.

I remember my mother explaining to me it was because we were Jewish and that there were certain things we had to be extremely careful about, e.g. we couldn't go into shops or swimming baths. If I remember anything it was a feeling of solidarity in the family at that time that these were rules I had to keep, partly because my brother was literally whisked off to Switzerland when he had in some way told a group of Hitler youths that we had 'forbidden books' in the house. He was sent to Zürich, and he was fostered there by a family.

I remember being very frightened at that stage. The pogroms against the Jews were increasing. My mother and sister went to Freiburg with suitcases full of our silver because every bit of silver and gold in the house had to be given in. In some parts of Germany, people's gold fillings were taken out. Why I remember it particularly was because my mother had to take a watch an aunt had given to me, a little gold watch, which I was enormously proud of and very attached to. (Watches seem to have played an enormous part in my life!) She handed this watch to the official who'd just taken the suitcases of all her silver, all the stuff that she got when she first got married and so on . . . It was just thrown onto a pile of silver, candlesticks, cutlery, plates, whatever, jugs, jewellery, all just in one big pile like a rubbish heap. She gave this watch to the man and said that it belonged to her daughter and he said, 'I have a daughter too,' and he looked at it and said, 'This is not gold,' and gave it back to her. I remember my mother coming back with this little watch, and it was only in later years that I realise what it must have meant for her.

I remember also being very aware of people disappearing, and asking my mother once where Mr so-and-so was. We were outside a tram and she made it very clear to me that I wasn't to ask that question, and then when we got home explaining that you mustn't ask questions like that because if you do then a little box will come through the post with your ashes. That was in fact what had happened to him. His wife got a box with his ashes. This was part of the terrorising that went on. And it was a period of great fear. Having a very vivid imagination, and a confused idea of who God was, I thought that sooner or later somebody would catch up with me and something terrible would happen to my family.

I think the other very traumatic thing that happened to us was that my sister's friend was one of the young people who was rounded up and arrested. She was at any rate left standing with a group of young people in the hot sun on a flat roof, because she had associations with a Jewish girl, my sister. It was a kind of punishment presumably. Anyway, she had a heart condition and collapsed and died. That was something that was not talked about a great deal but made an enormous impression on me, the anger and the fear about that. There was a lot of anger in me at that time, of the unfairness of things. The unfairness of the way that my father dealt with us and the unfairness of this whole business about being Jewish, that to be Jewish was dirty and unacceptable, and that in some way I was dirty and unacceptable. And yet there was anger in knowing that that wasn't so, and I felt a tremendous need to prove that I wasn't like that.

I think all those experiences, although they were painful, in later life were things that I valued. None of those things have been left as negative experiences. In one way or the other they've been woven into my life and are things I can look back on and say, 'Well I'm glad I had that experience because that helped me with so-and-so.' But at the time it was frightening.

There was also the rebel bit in me that became very devious

and very manipulative. I would go into shops at the other end of town and I had my parents' backing on this because I was fair haired and didn't look Jewish. I got a tremendous kick out of cheating the system, and quite honestly that is still with me now. Getting the better of the system when the system is tyrannical in any way is a very strong streak in me, and working and living for a more just society is very important to me. And anger is a very strong part of me, yes. It's one of those areas of my life which I find difficult to live with myself, and other people find it difficult. I would say through my AIDS work I've come to terms with that as never before, and can now see something creative in my anger. And I am in fact much less angry than I used to be. But anger I think stems from that time as something which was too dangerous to be expressed and therefore I would keep it within myself.

After this year my father decided that we should emigrate. It was after the murder of Jews in the Kristallnacht, which was a horrendous experience. My father had the idea that we would go to England, South America or Canada. He wanted as much space between himself and Germany as possible; he was very depressed, very angry. I think he was a very depressed man. And I think a lot of his anger came out onto us, the injustice and the disappoint- ment and the fact that his dream had been shattered. Whilst he was very powerful within his family, he was powerless against Hitler.

Soon after that, the immigration numbers for my sister and myself came up together for placements in Oxford, but because of my mother's illness Lotte stayed with her. My father had already been tipped off that it was time for him to leave, and had gone to Luxembourg. Lotte and I were scheduled to go out in a children's transport, and I can't actually remember leaving home, which is interesting. I have no real memory of leaving the house. I don't even know who took me to the station, which is strange. But I remember being very excited about going, I was actually happy to go. I was nearly twelve, and it seemed like a new start and somehow exciting. I saw my family life as something I wanted to get away from. I think a bit of me was always an optimist and thought that if I started a new phase of life then all this business about being Jewish and dirty and unacceptable would disappear. That was something that really weighed quite heavily on me, knowing that the outer label didn't fit the inner one.

I came on a train with two hundred other children to Ostend, and remember being given packets of sandwiches which had white bread, and we hadn't seen white bread for well over a year, and thought that that was wonderful. White bread and banana, I remember that very clearly. I remember also queuing up for this and seeing children behind me clutching little ones, and trying to quieten them as they were crying. The youngest on that transport was about two and a half, I think, and I remember feeling very grown-up because I was there on my own.

When we arrived in England people were very kind, but I remember thinking, 'This is a little bit like being in a cattle truck,' because we had our names put on us, we were labelled, and I hated that. We were in a large waiting room, waiting for people to come and pick us up, and it felt very much like an auction. My feeling of suspicion of anyone official was very much around. I remember going to spend a penny, and when I came out, holding out my hand for the attendant to take money from me, because I didn't know how much to give her, and thinking, 'I bet she's taken more money than she needed,' which was a nasty thing to think. But that was the kind of feeling with which I arrived: a lot of suspicion about people, and how they would act, and their motives.

I felt quite relieved when a very good-looking young man picked me up. He was the son of the couple who fostered me, a local headmaster and his wife, and for the first four weeks I was on my own. My sister then came over on the next transport and was about ten minutes away from where I lived. By that time I'd already picked up quite a bit of English, amazing how quickly one picks it up, and about six months later my parents came over, and I was immensely proud that I could take my mother shopping.

My sister and I never spoke German because by that time it was already not wise to advertise that you were German. War hadn't broken out but there was tension. And I think one of my biggest shocks and disappointments when I came to England was that I seemed to have come from the frying pan into the fire as far as my dream was concerned. It didn't matter being Jewish, but it *did* matter being German. Couldn't win. That felt pretty bad, and I think that was a shadow for me, oh, for the next ten, twenty years. I remember wanting to hide the fact that I was German and feeling that there was really nothing to be proud of when the experience during my lifetime was of Nazi Germany. I didn't belong anywhere, and also, in terms of language, I stopped learning German by the time I was twelve and so never developed an adult vocabulary, and yet I don't feel that English is my own language.

Fitting in socially in England was extremely difficult. My sister and I were sent to the same school in Oxford, a day school, Milham Ford, and Lotte, within a year of being in the equivalent of GCSE, got her exams and was in the first tennis six and the first hockey team and all that. I just couldn't cope with English education at all. The whole business about playing *games* was just beyond me. The seriousness with which teams were picked, and knowing that I would always be the last one to be picked, and the groans from whichever team had to have me. The idea of spending two hours running with a stick in your hand chasing a ball or trying to get away from it . . . I just simply could not understand! So that was a very difficult part of life, and I only lasted four terms at that school when by mutual agreement it was felt that it was time I moved on.

The person with whom my mother was living at that time – as a cook – helped to finance a place for me at boarding school. That was a happy move because it was a very progressive school and ran its own farm, on democratic lines, and the fact that we didn't have to play games but looked after the animals was very appealing, very attractive. I loved it, but I did virtually no work and failed my exams.

I think at that time I was still very depressed. I was confused about myself and the world I lived in. I was mixing with people who had stable homes and who were socially very middle class – people with whom I would normally get on, except you couldn't let on that your mother was a cook and that you were on a sponsored place and didn't have enough pocket money and couldn't have the holidays and do the things that other people did. So I stole things like bits of uniform in order to be like everybody else because the things my mother could afford to buy me were that much cheaper and looked different. I remember stealing things like pants and taking name-tapes out and putting my own in, and also stealing sweets. All the kinds of things that deprived kids do, and being quite compulsive about it, and extremely expert about not getting caught. I had become very expert at showing one part of myself to the public and living in a different part of myself privately.

Publicly I was the cheerful, bright, somewhat extrovert person, but by nature I'm really very introverted. I was very musical and that was part of my public bit. I played the piano, and I was very adequate. At college later on I was given lessons because Myra Hess came one evening and did some spotting and suggested I should have some. I took it as my main subject in college, but at school it was just for myself, though it meant that when there were parties and country dancing I was chosen to play. It was my thing.

As I said, my parents had come over to England, and the only way that they could stay was if they could find some kind of work, and as domestic work was the only thing that was available, my mother was given this position as a cook in a household with a family with whom she became lifelong friends. At the time it was horrendous for her. She had a little room in what we would have called the servants' quarters, and I think what that meant for her was something that even now she finds quite difficult to talk about, except that she knew it had to be done. She had not only the anguish of becoming 'the cook' but my father insisted that she should come every morning before she started her duties in the house, to clean up his room, and she went on her bicycle and cycled over to him and then came back in time to cook the breakfast for the people in the house. She was too frightened of what the consequences would be if she said no.

My father lived in a room on his own in another part of the town, half an hour's distance away, and got a job packing cardboard boxes, which for him, with all his inbuilt feeling about status being so important, was just as near to the last straw as he could get to. My brother was by this time also in England and was attached to the Land Army, agriculture. But very soon after the outbreak of the war my father and my brother were interned on the Isle of Man and imprisoned during the war years.

It was shortly after my father was released after two years, on health grounds, that the marriage broke up. I have a very traumatic memory of that time, again in connection with my father's violence. He and I were walking in the university park and something I said incited his anger, I don't even know what it was, and he hit me across the face publicly. I was fourteen by this time, and I was absolutely livid. I remember standing in front of him and saying, 'This is the end, I'm never going to see you again,' and turning heel and walking away. That was in fact the last time I had any . . . I saw him once across the road after that but that was the last communication I had with my father, and I remember going home and telling my mother what had happened, and being surprised that she didn't remonstrate with me. I realised she was quite relieved that I'd actually done that.

Looking back on it, I think for me one of the horrendous bits about that was that having taken the decision to sever the relationship with my father I was then landed in this female alliance of the women against the men, and I felt very separated from my brother. When my father's immigration papers to the USA came through, he asked us all to come with him, and my mother, I think for the first time in her life, stood up to him and said no. She and Lotte and I would stay in England.

She started working as a matron in a school: she felt she needed to do that in order to earn enough money to keep me at school. She had one or two jobs like that, and finally ended up as bursar at Chorley Wood College for the Blind. Throughout that time she maintained me. She saved money to buy me clothes, and for many years one of my treasured possessions were the volumes of Mozart and Beethoven sonatas which she'd bought secondhand for me.

I left school at sixteen and did a two year nursery training. I then realised I would need some qualifications so did a year's au pair in Cambridge – three children in a very chaotic family – and had tutoring to get my exams. It suited me admirably. I enjoyed the children and did most of my studies in the early hours of the morning because at that stage I also made friends with a group of students, so had my first experience of real boyfriends. That was a very happy year for me, very much sowing my wild oats. I had a fairly riotous time, but there was doubt in my own mind about whether I would get through my exams. I got in a real panic about that, and I remember thinking, 'If I don't get those exams then there's just no future for me at all.' I decided then I would commit suicide and had actually chosen a tree near a beach where I was going to jump off, and to my great relief my results came through and I had passed. I spent years afterwards feeling intensely guilty about that. I wasn't at that time a Christian but there was just a deep-down feeling that that was an aggressive act which I had no right to perform. I don't know whether I would ever have carried it through anyway, but I think it was the ultimate of years of depression.

One of the things I didn't mention about my schooldays was that I had long periods of depression when I would just curl up and go to sleep on my own somewhere. And I think that that suicidal period was really the culmination of all that had been going on with the upheavals in Germany, the disintegration of life, the fearfulness and the cruelty of it all. And not having a faith at that time, wondering, you know, what was the point of it all? There was no point at all. No point in growing up either.

But I did grow up, and having got my exams I got into college at Cambridge, at Homerton. And there I had my first really serious boyfriend. I was deeply in love with this person, and it was physically a very close relationship, though we didn't actually sleep together. Like many student relationships, we spent a great deal of time together, having more free time at that stage in life than I'd ever had before. We wrote to each other whenever we weren't together, and though we never went away on holiday together, if we went out to parties I would stay overnight with his parents. I felt the difficulty of not having a home at that time where he could come and stay, because I stayed wherever my mother worked, which was at that stage at the college for the blind, and uncomfortable knowing what my own social background would have been like had there not been the disruptions.

I certainly fantasised about marriage and having six kids with him, though even then I had a feeling that perhaps what I really wanted was children rather than getting married; partly because my own experiences of childhood and seeing my parents' marriage made me wonder if any of the three of us who went through that experience would ever be able to sustain a marriage relationship. I remember tussling very much with that, but longing to have children. And even as I say this I've always maintained that for me the most difficult part of the vow of chastity that I took later was not having children of my own. But at that time – I was about twenty or twenty-one – life was just exciting and wonderful.

The relationship continued for about four years, at the end of which he decided to marry somebody else, and that was a tremendous blow. It was sudden for him. He'd met somebody at a Golf Club ball and they decided to get married. It was a great shock, but at the same time there was also a sense of relief. Looking back on it I think that it wasn't only that I felt I wouldn't be able to enter into a marriage relationship because of all the brokenness in my own family, but somewhere there was a mysterious sort of awareness that I was being called to something else, though I certainly didn't want to know about it.

As part of my Social Studies course I did a year of philosophy. And while we were doing Greek philosophy I felt again a sort of urge to find out 'Is there a God?' and it was during that year that I was introduced by a friend to the Dominicans at Haverstock Hill, and had instruction there. This was not with a view to becoming a Christian, I just wanted to know more about it. But I did ask to be baptised at the end of the year. My sister had already been baptised into the Church of England, and I remember saying nothing would ever move me to do something like that, it was just clutching at psychological straws and I wouldn't need that. And when I did, it was a big blow to my mother, who in the meantime had followed my sister into the Church of England, because I'd decided to become a Catholic. I think she found that really hard – why was I being different?

But I needed to be different. I needed space for myself. I think I also felt that the Church of England had a very middle-class ring about it, and was for very good people, and I didn't feel comfortable in that. I was appalled by the history of the Catholic Church, particularly in the Middle Ages. But, I felt, a church that can survive all that is a church for sinners, and therefore there was room for me there. God must exist if the amount of evil that went on hadn't triumphed and destroyed that church. So somehow my belief in God and my awareness of not wanting to be in a comfortable middle-class club veered me very much towards Catholicism; it just seemed more in tune with my own inner chaos. I also liked the idea of a universal church. I liked the fact that at that time one could go to any part of the world and follow the mass. Globalism has always appealed to me because nationalism is not attractive to me. Looking back on it I can see the need to have the security of something that seems to have roots deep deep down. It was to do with security, undoubtedly. The boundaries seemed to be much clearer.

That year was a year of discovery. It felt like new horizons opening up. That's often been my experience at different stages in life. I really looked forward to the weekly sessions and didn't find faith difficult to embrace. I don't think intrinsic faith has ever been a real difficulty for me. Maybe that's yet to come. Once I'd started that year the belief that God was there was very deep.

I think there's a right moment in a person's life when you can actually respond to a gift, and having touched rock-bottom there had to be a coming up. But the extraordinary thing looking back on it, is that however painful it was – and that was one of the most personally painful periods in my life – I just have a sense of wonder of the process of life, and how right it is that I didn't enter into that marriage. At least it feels like that now.

But as I said at the beginning, for me the one regret, the one thing that I really miss as a woman is not having had children. I can say that now accepting it, but in my thirties I found it very difficult to accept, and I've found it hard to accept being single, though in a sense that is what gives value now to my understanding of the vow. I think when I made my vows it was almost with a sense of naïvety, but I remember a very wise older Sister saying to me: 'You sign your cheque when you make the vow and you pay it out in pennies for the rest of your life.' That rings true now, because at different stages of my life I have queried leaving, or longed to be in a particular relationship with somebody as a twosome. At the time I don't think I saw those feelings as part of a normal maturation process, but looking back I can see that that is what they were, and it's good. It's very painful, but it's good.

I think the person who was really the most formative influence at that time was a friend called Lucy who was twenty years older than I was. She and I became very close friends. She was a Catholic, and spoke to me about her faith, and we had great arguments about the existence of God and faith and the Catholic Church. It was really through her that I met the Dominicans, and it was also through her that I later entered the Society of the Holy Child Jesus. She had taught with these nuns and had taken me on a bet to Cavendish Square to meet them. The bet was that she could show me some nuns who were human, and I just thought they couldn't exist.

Having been introduced to the nuns here I had to concede that they were human, but I also thought that they were exceedingly upper class and snobbish. In fact that wasn't true: their attitude to education was something that I felt in tune with. It was very creative, very progressive. I was offered a post at one of their schools near Sevenoaks. There were only seventeen children in that class and most of them came from very wealthy homes and at that time I was teaching at a primary school in a deprived area with fifty-two children in the class. And I just thought 'That would be too easy a job, I'd be bored stiff.' On principle I didn't feel happy with it. So I lost contact with them for a couple of years, and then when I started thinking about religious life, Lucy said to me, 'Why don't you go back to Cavendish Square?' and I found myself saying – one of those rare moments that you some-times experience – 'If I go to see them, I know I will enter.' I went to see them, and six months later I was in the Novitiate.

The idea of becoming a nun really felt dreadful. Becoming a Catholic was in a sense extraordinary enough. Bad enough, if you like, because it meant a U-turn for me, breaking through a barrier. But nuns, I thought, were just the most inhuman creatures, and I felt too that my disappointment in my love affair – well, I felt

that nuns were probably all people who'd had that kind of experience and who were running away from things, and I wasn't going
to do that. But after I had come into the Church, I had much
more of a faith experience then, an experience of God as a person
to whom I could relate, and who related to me – in a mysterious
way but nevertheless real. In response to this great gift of faith I
wanted to give myself to God, and thought about various ways
in which I might do that. One of them was to do some work with
Voluntary Service Overseas, but that still had the feeling of a
partial commitment, and I really wanted to be able to commit
myself totally. Becoming a nun seemed the appropriate way to do
it.

Suddenly things made sense. I think the overwhelming fear of
the power of evil and destruction, and the feeling that Christ had
actually triumphed over that, was an inner release for myself. And
with that came a tremendous joy. I'd always loved everything in
creation; flowers and birds and trees and animals. They were
always very much part of my life, and even as a child I loved
finding the first spring flowers or making the first footprint on
snow. Somehow or other they hung together now. They weren't
just beautiful things to look at, but the work of a creator who I
was getting to know, and who knew me and accepted me, though
I still found it very difficult to accept myself. I think there were
decades of struggle and very often periods of doubt – particularly
just before my profession as a Sister. You know: was it all a make-
believe, was it all a sham? Did God really know me? I was aware
that there were parts of me that I didn't know myself, and I
wondered whether someone as broken and as disintegrated as I
had experienced myself to be would be acceptable in religious life.

One of the unconscious awarenesses of that time, from the time
of my own love affair onwards, was my uncertainty about relationships with men. In the family I always had the reputation of being
a flirt, and I think that said something about the kind of superficial
relationships I tended to have because I was frightened to enter
into something more deep. Apart from getting hurt again, there
was also that deeper fear of the experience that my parents went
through. So I think men proved to be a frightening force in my

life. I had a great need for closeness, but I was scared of intimacy, certainly scared of sexual intimacy. I think I fantasised a great deal about sexuality as a child, and coupled it with cruelty and viciousness, because that's how I experienced my father, and I knew that my parents slept apart, so the idea of sexual relationship being something loving and pleasant was not part of my experience. I also experienced men generally as being extraordinarily dominant, and the rebel in me resented that. Even though there was a much more liberal view about women in the 1940s and 1950s in England than we'd experienced in Germany, it was still very restrictive.

Before entering the Novitiate I'd lived with Lucy for five years, and that was a very close and satisfying friendship, and very difficult to give up. Having had that independence, to come into a Noviceship at thirty was an extraordinary experience, a watershed really. I often wonder now how I survived that. But I think the group of us that were in together saw it as a bit of a joke, a bit like being in the army – you put up with certain things in order to achieve the end that you've come for.

I felt unthreatened by Lucy in the way that I would not have felt, I think, in a relationship with a man. The physical sharing, the everyday arrangement of things, was very harmonious, and leaving all that was very hard. It was never a genital relationship, but it was very very close. And given the fact that she was twenty years older than I was, the break came at a difficult time for her. She lived with another friend for a while, in fact with a couple of different people, and we drifted apart.

During the first year of the Noviceship I wasn't allowed to have any contact with anybody. I didn't see my family at all, and in the second year I would see them for about three hours once in a blue moon. That was artificial. Dreadful. My mother, with her experiences of Nazi Germany, went through something near a breakdown during the first year because she thought that I would be indoctrinated, that I'd be totally estranged from her. When she came down we weren't allowed to have food together at first. We were never allowed to eat with friends, it was just ridiculous. She felt that we were probably just eating dry bread and water, and as a German-Jewish mother that was horrendous for her. Food, and feeding people you love, is so important for her. So not to be able to share that – it was so cruel.

For Lucy I think it was just a mysterious trying time. I went through a very confused time too, wondering was that relationship unnatural, was it wrong? And yet I felt that the love between us was so real and so right, of a very different quality to my love for Mick, the man that I had been in love with. We were seeking mutually for what was right for the other. It wasn't the quality of two sisters. It wasn't a maternal relationship, even though she was older. It was very different, and I missed her intensely, and felt a lot of anger about this being the right decision. Is this what loving God is about, that you have to hurt somebody else?

I felt called, and tried to resist that call. And yet I felt that the call was like an inner certainty that this is what I must do. If I wanted to know and experience love, then this was the way. It was an unknown way, it was mysterious, but faith told me that to take that step in the dark was necessary. That's what faith in a sense is all about – *not* knowing and yet trusting in the unfolding love. And it wasn't just that. Somewhere I had a part to play to bring love into the world to somehow redress the evil that I had experienced in the holocaust, and perhaps the reason for me being alive and having come through that experience was that I had a part to play and that it would unfold. Part of becoming a Christian was about that.

I had to allow God to show me the way. God was saying, 'This is what I invite you to. You don't have to take it, but this is an invitation. And yes it does mean leaving a lot of other things, a lot of other plans, and a lot of other people, behind. But it is a way that's open to you.' I think that that's the way I experienced it at the time, as an invitation. There was a choice about it, and it gave me an opportunity of proving my love to God and doing it without any advancement for myself.

There's a bit of me that has always wanted to be totally committed to what I do. The dream was that I was going to marry somebody and go off on a Scottish island and grow wholefoods and organic things and be wholehearted in that way. And a bit of that dream is still around. I love getting away from it all, and holistic living is very dear to me. But that love was a leap into the dark, and during my first few months I felt absolutely terrible. Absolutely terrible! I remember standing with one of my fellow Postulants at a window, watching the railway, and saying: 'We'll wait until Friday and then we'll say we'll go.' This happened week after week. Eventually the railway was closed, and then there was that awful feeling of the escape route being cut off.

At the end of the first six months the idea of actually making a commitment and receiving a habit was horrendous. The thing that I *really* hated was this whole symbolism of marriage. I've never ever been able to accept the idea of being married to Christ. I just can't go along with it, because I see marriage as a loving union between two human beings, not only for the procreation of children but for its own sake. I see myself in a total commitment to Christ but I *don't* call it a marriage, and I feel uncomfortable with the confusion of symbols like having to dress up in a white dress. I remember really hating it, and knowing how much my mother would hate it. It was just excruciating for her because, of all of us, she had always hoped that I would marry and give her the grandchildren she longed for, and here was this parody of a wedding. I don't know how she ever sat through it. It was one of the days which should have been a happy day but which I remember with real anguish. The whole thing seemed a kind of charade, except the promises I was asked to make, to commit myself to Christ, and that felt real, though the reality of it only got played out very much later.

The Noviceship period was two and a half years for me. The first year I was just longing to be sent home. I didn't want to take the step myself, but I would have welcomed it if I'd been called into a room and told, well, this isn't the right life for you. The second year I was dead scared of being sent home. I really wanted to stay, even though it was a struggle and so much of our lifestyle was totally foreign to me.

For instance, our letters were opened, and I thought that was horrendous. The incoming letters were read, and it smacked to me of the Nazi regime where letters and phone calls were intercepted. The whole business of somebody invading your life, your person, seemed to me appalling. The group living I found very difficult too. Having lived an ordinary adult life with all the decisions that go with that – all the freedoms that go with that – and then not being able to go out or have money to spend. Having had my own salary I now no longer had any control over my own money, and that felt very strange. It also felt very good in many ways, it felt very freeing, and that is something which I think the vow of poverty does, it actually frees you.

The other thing that I remember about the vow of poverty is that like all the other vows the teaching on it as I experienced it was really very negative. You *gave things up*, and that was the considered virtue. You owned nothing of your own. We had it written into our Rule that if we were given anything, however small, it was taken to the Superior. At Christmas-time, for example, if you received small gifts you would either ask our Superior if you could use them, or they would be put into a general pool and either used by the community or given away as gifts for other people, so you owned just nothing. And though I saw that as an ideal I did find that very difficult. What I found even more difficult was asking permission to use something rather than give it up. But on the other hand that made for some form of uniformity. If you're living with people, some of whom have got rich relatives or wealthy friends, and others who haven't, to avoid some kind of feeling of hurt and lack of equality it seemed a reasonable thing to do.

I remember towards the end of the Noviceship the questions came up about actually signing papers to say that we gave up the right to any dowry money, and money that might come through bequests, that this would be for the Society. I remember wondering, if I do come out and I give up superannuation, where am I going to be? I remember spending a lot of time thinking it through, and that was a point of knowing I was committing myself. So poverty at that time just meant doing without and giving up things I'd been used to having, and finding that quite difficult.

Once we started coming out of the habit and buying clothes, I would, for instance, think it was wrong to spend a lot of money on an article of clothing if I could get it in Oxfam. I think in some ways that was linked with the fact that as a refugee adolescent at school and so on, there was no money available compared with what other kids had. We had lived on a shoestring for so long that poverty meant something in those terms long before I entered. I had quite strong feelings about the standard of living in the community and I was often out on a limb about that: I think I was quite critical. I don't think I'd ever really sat down and worked out that doing without a colour telly for example was nothing to do with poverty. There were a lot of areas of confusion in my own thinking there. There was a time when a simple lifestyle meant that we never sat on an easy chair. That was something that only the older nuns did – and that was called poverty. And when I first started teaching with this order, I had a little cubicle in the children's dormitory. When I did have a room of my own I'd never think of putting pictures up as I have here. Again, that just didn't seem proper.

It has changed enormously. And yet perhaps all that was a necessary stage to go through, and there was some sense in that kind of abnegation; living in a very materialistic world it made a statement about things, which was important, and there was something positive in that. But I see poverty much more now in terms of identifying with the marginalised, with the third world poor, who have no voice, who have no power. It has much less to do with money now. In fact, I'd be quite happy to spend some money in order to have the time to do something else. I wouldn't think twice now about taking a taxi in order to get from A to B in order to spend more time with whoever I'm going to see. And tonight, for example, I'm cooking supper: I can do an interview from four to six because I can do a quick supper from the freezer, but if I actually made it from scratch we wouldn't be having this interview. One has to weigh up what is important in terms of energy. We're getting older as a community and it's sometimes good to spend money in order to make life easier for people in their sixties and seventies who are doing a job and coming in late in the evening. These days we haven't got the time that we might have if one person did all the cooking.

Poverty – poverty of spirit – has more to do with this being powerless, depending on God, depending on other people, giving up one's freedom of determination and choice and living much more in faith, giving up your own agenda. And that kind of faith, and that kind of love, has to do with letting go of what I'd want to do more. It means living in the readiness to follow what I think is my calling even if it leads me in a direction where I feel dead scared that I won't be able to do it. And in a sense the whole of the AIDS work has been like that. There are so many unexpected calls within calls in this kind of work, things I would never normally have chosen to do. Like last Saturday: I would not normally have chosen to have spent a whole day being involved in a workshop with people to make sense of homosexuality, and giving my own personal story in that. Now I think you can only do that when you're poor – when you've got nothing to lose. And I think that's what poverty is about for me now, a sense that I've got nothing to lose and I can put myself at risk and try and do things without being afraid of failure because it doesn't matter. That's what poverty's meant to do. That's where the real liberation comes, I think.

But at the time it was often a nonsense for me. Just like obedience, I just couldn't believe the pernickety bits and pieces that were called obedience – blind obedience. In our Rule we had a sentence – I can't remember it verbatim – which said that when the bell goes, even if you're in the middle of a letter, you put down your pen and go to wherever you're meant to be. That was obedience. A total handing-over of your life in its minutiae was obedience. I could see the principle of it in terms of that kind of self-emptying that Christ underwent when he became a human person, and yet, for myself aged thirty, that was incredibly hard. And I think what I struggled with was that it seemed almost destructive of anybody's personality to make decisions for them in order to show their obedience. It just did not make sense to me.

Neither did this emphasis on 'You keep the Rule and the Rule keeps you,' make sense to me either. Which meant that when the bell had gone for silence and somebody was upset and crying, you had the choice of keeping the Rule or being with that person. And so one was up against a whole lot of different issues from the normal way of relating to people as an adult. Throughout my religious life until perhaps about ten years ago, various Superiors would always say to me: 'The trouble with you, Eva, is that you have an authority problem.' And it was only when I was actually able to say to somebody once: 'Yes, you're absolutely right, I have, but you show me somebody who hasn't,' that I felt freed from that kind of label. I suddenly realised yes, I *have* got an authority problem and I *ought* to have an authority problem because there's so much nonsense about it, and everybody else sane ought to have an authority problem too.

The other thing which worried me a lot was the idea of the purification of one's own selfish desires. The idea of service, that we're there to serve one another, all that was fine. But the hypocrisy which surrounded a lot of that was something which really did bother me. For example, our lifestyle was meant to be a simple lifestyle. Now, round about particular feasts – you know, Christmas celebrations – like everybody else we would have extras, and yet we were never allowed to talk outside the community about those kind of things in case people got the wrong impression. Now those kind of pretences made for such false relationships with people that I couldn't see that as holy obedience.

What I *value* about obedience is the notion of common ownership and common life. But the extent of that! The word 'I' was totally obliterated, it was always 'our' things, and I think unless you had a sense of humour about that you'd never survive it. I mean to start talking about 'our' shoes! They're *your* shoes! Or 'our' books, or whatever. That is a form of trying to mould somebody into a way of thinking which I suppose had overtones of indoctrination I felt very uncomfortable about.

And chastity! Oh, chastity to me was just horrendous. Poverty was relatively easy, obedience was just a rebellious struggle, but chastity was so negative it just wasn't true. The drastic way in which that was presented to us really was extraordinary. It was much more to do with you abnegate this, you abnegate that, and any sexual fantasies you had, well you'd never share those with anybody because you'd be so afraid that you'd be out. Any sexual desires you had – well, I don't think I could ever have talked to anybody about that, so all that was internalised and that was very painful. I was very confused about it. And certainly when I came out of the Noviceship and started teaching I was quite suspect in my relationships with people outside the order. The kind of relationship I had with them allowed an emotional outlet, and there was a lot of confusion about what I felt I could do *professionally*, and what I mustn't do as a good nun.

So chastity really had to do with keeping the Rule, which I found extremely difficult, and I think I bent it from early on in all kinds of ways. I bent it particularly during the second year of my Noviceship when I really began to see God as a person, who was revealing himself to me through other people. And so my response to other people has always been a warm, loving, touching response, sexual but not genital, though at that stage I wouldn't have acknowledged it to myself as sexual. That only came much later.

I think in the sixties there were about eight or ten of us in the whole congregation (in England) who had what were called 'particular friendships'. It was very much frowned on by people who saw it as being potentially dangerous because it could arouse sexual feelings. It was also considered to be potentially destructive to community life. The word 'lesbian' would never have been used, and I remember thinking at that time 'I really don't know what that means, but this is obviously what some people are afraid of.' We were allowed to go away on holidays too. You weren't just spending your holiday time at another convent which was the usual procedure. So you could go out with a friend, but you also had to face coming back to a lot of disapproval. The idea was that you were not being as perfect a nun as you might be and that there was a lot of *dangerous* stuff around.

But it's been immensely important to me to know that somebody's sought a close relationship with me. Given my early experiences as a refugee, rejection, the feelings of not being acceptable, feeling different – that was reinforced in lots of ways in early religious life. And I've had a relationship since which has been difficult, and when it had to change I was hurt by that, I felt very bereft by that, I felt very angry about that. I mean it's taken three or four years to really feel at peace about that, and not to feel either that I or the other person has failed, which is often one's immediate reaction when a relationship breaks up. You think: 'What's gone wrong?'

So now when I deal with so many people who have to face that kind of brokenness, to have been there myself has become very important: to be able to own the broken bits in myself and to know that in time they will be healed. I'm going to meet that kind of brokenness if I'm going to love Christ who allowed himself to be broken for me, and if I talk about 'identifying' with people, then I need to identify with my own brokenness, otherwise it's just arrogant to say I identify with other people's. Brokenness is part of our humanity, whether we are nuns or whether we are not nuns.

The AIDS work I do has really changed my life. It came about at a time when what I had planned for myself was to do some psychiatric work with a GP, but it fell through. I went off on a three month course in spirituality, and a month into it I was looking at the passion of Christ and his experience of being mutilated and tortured while totally innocent, and I was aware that somewhere I had a hand in that. I became very aware of wanting to reach out to him, and feeling stuck in that, not knowing how, and then sensing the Lord saying 'Just go and do it.'

It's a long story but the 'Do it' became AIDS and I can tell you, I just didn't want to know! I didn't want to know because it touched the whole of that sexual area that I felt so unsure about, the homosexual area, and I just didn't know how to handle that. And yet it wouldn't go away, a little bit like the vocation to become a nun wouldn't go away, and I felt that I was on a kind of conveyor belt being sent from one person to the next – a little bit like St Paul after his blindness when he was sent to a certain address he didn't know and then passed on somewhere else. But with it came a real feeling of peace that I was moving in the right direction, however unknown, however frightening it was. And just coming back for a moment to the vow of chastity, a lot of my hang-up about chastity – though I couldn't have put it into words at the time – was to do with not knowing really about my own sexual identity, always assuming that I was a middle class, heterosexual woman, and since I've started this work it's really changed my life.

I think if you have deep-rooted fears, as I had, about sexuality, and particularly about homosexuality, to dare to own that there might be more to me than heterosexual woman had certain moral connotations which I would have found very difficult to take on board. The AIDS work brought me face to face with that area of fear because I moved into the homosexual community. Just going into the Terrence Higgins Trust and seeing mostly homosexual men, and some lesbians, was a culture shock and an emotional shock and a *religious* shock because I was now face to face with the thing I'd feared. And seeing that people were not what I'd feared but that here was a community of people who openly showed affection in the way that I had been inhibited from doing, and who were obviously caring, loving, good fun with each other, but could also cry with one another; all the social taboos seemed to come down once you entered the building. But I felt outside it, I felt rejected, until I gradually realised I was doing the rejecting. I was still thinking of 'them' and 'us'. And when I finally allowed 'them' to become 'we', that made a tremendous difference. I felt then that the very people that I had rejected were actually accepting me, and that was an overwhelming experience in terms of myself as a Christian.

I was also conscious that as a Christian I very often felt ashamed of the way in which the institutional Church responded to people whom it saw as "sinners". One of the first people I met at the Terrence Higgins Trust was an Anglican priest and I asked him what he was doing there. He said, 'I bury them when nobody else will.' The impact of that has never left me. And the shame that I feel as a Christian, that I belong to a Church where a large number of people feel that the wrath of God will come on homosexuals *regardless* of the quality of their relationships, and *regardless* of the fact that in the heterosexual community horrendous non-loving sexual activities and involvements take place. The hypocrisy of all that angered me and made me aware how involuntarily I have colluded with the system that calls itself Christian and allows those things to happen. I was appalled, partly because I realised that I had been totally unaware of the number of homosexuals who were in concentration camps, and the realisation that if you don't talk about a particular person or group of people you can annihilate them. There are many ways of annihilating people, and that really shook me rigid.

I also became aware as I worked with people that although I might think I was going in there to give support what I received was so much more. What I received was that widening of the horizon of ways of loving, that out of the uniqueness of different people God's love was allowed to come through to me and to other people because they were *there* – they had *not* been annihilated. Seeing, for example, the quality of love between two friends who are celebrating their twenty-fifth year together, or a bisexual man who'd been married and after fifteen years came out of that marriage and after a further five or six years is now in a relationship with another man. Seeing the growth in that person, somebody I got to know very well, and knowing how under institutional Christianity he would have been crippled for life – these are the kinds of things that made me re-think my vow of chastity. Chastity has to do with loving as you are, and allowing God's love to flow through you as you are and not as you want to be in order to conform to society. I have the image of an orchestra. We may not like the score, and we may not like our own particular score or that of the person next to us, but if we re-write the symphony by leaving out one particular section then we're really in danger of distorting the symphony of love that God created.

I think the other thing that I've learnt from this scene is that my stereotyped view of what it is to be 'a good loving person' has been very much influenced by the hypocritical, the standardised, and very often the political view of love. We're living in a consumer society where you have to succeed, there's no room for failure. And to be allowed to fail in a relationship, and allowing the other person to fail is to me a very important incarnational discovery of love. Christ failed. He failed totally at the end. And yet out of that failure came the resurrection.

The resurrection takes away a lot of fear of failure because it allows people freedom and a very different view of God. It can allow them to see the God of the second chances and the God of the seventy times seven. At the moment, I am currently in a very close relationship with somebody outside the community. And now, if I were to fail in my ideal of the vow of chastity, if sexual fantasies and longings and desires were around, I'd no longer run away from them because I know that the God who loves me is not a God who condemns failure. God knows that because I am a broken human being I may very well fail. There is within me, as there is in every other being, a longing for total union in love. However, I strive to love within the boundaries of my vows, and not in spite of them.

So in a strange way, although I say I chose to become a nun, I think it's only now that I'm beginning to choose. Because now I have the choice to leave the order and enter into a relationship with this other person, and there might be quite a strong pull to do that. The choice is to stay in the vowed relationship with Christ, and within that to love this other person, and I think it's the work with AIDS which has opened that kind of commitment for me: seeing people struggle to be themselves with the incredible degree of honesty and caring that is around, against incredible odds that can be life-threatening – and much more so than AIDS. One thing I have learnt is that AIDS is not the only life-threatening factor. What is threatening to the very existence of people are things like Clause 28, and prejudice and scapegoating and injustice. And when I think about children with AIDS . . . we're soon going to be living in an age where children with HIV will be undiagnosed in ordinary schools, so it is good for me to have had some experience of rejection and hurt, so I can be there not just alongside people, but also to fight for the rights of children and families. I can do that from the position of freedom that I have within a vowed life.

There was a lot of suspicion on the AIDS scene from people who knew I was a nun. There were people who were delighted to see somebody who was religious working at the grass root level. There were other people who thought I might have deserted the ship and was neither one or the other. Some people would say: 'How can you still be part of the Church, and you're certainly not part of the gay scene: where do you fit in?' I was seen by some, and still am, as a kind of impostor. None of these feelings would be expressed openly, but they are certainly around. Having said that, I feel more accepted on the AIDS scene than I've ever been anywhere else in my whole life. Partly I think because people who have been so scapegoated and at the receiving end of prejudice know how to not categorise people. Their own longing to be accepted as themselves enables them to accept other people. So there is a kind of honesty on the AIDS scene which isn't always around elsewhere. There's also much less status. I don't have a professional status label on this scene. I'm not the headmistress or the senior psychiatric social worker. I'm just Eva, and I'm accepted as Eva, rather than specifically as Eva who belongs to a Catholic religious order. And that I find very liberating, it liberates me to be myself.

In the last year I have actually become much more involved in the spiritual dimension of AIDS, in counselling, in giving retreats, in weekends for people who are HIV positive. A group of us have set up weekends away for people and they've been very meaningful, not in any specific Christian terms but just in allowing people to be themselves. I feel the gay community have given me 'permission to be me', within the framework of my vows, and I'm therefore able to allow other people to do that too. So I feel I've been given a kind of injection, a strength, from the very people I was most afraid of. And the lack of crap when you're dealing with people who have a limited lifespan is amazing: a lot of the things which engage our energies, and which are totally useless, fall away, and what matters then is relationships. What matters is when a twenty-year-old whose father used to beat him up in the hope of beating homosexuality out of him, would say, six months or so before he died: 'Do you think my dad will ever be proud of me?' and enabling that father to say that he was – not just to feel it, but to say it before the boy died. And the *difference* that made in that relationship. That's the level at which things happen, and it's good to be there. It changes everything. Your sense of priority alters.

You see a couple, one of whom is dying, and his partner goes home every lunch hour and evening to look after him, and by looking after I mean cleaning up every time he's sick and has diarrhoea. He took two years to die but he died in the arms of his partner, they were together, and that's a Calvary experience. And when you see love like that and then you hear the cries of, 'Get rid of the gays,' that's when you think: 'Whose side am I on?' Well, I know whose side I'm on: I'm on the side of love.

One of the things that I've come to appreciate in the religious life as I've grown older is this concept of process, that we're all on a journey. There's our own separate journey, there's the collective journey of us as a community and a religious order, and there's a pattern about that. If I look back on myself as a person in community one of the things that strikes me is that I've always been a very difficult person to live with. I can look back now with some compassion for myself, and see that given the circumstances of my life it was almost certain that I would find it difficult to live in community, to live with myself. And I think now, for the first time in my life, I feel comfortable in myself because I can accept my own brokenness without feeling it an irretrievable failure. The process of being in relationship with God and with others has brought me much closer into the mystery of what love is all about, and that has taken so much of the sting out of past guilt, feelings of failure, all the things that can cripple us.

When I started work with people who were HIV positive, it was a new experience for me *and* for the community I lived with. AIDS confronts us with two taboos – death and sexuality – and the *fear* around sexuality, the *fear* around death and dying, was something which I don't think anybody could have put into words but was almost tangible. It seemed to express itself in difficulties around communication at home because for the first three or four months the subject was hardly ever mentioned, and if I brought it up there could be quite an embarrassed silence. At the time I felt very hurt by that. I very quickly reverted to old patterns of feeling rejected, blaming myself, and yet not knowing how to put things right. And when that happened I separated myself out from the community. Although that has since changed, it was a period of great pain, great darkness.

Socialising with the community is difficult for me because most of my work in the evenings is on the phone. The very fact that they've given me a phone, and made this extra room available for me, has in some ways cut me off from them, but there's the awareness that this is their way of facilitating my work, making it possible. And just as I like that statue outside this building, with Mary standing *behind* the child, in a sense I feel very much that this is the position of the community with me, that they're behind me in a supportive way that I've never before experienced in religious life. There's a lot of interest in what I'm doing now, both from people inside and outside the community. The Congregation as a whole has become very conscious of the need to be involved with AIDS issues, and that is a cause for enormous gratitude.

Not only has the AIDS work influenced my understanding of sexuality, but it has influenced my relationship with God because until I was exposed to my own sexual identity, I'd always thought of God as masculine, as the father, the son. The possibility of the holy spirit being female, the spirit of love, of creation, hadn't really impinged on me before. The change now is seeing homo-sexuality and the feminine and masculine not as two separate things in little watertight boxes, but as very much a part of the whole of my being. There is the male and female in all of us. I therefore find it difficult to think of Jesus as being macho-mascu-line, particularly in terms of the caring/healing aspects of his character and his relationships with both men and women, and his freedom in them, like His closeness and intimacy with John. So I do see him as male but not in the stereotyped sense.

Towards God the Father there's been an enormous change. The very fact that until comparatively recently my feelings about my father were antagonistic and bound up with fear, still made it very difficult to relate to God as a father. It has only been in the last ten years, through talking about it, that I was able to separate out the feelings which belonged to my father, and to see God in a different way. The big difference now is that I do often think of God as 'She' and find myself very much in tune with the trend in theology which talks about God as 'She', and I interchange He or She quite happily now.

Christ's words 'Love one another as I have loved you' are the real challenge for me now. I couldn't in fidelity turn my back on Christ for whom my love has grown over the years. It would be a death-blow to myself if I broke that fidelity, and it would make any other relationship void. But I now know what it's like to struggle, and I'm glad, because I am more alive because of it. So I think in a way the gift of my sixties has been to learn to love responsibly. For the first time in my life I have some understanding of the pain of loving within my vows, as well as the peace and joy of desiring to fulfil them.

You asked me how I think people see me, see nuns. I think many people, and perhaps some men in particular, see us as powerful people, and we are regarded by some of the clergy as a threat. Nuns have very often been innovators. I think the very fact that many Sisters have been in, and are still in, leadership positions in education and reform, means that we are aware of the way in which society and the Church have, for centuries, colluded with attitudes which diminish women. That awareness makes us potentially powerful. Our vows are really about Kingdom values – social justice, preferential options for the poor, those kinds of issues, so we present a threat to some people who do not share our priorities. But the role of women as described in the gospel according to St Paul, is not acceptable to many women, including those who are in religious congregations. There have always been women in religious communities who have exercised a freedom which was staggering to the male world – particularly so in a male-dominated Church. Our own foundress, Cornelia Connelly, was a very controversial figure. So we are still a long way from 'equal opportunities' in the current structure of the Roman Catholic Church.

But I think it goes even deeper because it also has to do with the whole question of sexuality and spirituality, and people do not often feel comfortable about that. I think that some priests, for example, feel very threatened that their authority will be diminished if there is more shared teamwork ministry: it presents an enormous problem to those with a very narrow view of the roles of men and women.

There's also a strange projection of 'the good nun' that people put onto us, and 'the good nun' is compliant, she's like those dreadful statues of Mary, and that suits people. It suits the bossy male, it suits the powerful, authoritative Church institution and it fits in with the reactionary view that a woman's place is in the home and that she brings up children or is compliant in other ways in her service to the Church. People take up these artificial positions in order to maintain their own position of power, their own role in a very male-orientated world and Church, and anybody who has different ideas is a threat to authority.

So I just hope I live long enough to see the ordination of women. It makes such enormous sense to me. I feel equally strongly on the marriage of clergy in the Catholic Church. In terms of ministry it seems to me vital that the creative gifts of women and men can be used as needed in a society that cries out for that. When I think of the whole area of reconciliation and the work that needs to be done within all the churches, the role of women there as ministers is vital; and the role of women amongst the laity is vital too.

I remember watching the film of the installation of the first black woman bishop, and it was a deeply moving experience. It filled me with enormous sadness that this is not a universal practice, particularly in terms of black women in the Church: the Church is still so white. So for me, being a woman or being black are not separate issues; they're both part of the whole issue of allowing God's creativity in the diversity of colour, race, sex to be the Church. It's not for us to decide who we want to choose out of that medley of creativity. So I would campaign for the ordination of women, and my hope and my belief and my experience in practice is that it will come from the grass roots and not from the top.

I hope for a re-shaping of the whole concept of ministry, so that the original gospel truths can be lived out to meet present-day needs. I certainly no longer in conscience feel comfortable with the practice of the institutional Church at all times, and I know that there are many, many people, also within religious orders, who feel as I do about that. I remember thinking recently, thank God I'm not teaching sixth formers, because I would find it very difficult to teach the traditional Catholic doctrine on birth control. Certainly on the AIDS scene I have no problems about safer sex and condoms. Condoms are not one hundred per cent safe, and they are *not* the answer to the AIDS problem, but it is far better to practise safer sex than not to practise it.

I believe in the essential structure of the family as an ideal. I also know, and have experienced, a great deal of the brokenness within families and relationships, and hope that I can take the stance of not judging but seeking to understand that brokenness.

So as far as divorce is concerned, my psychiatric training would lead me to say that there are some people who should not live together. There is also, I think, a necessary process, both for heterosexuals and homosexuals, where people cannot make it the first time round. People have to learn how to live in relationships, and need the support of the Church, not the condemnation and the judgmental attitudes of the Church in that process.

For me the God of the second chance has become so important in my own life that not to recognise that in the lives of other people makes no sense. After all, I think that is the way that Our Lord dealt with people. I am aware that such views can be refuted by quoting Our Lord's teaching on marriage, as in the gospels of Luke and Matthew, but as well as the fact that our time and society is a different one from Christ's, I believe that the most important thing about Christ was His compassion. He understood the complexity of our broken human relationships and is, above all, the God who forgives not once only, but as often as needed. He is not a judging God.

My experiences in Germany and during the war brought death very close to me, but I think it wasn't something I was particularly conscious of. That changed radically in my work with AIDS, and the way that I think about death now is as a kind of paradox, as the light and shadow part of myself. I often find myself centring on a line from an Ignatian prayer which says: 'On each of my dyings shed your light and your love.' I see death and resurrection very much as a process in my own life, and in my own experience, in my own daily dying, the pain of that process is something that I'm very conscious of. The death of relationships. The new growth of relationships. The death of my ambitions and the letting go of things that are no longer important. So much freedom and new life has grown out of that.

But actually seeing people die . . . Even with all the violence in the early part of my life I had never seen a dead person until a thirteen-year-old girl at the school where I was teaching died of cancer, and there was a peacefulness about her which I would never forget. Seeing a couple of our Sisters after they died I had much the same kind of feeling.

But then my brother's death really brought death home to me. He and I were very close and it was an extremely difficult time when he was dying. He came home to die, to England, to my mother's, and he died in her home, in the room that I use when I go home. He had cancer, and I was the first one that he told. He came home from California and had about two or three months at home. That was traumatic; the diminishments of death were traumatic, and it was an extremely painful time for my mother. I mean, to be eighty odd and to see your son dying . . .

His death brought me very close to what death is all about. It made me realise the horror of death too, and my own fear of it. Dick was a very spiritual man but he didn't belong to any particular church and he had had an extremely difficult and painful life in many ways, so there was a lot of unfinished business in his life. But I was also aware of his letting go, and the last words he said have always been very precious to me. He said – the three of us were there, my mother, sister and I, and we three have grown so close now – he just looked up and he said, 'Thank you so very much.'

That death touched me very very deeply. Losing him was the closest personal loss I've had, and my anger with God, my anger with all the unfinished business and sadness in his life – that was with me for a good year or two. And each time I see the horror of physical mutilation, physical diminishment, on the AIDS scene, it's a deep anguish. Though I can echo what a father said when he saw his son dying. The boy's mother and lover were supporting him with their hands behind his pillow and trying to lift him to ease his breathing, and the father was at the foot of the bed. And the father said to me the next morning: 'You know, you may think this is silly, but when I looked at our George I looked at Christ.' And to me the whole thing was just a Calvary scene. It is repeated many many times, and it's always awesome and a privilege to be there. In all the grief work of the following year, 'being there' becomes the kind of central focal point. I think that 'being there' has become a crucial, meaningful, living phrase for me. Because being there at death also means that we can share the faith in resurrection, which may not come for a year or two –

often longer – but there usually comes a point sooner or later when it happens for somebody bereaved, somebody grieving.

I remember a young man who was dying, and his father had not allowed his lover to come into the house, and when finally he did so, when the lover was with the young man, shortly after that the young man died. He'd been waiting for his lover. And so much reconciliation comes through the person who has AIDS. It was the man who was dying who enabled the father to get over that hurdle of fear and anger. And the same father, when it came to the meal after the funeral, publicly asked that man to come and sit at the table with the family: that was new life for that father. So death to me is very life-giving. And there are so many signs of the resurrection. So much reconciliation comes from the cross, and if one didn't have faith and hope and love then it would be devastating.

What never ceases to amaze me is the quality of love which many gay couples have for each other, and this is what makes me so angry about the stance of the Church. It *really* makes me angry. That phrase of the early Church, 'See how these Christians love one another,' is what I see, whether they're Christians or not in the formal sense. It's such an example to a judgmental Church. And I'm not only talking about the Catholic Church now, I'm also talking about some of the fundamentalist evangelicals; about the minister who will say to the nurses, 'Don't pray with Catholics because they're not Christians,' or the ministers of a well-known church who won't bury people who are known to have died from an AIDS-related illness. That's still happening. Oh, the wrath-of-God brigade and I are poles apart.

If I were challenged on this point – as I am sometimes – I hope I would have the courage of my convictions. I hope I would not be pushed to make a decision about whether to remain a member of the Roman Catholic Church with the views that I have about homosexuality, because then in conscience I know I might have to make a decision which may or may not keep me within the institution. I *hope* it would never come to that, because after all, there are so many signs of hope, albeit small signs. I've recently been to Bodmin to see a new purpose-built home for people with AIDS, and a Congregation has given its property and resources to enable that to happen. Well, that's a sign, and it's a mustard-seed if you like, but it's the way things grow.

I think the other thing that I want to put on record is that working with the marginalised, working with people who I feared in many ways – they're the very people who've enabled me to know that I'm lovable. Being lovable and able to love is a relatively new experience for me, and I think it's one of the joys of growing older. I really enjoy growing older because I can look back and see the link and the sense of things which, when you're in the darkness and the confusion and the mess, you cannot see. Looking back, there isn't anything in my life that I regret because it makes so much sense in the present. And I would say that even of my failures. They're part of it.

I fear diminishment like everybody does. But I've no very strong feelings about my own death, because I can genuinely say: 'Into your hands I commend my spirit.' It's not something which predominates my thought, because I am much more conscious of the daily dyings, the daily letting go. And out of my Jewish experience has come so much opportunity: my hands have been opened to receive something else. That's something I've learnt from people with AIDS too.

So what I feel now is a growing experience of God's love as unchanging, constant, eternal, and that is what I want to *share* with others; that living is actually good, and being alive is very precious and a lot of fun. I don't think I've ever laughed and cried as much as I have done in the last four years – and there's been a great deal of laughter. Neither have I had such a sense of real hope, for myself and for other people, and that's exciting, there's a kind of new birth feeling in that. So if somebody says to me: 'Who's God for you?' then He's certainly the God of the second chance and the seventy times seven. The continually forgiving God.

FELICITY

Community of Poor Clares, Arundel, West Sussex
ROMAN CATHOLIC: ENCLOSED

Age: 42
Nationality: English
Age at entry to community: 18
Number of years in community: 24
Previous employment: Junior Matron at a preparatory school/
Trainee nursery nurse
Dress: Habit

Felicity has the sort of robust looks and complexion that are more suggestive of recent and prolonged walks in bracing weather than a life of shelter. She wears a full-length brown habit with a white wimple (the bit that goes around the face, beneath the veil), and no shoes, even in winter.

Founded in 1212, the Community of Poor Clares is one of the oldest female religious orders. It places enormous emphasis on poverty and simplicity, and is probably the 'strictest' of the female orders after the Carmelites. The community attempts to support itself by printing religious texts and making vestments, but it is far from wealthy.

Felicity and I talked in a bare room in a modern extension of the nineteenth-century convent. Apart from the chairs in which we sat, the room contained an art deco sofa, a table and an artificial potted chrysanthemum. It was extremely wet and cold outside and not much warmer inside, but perhaps the trick of staying warm is to eat the vast teas that are provided every day, and which were wheeled in to us on a tea trolley by another nun. Felicity seemed oblivious of the chill – 'you get used to it' – and seemed positively to relish the physical demands of living a life which, despite its teas, is very austere. She seemed also to relish the opportunity for physical challenge, and she told me with a mixture of delight and embarrassment how, when a garden wall was being built with her assistance, she managed to turn over a large – and very expensive – JCB digger.

Felicity seemed to enjoy being interviewed very much. She answered all my questions slowly and carefully, and when she had finished speaking would wait eagerly for the next one. She spoke with extraordinary clarity and simplicity, something I found both refreshing and slightly disconcerting.

Felicity

I suppose if you wanted it very simply, I'm a 'sticker'. If I commit myself to doing something I will do it. Very difficult to work out what one actually puts down as temperament. I think I'm basically a happy person, although I've gone through some very unhappy periods. I've always known myself as a deeply loving person, but gone through long periods when I haven't been able to express it adequately. It's always been an ideal, even as a small child, to live up to my name, Felicity, because what's the point of having a name like that if you can't live it?

I'm stubborn. I mean you can call it stubborn or strong-willed depending when you're looking at me! Which I suppose goes with being a sticker. I'm not – is the word ebullient? I don't bubble easily. When I bubble I do it properly. There have been periods in my life when I've looked at other people and said, 'I wish I could enjoy things the way they do,' but my enjoyment is a much quieter, deeper thing. And there are times when I look at the person who acts the clown and think, 'Wouldn't it be nice to be like that,' but I'm not. A clown does pop out occasionally, and that startles everybody. Which is quite fun. I get quite a kick out of suddenly producing something that people aren't expecting. They say: 'That's not like you!'

But my family? I suppose you'd have to say middle-class. Big. Eight children over a large age span. There's twenty-one years between the eldest and the youngest and I'm in the middle. Mum was always at home and my father was in the prison service, borstals. Dad's work took a lot of his attention.

We were all people who liked our own space. I was very much a tomboy and I don't remember my mother ever trying to make me be otherwise. I know it exasperated her because of things that she's come out with in my adult life – like once when I was telling her about a Sister who'd been explaining to me about different norms of politeness at table and I was saying what a country bumpkin I'd felt. And Mum turned round and said well, you *always* rejected these things. But beyond saying, 'You must wear a skirt in the evening,' she let me do what I liked, which was mostly the sort of things that a boy would have done.

I think I probably identified much more with my father as a child, although I'm actually more like my mother. My father is very idealistic, yet even with his ideals he was always very loving. We always lived on the premises of his work, so he didn't go out to work in a sense that a man goes out to the office. He would often leave the house before we'd gone to school and sometimes he'd be very late in, but then he might have a long gap at dinner-time. Inevitably with a job like that you had to be someone with a fairly powerful personality, and to some extent his disciplining of delinquent boys rubbed off on us. Sometimes he would let out a roar that would leave you quaking, and looking back he obviously lived a lot on his nerves; if the telephone went, he'd leap as if he'd been stung, because a boy might have absconded, and these boys were as important to him as his own children.

Although I jumped if Dad slammed his fist on the table and bellowed, I wasn't afraid of him. I could relate to him in a way that a lot of my brothers and sisters couldn't. I would be quite happy helping him sow seeds in the garden or cleaning the car just to be with him. That was how you were with him – doing jobs. And most kids don't like doing jobs, so I had the monopoly there and spent more time with him. He was strong, and knew all the answers, and this was what I liked. That's just my temperament I suppose.

As a child, I never really *observed* my mother. I mean, Mum was there. The house ran, meals appeared, clothes were repaired, the love was given, and it was all taken for granted. Maybe the first time I really began to notice Mum was when I was about fifteen, and I suddenly noticed that Dad would ring up and say, 'I'm sorry, darling, there're two people from Head Office here and I'm bringing them home for dinner.' She wouldn't be bothered by that, she'd just fit round it. Dad was the most important person in her world, and she would accept almost any inconvenience to help him. She would do as much for us, and this self-sacrificial love stretched beyond the family too.

My father's faith is very much the Catholic faith of the early century – very clear cut, with great emphasis on keeping the rules and doing it right. My mother, who is a convert, has a faith which even as a child I was aware of as being less rigid. I remember shortly after I'd made my first communion (in the days when you fasted from midnight until after communion the next morning) I came in one Sunday morning in a great to-do because I'd been lying out in the garden chewing a piece of grass. She said, 'For goodness' sake, dear, I'm sure God isn't going to get worked up about things like that!' But her faith was just as important to her as my father's was to him.

I went to seven schools. The first was the local village school which was ye olde village school with juniors and seniors. The next was a very posh girls' convent school somewhere in Cambridgeshire. Our milk was heated up at breaktime and you had your own cutlery, things like that. Then we moved again just before I was seven and I went to the local Catholic primary school. It *had* to be a Catholic school as far as my parents were concerned, though this mellowed a bit with the passing of years. By the time I was at my third school my reading was pretty backward, and the headmaster used to give me remedial reading.

I was always a bit of a loner. If you change schools as often as I did, you spend your life catching up. This left me little space for developing friendships, so I grew to think of myself as different. I also grew up much slower than other girls so that when my peers were beginning to talk about boyfriends and pop music and this sort of thing it was still a different world to me. I enjoyed books, I enjoyed being alone. I still do. So, sadly, I look back on school as almost a waste of time: most of the things I learnt I've forgotten.

I left after 'O' Levels. Again, the family was moving, and I had discovered that we were there on half-fees. So when my parents said to me, 'You can stay on in the sixth form as a boarder' I said no, thank you. I felt they obviously couldn't afford it. They *would* have afforded it, but I decided to do nursery nursing instead. I went to the Careers Officer about it, and really the only thing I said was, 'I don't care where it is as long as it's Catholic,' because my faith was very important to me.

I couldn't imagine life without faith. Because I didn't have other relationships as a child my faith probably had more chance to grow, and I began to know God as somebody real, somebody who could touch me – not with words, but very deeply. I remember lying out in the middle of a field once, and looking at the sky and thinking, 'God made all this,' and just getting lost in the vastness of it. But at that point I wouldn't have said that I prayed. It's only with hindsight that I can see that that's what was going on.

Because we moved a lot, I stopped trying to build relationships with other people. It wasn't a conscious thing, but I did. And only when I came here and had a long period of life with the same people did I begin to realise that I could know people in a way that I'd never known people, though it took a long time. The first order I entered with, being a missionary order, also moved a lot, so the childhood pattern of constant moving was continued, and I was aware then of being a lonely person, of constantly feeling different.

After all, we were different as children because to the borstal kids we were the Governor's children. We were different because we were Catholics. We were different because we went to different schools. Because I grew up slowly I was even different from my own sisters. I was also different from my siblings because I was closer to my father; it's never a good place to be, you know – to be special to a parent in a large family. I was different because I wasn't teasable, and you can imagine my brothers and sisters making hay with that one, so it was much safer to get a book and retire, preferably at the top of a tree! And that was one thing my mother did get angry about. Frequently she would haul me out of my room and say: 'Stop living in books! Come downstairs and *be* with people.' I suspect I probably puzzled her.

I wasn't conscious of having a religious vocation when I was small. I was a religious child, but I wasn't pious: pious to me is something ugly. I had as a smaller person thought I would like to be a nun – not quite sure what a nun was beyond those shadowy things that floated round the school – but this was possibly because my eldest sister entered a religious order, although she left within a few months. So I thought about it for a while, but in my mid-teens the idea faded in favour of a big strong husband and a large family.

In 1965, when I was seventeen, I started work at the Southwark Catholic Rescue Society's Residential Nursery that was run by the religious order I later joined – the Franciscan Missionaries of the Divine Motherhood, or FMDMs. I'm not sure if I'd begun to wonder about a vocation before I got there but the question certainly became very real once I did, and frankly, my reaction to it was negative. I thought, 'Oh no, not me; I want to marry and have a family.' But the question continued to nag me. I spoke to no one about it and struggled alone instead. I had my own bedroom there, and I think the nuns were bothered by the amount of time I spent alone, so I was moved to share a room with one of the 'problem' students. I think they hoped that she would draw me out and I would quieten her down!

Anyway, one day, while I was sitting on my bed watching her backcombing her jet-black hair, I asked her what she would do if she had a problem she couldn't solve. She stopped what she was doing, looked at me and said, 'I know what *your* problem is' (or something like that), and disappeared. Well, I *thought* I'd been very subtle, so I was baffled when she returned shortly afterwards with a load of literature about religious life. I never even asked her where she got it, I was just so amazed!

Then, one day, when another girl and I were working with a group of little ones from the Nursery, the Sister in charge asked the girl if I would be going with her, and she said yes. So I asked *where* I was supposed to be going, and it turned out that this girl was going to the Clothing service of an ex-student as a nun with the FMDMs. So I went. I simply allowed myself to be organised. I think I always have done.

The day we were going, I went into the chapel and made a sort of deal with the Almighty. I said that if He wished me to be a nun He must fix it that day: because that seemed impossible, I thought I'd successfully squash this nagging question once and for all. So we went to the ceremony. So far so good. But after it, I was ushered into the presence of the person who was responsible for 'promoting vocations'. My friend had told her I was interested in religious life, though I'd never said anything to her about it!

Well, the poor Sister spent about half an hour trying to get some sense out of me, and I kept hedging. Finally, she said would I like to see the Mother General. The title meant absolutely nothing to me; I just wanted to get away. But instead, like a petrified rabbit, I said yes.

I arrived at the General's office and she looked me straight in the eye, and said, 'Do you want to enter this order with Christine?' Christine was this other girl, and she was entering in a month! Well! I was stunned, so I hedged again, but it was: *'Do you or don't you?'* Not very long afterwards I emerged with the whole thing arranged. *Not* a very auspicious way!

The thing is, though, I came out walking on air. It was like I'd been given a fantastic gift. I'd been told to leave the Nursery as soon as I could and have a couple of weeks at home. The Superior at the Nursery wasn't particularly surprised, and said that my father had warned her that this might happen. (My father said she had warned *him!*) Anyway, it seems that everybody knew except me.

At the time I wasn't aware that there were different sorts of nuns – contemplative or apostolic, enclosed or open order. I simply knew I was going to be a nun – and that was enough. But that order wasn't right. By this time I was working at a residential home for teenagers, though as a Novice Sister rather than a lay person, and I began to wonder whether perhaps I wanted a more enclosed, contemplative lifestyle. But we were told that apostolic Sisters like us often went through a phase of wanting to be enclosed Sisters like the Poor Clares; in fact, it was termed 'Poor Clare-itis', so I put it down to that.

However, the question of becoming a contemplative nun grew and grew. Again I struggled alone, until just before I was due to take my Final Vows; then I thought, 'I must test this thing: it's now or never,' and I finally told my Superior. She just told me I was conceited to think such a thing, so I assumed I was wrong and took my Final Vows after all.

However, the question kept returning, and I find it hard to answer why. It wasn't so much a reasoning as a sort of magnetic attraction, I didn't know what enclosed contemplative life would be like, only that I wanted more solitude, silence, time to be alone with God. I wanted less escape routes, less comfort, less material things. I felt that what I was doing in childcare was so minimal in terms of child neglect and abuse; I felt that I hardly touched the pains of my family and friends; and I felt that these things could be better reached through prayer. I somehow needed to give myself in a fuller way to God.

Periodically, I presented the question to my Superiors, and it was put off one way or another. But finally I had to do something. I came here, to Arundel, for a retreat and I loved it. When my next retreat was due the blessed question was still there, so I rang here and said, 'Do you think I could come again?' and they said yes. I said, 'Do you think I could actually spend the retreat in the Sisters' enclosure?' The voice at the end of the phone said: 'Are you thinking of transferring because I can't allow you into the enclosure otherwise.' So I took a deep breath and said, 'Yes, I think I am.' I put the phone down and went to my Superior and said, 'I've done something terrible. I've just said that I was thinking of transferring.' She said, 'Well that's all right. You haven't committed yourself.' But for me, when a thing reaches verbalisation I am committed. The decision is made.

So I came here to Arundel, and stayed for a week, and it was very clear to me that this was what I wanted. I went to the FMDM's Mother House (our term for the head community, if you like), and asked to see the Superior General – the head of the whole order. She took me into her room and said, 'Now, what did you want to see me about?' and I said, 'But you *know*.' It was all so sort of cold and clinical. I blurted out that I thought I wanted to transfer, and she said, 'Well, if that's where the holy spirit's leading you then you must follow the holy spirit,' and I was out within five minutes.

I was *stunned*. Absolutely stunned. Very quickly I could see that on her part she wanted to leave me absolutely free, she didn't want to influence me one way or the other, but her attitude hurt for some time, although now I realise there wasn't any other way it could have been done, she was doing the best thing.

Then I had from Easter to December to wait. When we took the children away on summer holiday I tried to explain to them that I would be leaving. They'd had so many people leave them,

I was terribly conscious of this. I had one adolescent who was extremely difficult. She was the sort of child we wouldn't normally have agreed to take because we weren't really equipped, but she'd been in several children's homes – all run by nuns – and created such havoc that the social worker couldn't find anywhere else to take her. I'd agreed to take her, but when I was coming here to Arundel nobody else in the community felt they could take her on, so I had to seek another placement for her. And one day my assistant said to me: 'When you accepted that girl you said you thought it was the will of God. Now you're going off and you say you think that's the will of God too. Is this just a nice way of saying this is what you want to do?' I said, 'Well, I don't *think* so,' but then it's very easy to deceive yourself. It's very easy.

When I came here, I had to start from scratch and go through Novitiate training all over again, and my conception of the religious life began to change. When I was first here, I was given a book called *The Map of Life*, and I can't remember what it contained but the phrase has remained with me: my image of the will of God was that there was a certain pattern for me. I don't mean a mould, but I thought it was all set out, and I just had to fit into the right slots, so to speak. Gradually, I began to see God's will as something far freer and far less clear-cut. God has no pre-determined vision of what is the best for me in each bit of life. For example, I don't believe that God wanted His son to die; I don't see how you can talk about a loving God who wants His son to die . . .

I hope I'm not going into heresy here, but right from when I came here, I had this sense that God wanted His son to come on earth and respond to Him as a perfect human being should respond, as the first man or woman could have done if they hadn't experienced sin. I had the feeling that Christ must have been searching all along for His Father's will. He said, 'My food is to do the will of My Father,' and that seems to me to have been an attempt to respond with truth and love to every situation in life. This inevitably led Him to death because human beings can't handle truth, being sinful; sin is the denial of truth. I mean, you still see it today. The person who stands up for the truth lines himself up for the firing squad.

So God's will seemed to be more like that for me as time went on; a *constant* searching for the truth, which for me was tied up with coming here and becoming a contemplative. And I still don't know anything about what I've got to do, except that as each thing comes up I have to try and respond with truth and love – and inevitably fail at times, because I'm a human being.

My pattern of living is built around the Roman Catholic expression of Christianity, and I haven't ever considered living by any other pattern. There have been times when I've suddenly thought to myself, 'What happens if it's all a load of old phooey, and I drop dead and there's nothing?' But it seems to me that if that were the case then there's nothing lost by my way of life. I'm happy. I've got – I was going to say 'all I want', but there are times when one inevitably wants what one hasn't got in this way of life. But that happens in any way of life, so I've thought to myself, well, if I'm not losing anything I might as well carry on. And on occasions when I've felt empty, this has been just what's kept me going until I come out the other side. And I inevitably find I've changed and grown every time I do.

Similarly, my understanding of the vows is constantly growing. Take poverty for instance. You start off with something very simplistic – Thou Shalt Not Have – and it grows into something very freeing: Thou shalt not be tied – by anything, though I do appreciate that a lot of people would see me as tied. When I first came here one of the Sisters from my old community said, 'I just couldn't live there, there are so many material limitations,' and even at that early point I thought, 'Well, that's funny, I'm freer here than I've ever been.' It's not material limitations that make you free or not free.

I see freedom as – well, put it this way: here I don't have to be just what other people expect me to be. Because as a community we're very accepting of one another, people are much freer. Watching people enter and slowly, slowly shed all their defences is wonderful. If you happen to be a person with a flaming temper, well yes, obviously people duck when it arises, but they don't love you any less. So perhaps the reason we've got a fair number of 'characters' here is because people are free to be just who they are. You know, if a person's in a mood here, they'll turn round and say, 'Oh yeah, of course, her period's due, she'll be okay next week,' It's very earthy, but it gives you a freedom, whatever sort of temperament you are. And that's a freedom that the majority of people do not have. You know, from listening to people and talking to people, I can tell that there are so many things that restrict or tie them, whether it be dress or the latest car or doing what other people do. Whatever. So yes: I reckon I'm much freer than most.

I can accept that people see this life as limited, but whatever walk of life you're in you are limited. There are things that I can't experience because I live here: there are things that you can't experience because you *don't* live here. Whatever choice I'd made in life it would have eliminated numerous other choices, and one just has to *make* a choice. If I'd decided to do ballet dancing I would have had to limit my diet, I would have had to make sure I got all the exercise I needed, and worried all the time that I wasn't going to get bad legs.

Of course it would be nice to get about sometimes. Of course one inevitably feels, wouldn't it be nice to walk down the road in something that nobody's going to look at twice and just do my own thing. It would be lovely to get on a bus and go somewhere. Or go on an aeroplane. I've never been on an aeroplane. And there are times – there are times when you would give anything to have a fella put his arms around you. Though there are not many things I find I really want, actually. When I first came here I wrote to my parents and said I'd give anything for a good long walk, and we do have grounds, but I can't walk around the garden for three quarters of an hour, it would drive me potty. I weed the garden instead because I enjoy that and it's exercise. In fact, there's plenty of scope for exercise in a certain field. We would play rounders round the garden. We don't, though some of the community would like to. Some of the Sisters went through a phase of jogging but soon got fed up with it. The garden's quite large, though when you've got forty people hanging around, and you've suddenly got fed up with forty people, it can seem really small.

I would give *anything* for a swim. Certainly there's nothing wrong with swimming, but I suppose one would say that a purely pleasurable reason wasn't a good enough one to go out of the enclosure, because you've chosen a life that is vowed, or bound, to enclosure. A few years ago, though, we were given permission to go for long walks. When we first got the permission on a trial basis *everybody* was going out; there were nuns walking on the Downs practically every day of the week. Now hardly anybody goes out except if they really feel a need, which, within the context of our discipline, is good, because there's a difference between a need and a like. If I needed to get out too frequently one would have to say, 'Are you in the right place?'

Your questions interest me, you know, because enclosure's a sticking point for you, isn't it? It's a sticking point for many of my own family too. My brother rang me up once and wanted me to go to his son's wedding, and I said, 'I'm sorry, Martin, I can't,' I said, 'Why don't you come up and see me?' So he said, 'I want *you* to come and see *me*,' I said, 'I'm sorry. This is a choice I've made. Why don't you come up at half-term?' So he said, 'If I do, can we go for a walk?' and I said 'No. We can't.'

But he knows I've been home when my parents have been ill and he can't put the two things together, that leaving when someone is in need is completely different from leaving for pleasurable reasons. He thinks this life is totally wrong anyway. He thinks that I would be much better employed spreading the word of God by caring for children as I was before. And I say, 'I think there's a value in prayer. I think there's a value in giving my God all that I've got in this way.' Other people give back to God what he's given them by using it in a tangible sense that people see, and that's good. It's just as good. But there is that intangible part of our being – our spirits – which happens to be where I've been led to respond.

We all respond to different bits of our human make-up, and I think as an apostolic nun I was conscious that by working with disturbed children I was affecting the lives of a handful of very unhappy people, and it seemed so piddly. I felt that by prayer I would reach a lot more. I was also increasingly conscious of a need for more time in prayer, and I suppose there was always this niggling for something more. I would think in any spiritual life that's being lived at any depth this is going to be a reality. I remember reading a book on prayer, and this chap saying that one would always be saying 'neti neti,' which means 'not enough, not enough', I've always had that sense of 'not enough' with God, although the 'not enough' now is a 'not enough' in my giving rather than my receiving. It's a sense that I'm reaching for something that I'm still not big enough for.

People often ask me how this way of life can benefit other people. In fact I recently had the same discussion with my youngest brother and his wife about what good are we doing in here. They were talking about petitionary prayer, and I was saying that I don't actually spend a lot of time in petitionary prayer. To me there is, as it were, an economy of love, so that the very fact that one member of the human race is making a particular concerted effort to open themself to love, to God, automatically has a spin-off for the rest of the world. I suppose you could put it as an economy of good and evil. Every bit of good, every bit of response to God that a person gives affects the whole world. I may not, in an active, visible way, be giving love or charity or whatever you want to call it, but I'm somehow exposing the human race to more love.

The same goes for peace. By the very fact that I strive to build up peace in my own world, my own life, my own little environment, I am adding peace to the world. Obviously people have got to work for peace on bigger levels, but their working for peace is their expression, their addition of peace to the world. My working for peace is just as effective. Not as visible, and I'm aware that many people don't believe in it, but I can't do much about it. I can only live by the truth that I know. Even if everybody did that, the world would be a very different place.

As a community we're actually very open to what's going on in the world, in society, in Arundel, because we believe it's important that we should be. How can we pray effectively if we're not aware? We have the experience that comes in through people who visit. We have the experience that comes in through people who join us. You might say that this is a very *limited* amount of experience: yes, but we have an *un*limited time to absorb it, and, if one could measure such things, I would bet we get more out of our experience, because we're not bombarded with it. With most people, experience slides over the surface because there's just too much.

In a community like this there is time and space for people to grow at a natural pace, and I suspect that this has something to do with being enclosed. You know, one day I was doing the kitchen with a Sister who'd just taken her First Vows, and she was saying that despite having made them she still didn't feel part of the family. I said to her that in a place like this where people come in and then you live together for the rest of your life, you have to grow as a family. It's not like going to a job where there's a rapid changeover of staff and you do your bit and then move on, because acceptance here is something much, much deeper. You accept the whole person, warts and all.

In practical terms, this means that when a person's coming up for her Final Vows we discuss it as a community; whether she's still suited, whether we're still sure. And often people pick up flaws. They may say things like: 'Her attitude to obedience is very strange, she always seems to be finding ways out and manipulating things to get her own way,' and one of the older Sisters will say, 'Yes, but you see how much she's changed in five years. Give her another few years and a bit more responsibility and I think this'll grow out.' So we think in terms of years here. And I think that enables somebody to grow rather than to be made.

I suppose in answer to all your questions – you know, do I get frustrated and bored? Do I ever feel trapped? – I have to say that ever since I've been here I've felt more and more alive! And I know it might seem odd, but it's true! When I came here it was like coming home. It was quite a fantastic experience.

I was thirty, thirty-one, when I transferred to this community, which is a point in a woman's life when she really starts blossoming anyway. I suppose the two things coincided, and I now had the time to sort out a lot of things on the emotional, psychological, level that I'd never had the time and space to sort out before.

I gradually found I had all sorts of talents. Having grown up thinking I was a pretty dull average, I suddenly found that I'm actually very gifted, and this was frightening. All sorts of practical things that I tried to do – I could do most of them! Which meant that I ended up with a lot of work. I do a lot of the electrical and building jobs around the house now.

On the social level I was gradually more able to relate to people, I was less prickly. And I began to realise, I'm not the lousy person I thought I was, I'm actually reasonably nice. That too was a terrific revelation, and I started making friends. Well, I'd never made friends since I was a child. Now I almost feel I've had an advantage by having that gap where I didn't know close friendship, because a close friend is something beautiful and special and a total gift, and I really value it.

But it's not all been easy. When, at the beginning of my religious life, I made the vow of chastity, which meant I wasn't going to get married or have sexual relationships (as the two don't always go together!) it never really impinged on me. However, maybe a year or so after I came here – how can I put it? – I began to be aware of a sort of physical *restlessness* inside me. It was a pain: it was a real ache. My body at times screamed out for satisfaction.

About that time, I remember talking with my youngest brother and his wife about it, and Sheila said to me, 'Now you see all this, do you think perhaps you're in the wrong place?' And I looked at her in amazement, even though this was in the middle of the pain, and I said: 'But *no*! I gave God a bauble that was no more than a glass bead. Now I find it's a diamond and I want to give it even more.' And it was really like that. There was the pain of not being able to satisfy very natural urges, but the wonder of finding out that this was something beautiful. I mean it wasn't a negative 'giving up', it was a returning of this precious jewel. And I think the very fact that I don't express my love through my body highlights my ability to express it in other ways. I mean it's part of the growth I've been very aware of in these last years.

I've never fallen in love, though I would think the nearest to falling in love was with a priest friend who supported me a lot over the transition period when I changed communities, and I suspect that was as much the support he gave me as anything else. I did experience a lot of emotional feeling in relation to him: I don't know whether I would go as far as saying it was sexual feeling. I talked to him a lot about my fears about uprooting and moving, and when they got too big for me I would be trotting down to the presbytery to talk it through so often that eventually my Superior hauled me up and said, 'Do you know that people are talking about the amount of time you're spending down there?'

But throughout that period I was convinced that however much I was falling apart on all sorts of levels, this man had such a respect for my vocation, and his, that nothing could go wrong. When I was leaning on him emotionally I was very conscious of God's presence. I remember at one point sobbing on his shoulder and knowing the satisfaction one can get in that position, and thinking 'Uh-uh, what are you up to?' And I thought, 'Well, it's okay, because God's here: it's okay.' I mean I wouldn't advocate that people go throwing their emotions around, but I think we're all human, we all have needs, and I don't think you can be human and avoid walking in grey areas.

Enclosure? I was wondering when we'd get on to that! It's a much vexed question. The old rules talked about doors and locks and walls and goodness knows what, but this isn't enclosure. There was a small child I wrote to once, one of my nephews or nieces, and what I said was: 'For me it is very important that I grow close to God, not just for myself, but I see it as being important for the world. If I want to grow close to someone I want to spend a lot of time with them.' I can relate to someone at a cocktail party, but that's going to be quite different to a relationship I have with someone I sit and spend time with. Just like us sitting here today: if I want to give you my whole attention then I must shut other things out. Well, I want to give God my whole attention, not so that I'm cut off from other things but so that I'm actually more receptive to them – rather like the blind person who develops a terrifically strong sense of touch. Not having a lot of communication with people or other outside stimulation means that I'm much more sensitive to what's going on around me. So that is why we need enclosure. It's not a shutting out. It's an effort to have this still centre which can reach out and be responsive to the less tangible things that go on in life.

Lots of people say: aren't you just escaping? And I say: try it. Just try it. I mean that dead literally. *You* try living in the same building with the same people, who get to know your every –

you know, even the way you move your eyes or whatever. You have to be extremely sane, both mentally and emotionally, to put up with it, because it's very hard. And if that's running away . . . Basically, I think you have to face yourself at a much more real level in here, a level which our society doesn't even *prepare* us for.

You could argue that we miss out, but then I don't have to go to the Downs to see the beauty of God's creation. I'd certainly see another aspect of it there but then I haven't seen Niagara Falls either. I mean, am I lacking as a person because I haven't seen Niagara Falls? And equally, coming back to this economy of love, I am loving the people around me. It's not the *number* of people I love, it's the amount of love I love with that is important. We, as part of the human race, are taking time apart, and if you see us as part of the human race as a whole, then it is a tiny bit of time that is being given to God.

However, when I came here a lot of people talked as if I was embarking on a higher type of life, but it's not, it's just different. I don't think the apostolic and the contemplative life can be compared, I think they're two faces of the same coin. And it's actually the main reason I agreed to work with you, because it's something I feel very strongly about, and I feel is misunderstood. You know, it's not a case of the worker bees and the drones, or even the worker bees and the queen bee. We're all workers: we just happen to be working in different ways. It's better for me to be here than elsewhere, that's all.

Still, many people find this kind of life practically impossible to accept. I suspect that as human beings what we don't understand we tend to write off, simply because it's easier to handle things like that, and a way of life that is radically different questions people. And they can either stand and face the question or else they can say, 'Nuns: they're mad.' And it's often easier to say, 'They're mad.' But people can be totally different and still be absolutely sane! It is possible to say: 'I don't understand you, but I accept you. I don't understand what you're doing but I can see it's obviously got a value because of what it's making you.'

Some people might feel sort of jealous of my conviction, that I know what I want, where I'm going. But then, they haven't seen all the convolutions that have gone on inside me. You know? Conviction isn't there all the time. It can be removed for anybody. Even Christ on the cross cried out, 'My God, my God, why have you forsaken me?' and he *meant* that, I mean it wasn't just a pious quotation then. He experienced the feeling that God wasn't there, that God was *not*. And I suspect we all have to experience that because the meaning of faith is 'believing without understanding'. And I suspect that faith's at its strongest at the point when you hang on to nothing so to speak. I haven't been that far myself, but I was listening to a cassette the other day, and the priest who was talking was quoting St Thérèse of Lisieux, saying that in the last year of her life that was literally what she felt – that there was no God. And there's a fine balance between what you feel and whatever it is that makes you hang on: it's certainly not an intellectual conviction that keeps you going. Faith is an intangible something that makes you continue along this path through the religious life – even when the path is seemingly non-existent.

There's a quotation I've been trying to remember while I've been talking to you this week, and I think it's from James Michener's *The Source*. There was a bit in there where he said: 'Man is born with his hands clenched and he dies with his hands open.' And to me this is what the religious life is all about. It's about a letting go on all sorts of levels, and the vows we take are the expression of that, a starting point.

The *end* in living a life of poverty like this is to make a person free to relate to God, and to others. The end in itself is not destitution. It's a having – I was going to say 'without possessing' – but it's a having without *being* possessed. None of us is totally free, of course, however much we might like to think we were. But there are all the non-material sacrifices of this life too, like being thought well of, or being remembered or noticed or important. I see the striving to free myself from *these* things as part of poverty. But when I started, poverty was simply a material thing, a paring things down to the nitty-gritty. And then I realised how proud I was of the fact that I had less than most people – which rather spoilt the picture and made realise that somewhere I was missing the point!

Poverty for us as Poor Clares is actually referred to as 'the *privilege* of poverty,' because Clare really had to fight for us to have no material possessions. In her day every monastery had to have endowments, and she only got permission on her deathbed not to have them. She said: 'We don't want material security. We want security in God.' And that's something we still try to cling to. Of course, it's very difficult to work out *how* you do this on a material level. The print room has recently got a computer because it saves a lot of work, but the ultimate reason for getting it was that it actually produced better work for the people we're working for. We try to use this sort of criterion for the work we do, but in other areas we try not to have the best.

On a personal level we all have different needs, and if you saw different people's rooms you would see how different their needs are. I have a bed and a locker. The bed is something I made out of an old divan, it's got drawers underneath, so most of my clothing sort of fits in there. And a chair. In terms of possessions there's my rosary. I bought it when I was fifteen for three and six. I think that's all actually. Oh well, yes, my clothes are mine. I've also got a very well-stocked toolbox, and in a sense I would call my tools mine: if somebody borrowed something without asking they would suddenly become very much mine! Which is when I know how un-free I am! My watch? Well, actually my watch packed up, and Mother Abbess gave me this two and a half years ago, it's one that her father left her. It's mine in so far as I'm using it, but I'd never have a second one.

I mean if I walked out of the house, which is perhaps the easiest way of looking at what's mine, I would obviously take – I was just trying to think what I brought when I came here. I know people were surprised by how little I brought. Clothing, breviaries, a Jerusalem bible, and four years later I gave that to a young girl going out to Uganda where they didn't have anything as sophisticated. Yes, that's about it.

Some funny things have been a great wrench. I prepared some children for confirmation this year, which I have done for several years, and I always give them a little present of some sort. We used to have a repository and I've always been able to take things from there, but we've ceased to restock it. Well, I had a black wall-plaque of Our Lady, a head and shoulders, which a child had given me years before. It's very beautiful, and I thought well, I could give that to one of them, I don't really need it. And it was *weeks* that I sat thinking about it. And in the end I thought, 'Look, take it off the wall and put it in the cupboard and get used to the gap on the wall.' So I did that. But it was hard, and I was surprised at how hard it was.

To some extent we each have to find the level that suits us, whilst striving for the ideal as honestly as we can. Financially, we are supposed to support ourselves, though the amount of money we earn as a community would never support us. We all work hard, but if you live in a place this size, maintenance eats away most of the money. It costs so much just to heat. We do have heating, don't get me wrong – look, there are pipes there – but you're not the only one who thinks that our heating is non-existent.

In terms of security, we pay people's insurance stamp until they've taken their Final Vows, but not afterwards. We don't build up financial securities. Most people would say this is ridiculously improvident, but it works: we're never without. Certainly a lot of the time we're the wrong side of the red line, but time and time again, just as we're scraping the bottom of the barrel, something happens. We don't go out questing as used to be done in the past because it's not encouraged either by the Church or the state, but somebody always leaves us a legacy or whatever. Last year, for example, we had to have a lot of repairs done, including having the steeple completely reshingled, and we were getting in quite a panic. Within the diocese there was a fund for contemplative communities that we had actually founded, and we'd never touched it, although apparently the diocese have been paying our heating bills out of it for a while – we didn't realise that. So we pitched into this very reluctantly, very shamefacedly almost, but when everything was completed and the last bill paid, the exact amount was given to us by someone. And the bursar said, 'You see. Trust God and He'll provide.'

So I think religious life will remain. I think God will always provide for it, if you like. Because it is a human institution, it is constantly evolving, but I think there will always be groups of people who choose to live in community as a way of creating a space in which to grow close to God. And I wouldn't be surprised to see this form of religious life remain as a basic structure, because the basic setting apart of a place for silence and prayer will always be necessary. Just from looking at history you can see how mankind has always had this need for God and prayer.

I was going to say 'prayer is just sitting and being' but I don't think that'll satisfy you. I think prayer is very much a relationship between two people, the second person being God – and if you ask me what God is I'll say 'I don't know'! God *is*. And like any relationship, it will grow slowly. Although you get some relationships which burst into being, most relationships have to be worked at, and it's no different with God. It has peak periods, and then there'll be the times when God's away and you're sitting there alone and wondering when on earth he'll be back – or *if* he'll be back.

I've come to an understanding of prayer, in fairly recent years I suppose, as total gift – as the love of another person is total gift. I can never demand it. I can never expect it to feel good all the time. I've been conscious that prayer can be a really sort of 'wow' experience, you know, when you come away and you think, 'Goodness, what happened?' and there's no way that you can ever *make* it happen. All you can say is, 'Here I am, Lord.' The more you learn to sit with your hands open, so to speak, in the assurance that He will come – and there can be months at a time when you do that – the more you can do that, the better.

But God *cares* about you, He really does. He *wants* you to be able to share your happiness and your sorrow with Him. He's waiting for us to say, 'I love you, I need you.' He wants us to be able to sit with Him and say, 'I'm cheesed off today. Everybody seems to be being rotten to me, and I know it's me being rotten to them and I don't know what to do about it.' He wants us to sit there and know that however grotty we feel He loves us just the same. But God never suggested He'd give us a soft option. He never said, 'It's all going to be nice and tidy and mapped out and you say please and I say yes.' What He did say was: 'All things will work together unto good' for those who love Him.

Actually, I've found talking to you – I said to a couple of Sisters this morning – has actually proved to be a very spiritual experience. I've found myself more conscious of praising and thanking God for my vocation in this week than I'm aware of ever having been, simply because I've been forced to look at it and say, 'This is what God has done.' That's partly why I'm so tired I think: it's something much bigger than I'd anticipated. Talking has made me conscious of how a lot of the things I've been struggling for for years have actually become a reality for me without me realising. Suddenly they're there, and only because I'm forced to put them into words do I see they're there. Like struggling for a better understanding of obedience – I remember it went on for months and months, and I prayed and prayed, and nothing happened. And suddenly I realised it was just there. And I think all spiritual things – you can open yourself to them, but you can't demand them.

However, when I look back over my time in religious life I can see how I've grown. You can never see it at the time. When you're in the middle of the mess you're like Job and you say to God, 'What the hell do you think you're doing with me?' And in a sense I would imagine that a measure of maturity of your relationship with God is in your ability to be completely open with Him, and not always saying 'God I praise you,' but sometimes, 'God, I wish you'd leave me alone.'

I don't think you can avoid pain. Ever. The reality of choices means that you can't avoid pain. I can't avoid pain by being here, but I've never experienced loss of faith. I've been very lucky. There've been black patches for me – sometimes very black. When I was sorting things out on the psychological and sexual level about nine years ago, I did wonder if everything was just going to collapse, but I live with this conviction that everything comes to an end, and it wasn't going to be grotty for ever. This was still the right place for me.

Have you read *No Hiding Place*? It's about a Dutch girl who was in a concentration camp, and she was in a bunker with hundreds of people, and they were infested by fleas. Well, they were able to read the scriptures because the guards wouldn't come past because of the fleas, and her sister turned round and said, 'Praise God for the fleas,' while everybody else was cursing them.

And most of us, in a situation, aren't big enough to see the good it's bringing. I mean, we can't see beyond our noses, but I think it's a reality that all things do work together unto good.

My personal future? I want total union with God. That's all I'm aiming at. As simple as that. And part of that is a struggle to learn to live now, totally. If I'm thinking about tomorrow, if thinking about tomorrow makes me fret, it's withdrawing me from what I'm seeking. You know, it's like that bit from the psalm: 'Do not fret, it only leads to evil.' It's very real.

FRANCES DOMINICA

All Saints Convent, Oxford
ANGLICAN: APOSTOLIC

Age: 48
Nationality: English
Age at entry to community: 23
Number of years in community: 25
Previous employment: Nurse
Current employment: Hospice nurse/Public speaker
Dress: Habit/Ordinary

I interviewed Frances in a large room on the ground floor of the splendid Victorian convent where she lives. It used to double up as her bedroom and office, but since the addition to the religious community of Kojo, a small Ghanaian boy, the room had become filled with toys, childish paintings and an extra bright red sofa bed. The mantelpieces were covered with photographs of children who have lived – and died – at Helen House, a hospice set up for terminally ill children in the grounds of the convent. It was the first of its kind at the time, initiated by Frances herself, and is now internationally known and respected.

The Society of All Saints, of which the Oxford community is a part, was founded in the nineteenth century to work with the poor. Since its foundation, it has survived mainly on legacies, although it receives a certain amount of income from investments and pensions. The Oxford community of eighteen women (and a number of domestic staff and gardeners) runs a clergy retirement home and a drop-in centre for the homeless. I found the place slightly disorientating to begin with, but this was hardly surprising given that on my first visit I stumbled over a Fisher Price toy garage in the hall, and straight into the unsteady path of a Trollopian clergy widow.

Frances, a tall, fair, slim woman, rapid of speech and manner, is sociable and effusive. She is also very busy. Her telephone rarely lay dormant for more than fifteen minutes at a time, and I lost count of the number of people who put their heads around the door to ask her questions like: 'Are you doing any hospital visits later?' and, 'What colour is Barry supposed to be painting the bathroom?'

Frances was generous and open with me, but she is a skilled interviewee – smooth, efficient, gracious, and fluent. Thoroughly used to public speaking and exposure, she unintentionally left me very little room to manoeuvre, and although I enjoyed my time with her, interviewing her was occasionally like reversing into a tight parking space.

Frances Dominica

I hope in here's okay. Gosh, it's not very warm, is it? Do you want to move? Because we can, you don't have to be polite. Tea? Coffee? Barley cup? No, I don't, but you can give it a go: one of the Sisters here swears by it. Kojo shouldn't be back for a couple of hours, so we'll have some peace I hope! Where do you want us to sit? Right, kettle off, barley cup coming up. Are you *sure* you're warm enough?

Okay: family. Would you like me to do this historically, or would you like me to tell you where we're at now? It's best historically really, isn't it?

I was born in the middle of the war, and my father was in the army, so as far as I was concerned, a family consisted of a mummy and a grandad and the children. We lived in Scotland with my grandfather, and he and I formed a very strong relationship in those early years, which lasted till his death aged ninety-five. He was probably the most formative person in my life. He was one of those old-fashioned lawyers who was pastor and doctor and lawyer all rolled into one, and he was an elder of the Church of Scotland, and I guess, although he rarely spoke about God or his own faith, it was from him that I caught my faith. I don't think faith is taught at all, I think it's caught, and if I caught it from anyone, it was from him.

My mother, by profession, is a musician, but the war put paid to her career, which was tragic really. At the end of the war, she found herself saddled with husband and child and a detached house in suburbia. My father's a chartered accountant, retired quite some time since, but his job brought him to the City, so we moved from Scotland to Surrey. Two and a half miles from the nearest shop, no car, and my mother pretty fed up because all her musician friends were in central London.

My mother was a very strong personality and we adored each other: there were a good many conflicts because of our personalities, but we did. When my father came home from the war when I was three and a half I was quite resentful because he was intruding. Now of course, we have a great love for each other, and a great mutual respect, but I think my father must have been very long-suffering, in that my relationships with my mother and my maternal grandfather were very strong indeed. My father never complained about that, and when my brother was born so sick, he and I grew very close because inevitably my brother and my mother were together a lot. The other thing is that my brother became a professional musician for a time, and my father and I felt terribly inadequate and second best, and sort of stuck together, told each other that we'd got gifts as well.

They're both alive still. My mother will be eighty in October, my father's a few months younger. My mother is one of those incredibly dynamic people who still runs rather than walks upstairs, and will drive two or three hundred miles a day and then organise dinner for four, or whatever. She is quite formidable. Woe betide you if you get up against her – as I well know from later experiences. My father appears by her side much older. He sits and does the crosswords, and potters off to the village to do the shopping and this sort of thing, and by comparison with many seventy-nine year olds he's not bad at all, but everybody compares him unfavourably beside this dynamic woman who's his wife. Quite tough.

My parents were not religious. My grandfather was, and one of my earliest memories is of going to church with him, Church of Scotland. I used to studiously refuse to go to the Sunday school or the children's service, because I just loved sitting beside him. I believe we far too often try to explain religion and religious belief and faith to children, and that actually what I was picking up in church was the unspeakable, the mystery, the awesomeness. I was aware that it was from this source that my grandfather got his enormous energy and ability to go out to other people, in his very quiet, steady, reliable way.

I also remember, by the time I broke the awful news to my family that I felt I had to test my vocation to religious life, he was pretty much bedridden, and everybody expected it would kill him, because religious life equalled Rome to anyone in the Church of Scotland, Rome really was *absolutely* beyond the pale. But he said, 'If you really believe that is what God is asking of you, then you have my blessing.' That was the most *amazing* gift, because subsequently, over the next few years, my parents found it too painful to see me, I was forbidden to go to the house when they were there. But I used to be allowed to go and spend a day a month with my grandfather, and he was always marvellous to me, he never tried to persuade me to come out.

I think on the whole my childhood was very happy. There were tensions, perhaps because of my mother's thwarted professional career, and the post-war years were not easy, anyway. But they were very good parents, looking at it objectively.

I was quite a shy, retiring child, so I didn't have that many close friends of my own age. I wasn't one of those effervescent, extrovert characters. From the age of three I knew I wanted to nurse, and when I was five my brother David was born very sick, and he spent six months in Great Ormond Street Hospital. He survived, and is now ordained, and married with four children of his own. They live in Switzerland. And that's my complete family.

When David went into Great Ormond Street, I decided that was where my training school was going to be. I don't know why I wanted to nurse, I suppose something in me just wanted to care for people who were sick. All my dolls and bears and rabbits and things were always sick, and they never got better – which didn't speak very highly for my nursing skills!

School, I have to say, was always a pain. I never enjoyed it. From four to seventeen, when I left, it was a question of marking time till I could do what I really wanted. I was unhappy at my first school, and relatively happy at my second. We had two houses there, Fry and Nightingale, and both those two women inspired me enormously. In fact, when I was in Fry House at the age of eight, I was determined to become a Quaker, because I thought Elizabeth Fry's way of life was wonderful, it really did inspire me. But school seemed so – what can I say? – so off the mark, really. It didn't enable me to be the person that I felt called to be, it seemed irrelevant and trivial.

When I was eleven I went to boarding school, Cheltenham Ladies' College, but I was never a success at school. Academically I'm not gifted. My criticism of that school, I suppose, was that I don't believe anybody, except maybe a couple of the staff, recognised my potential or helped me to develop it, and I believe that that is fundamental to what education is about. Never mind whether you're gifted at academic work or sport or drama or whatever: if you're not helping an individual to discover what they have got inside them – and everyone's got something – then you're not actually educating them.

It *sounds* as if I'm very ungrateful. My mother sometimes gets at me because she was at the same school and loved it, and I know that they had to make lots of sacrifices in order to send me there. But I *am* critical. I've visited hundreds of schools to talk in the last ten years, and I'm very often surprised by them. What makes a good school is an indefinable quality really, and it doesn't matter whether the parents are paying ten, fifteen thousand a year, or it's a state school in a grotty area of the west Midlands or somewhere, it's nothing to do with that.

Is that drink okay? It's not very nice, is it, I didn't think you'd like it. No, honestly I can make you some tea. No trouble, the kettle's still warm.

So, school: well, I think if you were tremendously extrovert, you probably benefited at Cheltenham. Even if you excelled at being naughty, you got noticed. But I didn't even excel at that.

When you were about thirteen you got confirmed at school, but I did not want to be confirmed when my contemporaries were. I didn't feel it was right. Not that I didn't believe in God – I did – but I wasn't at all sure I wanted to go along with the swing of things. I always had a relationship with God, but it didn't very often lead me voluntarily to church. So I didn't get confirmed until I was sixteen.

I don't think I thought about God very much. I was just conscious that God was there, and God was important and basic in my life. I suppose the things I longed to do could only be done from the position of being rooted and grounded in Him – to use a Pauline expression. I loved to read biographies of social reformers, and almost invariably they had a strong religious belief, so I suppose it was that that really got to me.

When I was confirmed it was a very emotional experience, and it was something I didn't, and still don't, feel very comfortable with. The emotion, I mean. I remember crying and crying, but I didn't know quite what it was, I couldn't rationalise it. And to this day I don't like God to be dramatic, or to make me emotional, which is quite funny really, because He has caused drama in my life. I don't know why I dislike it so much: I suppose I relate it somewhere along the line to attention-seeking.

Perhaps it also had something to do with the fact that as a family we weren't unduly emotional. Well, there were occasional rows. My mother and I used to row, usually over my brother. I used to accuse her again and again of being over-protective of him, that she was just spoiling him. She used to say that she wasn't spoiling him, she was just giving him a chance, because he'd been such a sick child, but we could never reconcile that, really. He went to an international school in Switzerland, and then when he got frustrated with it he was allowed to come home, and he had a tutor at home. Then he decided he wanted to take up the piano, so he got the most fabulous Blüthner given to him. We weren't a very wealthy family, really, and it just seemed to me out of proportion. It seemed as if anything David wanted, he got. He probably didn't, actually, but that was how it felt then. I hasten to add that it never came between us and we were always good friends, he and I. We still are.

Anyway, I'm digressing. I left school at seventeen and a half, and I had a year before I started nursing. I spent part of that year going up to a settlement that was set up by Cheltenham in Bethnal Green, going to schools and youth clubs in the area, and visiting the families in the tenement blocks locally, collecting threepence or sixpence a week from them for the Children's Country Holiday Fund, so that their children could go on holiday.

I really enjoyed it, it was a good time. Then after a long summer holiday, I started nursing, and just knew that this was where I belonged. It was absolutely wonderful, more than I'd dreamed. From the day I went in, other people seemed to recognise that I fitted, and I excelled from the beginning. Friends have said since then that they got together in the early days and said, 'Frances is going somewhere, you know.' Well, that was a new experience after eighteen years which had been clouded by a sense of failure. Instantly this was success.

Oh, dear, I'm sorry about all the noise, that's Kojo back already. He should be at school – he goes to a Montessori nursery – but I hadn't reckoned with Bank Holiday when we fixed this up, so he's been shopping with one of the Sisters, and they weren't due back until 11.30.

No, no, it's okay, we'll carry on.

I trained at Great Ormond Street, the sick children's hospital, and through my nursing career I made many, many friends who stuck. I really discovered my people and my place and I had ideas of offering myself to one of the voluntary agencies and going abroad at the end of my training. This was all part of the 'heroine' thing, not so much seeing myself as a heroine, but just being inspired by other people who did pretty heroic things. Some of the training staff from Great Ormond Street were going to Saigon, nursing children wounded in the Vietnam war, and that really inspired me. I would have loved to have done that.

When I was in the middle of my thirteen months' general experience at the Middlesex Hospital an Anglican priest was admitted. At this stage, I was not churchgoing. I still talked to God a bit, but church wasn't where I found Him, church was pretty boring. Anyway, I nursed this chap for about six weeks, and he said, like so many patients, 'Do keep in touch and come and see me,' but you can't, not with all of them. Then he came up to out-patients one day and said, 'Oh, do come and have tea,' so I did, and he took me to his church, and I have *never* in my life been into a church like it! I mean, you couldn't see one end from the other for smoke and plaster statues everywhere!

So I started going there. Extraordinary, really. Unlike anything I'd ever experienced, apart from the odd glimpse into Roman Catholic churches on the Continent when I'd gone on holiday with my family. But I went quite regularly, weekday masses as well, and my family went nearly spare, they didn't approve of this at all, I'd got 'religious mania'.

It was like falling in love, it really was. And I don't know now whether it was falling in love with God and the worship in the church, or whether it was partly falling in love with the priest, who was celibate and as gay as they come. He's dead now. No, there was a glimpse of something which I wanted, and I was prepared to go all out for it. Then I started doing daft things like offering to clean the brass and scrub the altar steps, you know the sort of thing. This all coincided with my very great friend and flatmate leaving training early in order to marry a Dane, so I went to live in a room in one of the parishioner's flats instead, and it was a whole change of lifestyle.

Anyway, after going to that church for about nine months there was a pilgrimage to Walsingham, and I went. And again, it was a highly emotional experience for me. It's not my sort of place, and I haven't been back since, but a big bit of me went out to that whole emotional side while the other half was repulsed.

It was really strange. On the Sunday morning, the parish group went to mass in the parish church, some bishop or other was preaching. The service was at eleven, and I was sitting there waiting for it, and at two minutes to eleven I thought, 'Oh my God: I have to try my vocation to be a nun!' Well, you can say all sorts of things about that! After all, I was highly emotionally charged over the weekend, and yet the experience of being called was very real, and it's just how I don't like God to be – very dramatic. I remember sitting there with tears streaming down my face; you know, *Save The Children Fund* and subsequent marriage and five children of my own, and five adopted, all out the window, because I knew from that moment that I had glimpsed the thing that I had to do. I knew everybody would say, 'Oh, she's just trying it, it won't last,' and I knew in my heart that it would, and that here was my – my *gateway*, if you like.

It was incredibly sudden. Yet when I phoned the parish priest a few days later and said, 'There's something important I need to talk to you about,' he already knew. He said it was either that I was going to get married or I was going to try my vocation. I had actually just met somebody, who saw our relationship, admittedly, much more seriously than I did, but for both of us it was quite a profound experience. I mean, thank *God* I didn't marry him, or anyone else!

Anyway, I made the mistake of telling my parents in the very early stages – I was so naïve. I thought they would be pleased for me – but they expressed *absolute* shock horror. They fought it tooth and nail; my mother, characteristically, much more vociferously than my father, but my father hated the idea from the start, it repulsed him. My mother was just *so* angry, *so* upset. It was like I'd thrown everything back at them that they'd given me over the years. You know, they loved me, I was gifted, I'd discovered my gifts at Great Ormond Street and what was I doing? I was going to be walled up behind some terrible – no, that's a mild adjective – but in some *ghastly* convent place, and just throw away everything I'd ever been given, either by them or by God.

So they reacted very strongly indeed, and my religious fervour got stronger as a result. I dug my heels in, and I was absolutely determined. It really sorts your friends out too, that sort of thing. Some people would say, 'I think you're nuts, but I still love you.' Others would say, 'If that's what you're choosing, then sorry, but I can't be doing with you.' One friend from school said to me: 'I've always wanted to ask you to be godmother, but I couldn't inflict a *nun* on my boys.'

Fortunately, there was a select band of really fabulous friends with whom I could go and lick my wounds and so on. But the war between me and my parents just waged, and, *oh*, it was grim. After I entered the community they forbade me to go to the house. They couldn't bear . . . they couldn't bear to see me – 'Don't come near us, we can't bear to see you.' – For months I wouldn't hear from them, and then I'd get these *appalling* letters from my mother. Appalling. She used to write and say things like: 'What are we supposed to tell our friends?' In one letter she said: 'I've decided to think of you as dead because that's less painful than thinking of you as a nun.' So it was several years before I was able to see them, and in the meantime, all sorts of things happened.

My mother said she would never darken the doors of a church again, but she's weakened now, because every time one of her children is preaching, she'll come. My father became a church-warden, and is still very committed. It affected them in opposite ways: he went in to the Church, she went out. I think my father would have made much more attempt at reconciliation had it not been that he felt he should be loyal to my mother, and also, life with her would have been intolerable for him if he'd agreed to see me.

My brother, meanwhile, was struggling with 'A' Levels at home, and my mother would say to me: 'You'll kill your grandfather of heartbreak; your brother will fail all his "A" Levels; our marriage will come to an end.' I can't remember all the other things that were going to happen, and in fact, none of them did, but it was quite hard to live with the knowledge that while you felt you were doing *absolutely* the right thing, you were causing considerable pain to the people that you loved most.

And it's funny the things you remember, but once I was walking along the retreat corridor in the convent, and I caught a whiff of somebody's perfume or talc or something, which was the same as my mother used, and you know the way your stomach turns over when that happens. Strange how very strong is the memory brought about by the sense of smell, isn't it – stronger than anything else, more poignant than anything else. And I remember she'd said to me: 'If ever I'm ill or dying, you're not to come near me, you're not to come to my funeral, I don't ever want you anywhere near me again. I forbid you.' And I remember thinking when I smelt that perfume: 'I'll never see her again and she's my mother,' and being devastated by that, and yet knowing that I had to carry on because it was what God was calling me to.

Then when my brother was being ordained, I rang our priest at home and said, 'Is there no way they'll let me come to his ordination? I promise I won't come anywhere near any of the family. I'll sit at the back.' He said, 'I'll do my absolute best for you, Frances,' and he came back to me later and said, 'There's no way they'll let you come.' And that was painful.

Now – well, we'll come onto now tomorrow, won't we – but now my parents are my strongest supporters, they'd throw a real wobbly if I came out. Our love for each other has proved strong in the end. But there's whole lots in between. It was a very hard experience but perhaps it had to happen in order for me to become my own person. I had to experience that total separation. It was a very sobering experience, and in the end, a very productive experience, I suppose.

*

During my first years in community, I was mostly doing very boring, menial tasks, which I guess Novices today wouldn't accept all that happily. But it opened whole new worlds for me; whole new vistas. It was just amazing, because it was like falling in love all over again, but falling in love with God this time. God just gave me so much, and the fullness of the religious life sustained me. My friends used to say, 'You'll never survive not having children of your own, not being married,' and yet every fibre of my being was being used in the community. Gifts that I hadn't known I possessed were being discovered and drawn out and used, sometimes on very superficial levels, things like cooking and flower arranging. But the thing was, I could actually do things I didn't realise I could do before. One Easter I suddenly found myself with fifteen big flower arrangements to do in chapel, and I know it seems very trivial but there was such joy in being creative like that. And after I'd been in community about nine months, the cook went sick and I found myself cooking for ninety, which was pretty horrendous because you don't even boil eggs for ninety like you boil them for three, but again, I could *do* it. I wasn't hopeless.

I never had any doubts from beginning to end. I don't find it difficult to conform, and I was about the last of the generation who was told: 'Swallow everything whole for the first ten years and then start asking questions.' As far as I was concerned, here was a great tradition, which I wanted to be part of. Some of the customs were incredibly Victorian and old-fashioned and lacking in logic, but that didn't worry me, because it was a means to an end, and I was prepared to give anything for that end. I'd glimpsed a vision, and I was going to go for it.

Oh, I'm sorry, I thought we'd avoid disturbances today.
Come in Bryan! Yes, later would be better.
Sorry. Builders. *Chaos.*

Yes, so I never had any doubts. We had a home in those days for a dozen or so disturbed, maladjusted children, and I worked part-time there. And one day I thought to myself: 'Okay, I'm not in Saigon nursing children, I'm not with *Save The Children Fund*.

I'm not doing what the world would see as heroic, but if I can reach even one of these children through love, and change their lives because of that love, then that's enough.'

Of course, you can't really communicate that to family and friends who are appalled by what you're doing. Here I was, not in Saigon, but an hour's drive from home, and – as they would say – walled up in some dingy convent with pathetic kids who should never have been there anyway, because it was totally unhealthy for them. But it was right there that I caught a glimpse of the irrational values of God; where I realised that loving one person well might be all that was being asked of me.

Because I was so happy, I don't think I had to struggle with the vows at that stage. Poverty was certainly a joy, because it was as much simplicity of lifestyle as anything else, and I was never somebody who liked to be cluttered with possessions. Present-day living is much more difficult because we have our own little bits and pieces – well, you can see them all around the room: people give you things and you don't necessarily have to give them away, so life now requires a lot more personal decision-making about what's luxury and what's necessity. When I entered, you were supposed to be able to pack all your possessions within half an hour to go anywhere in the world.

We also wear our own clothes now, when we feel its appropriate. People outside can be put off by habits, and so we agreed about twelve years ago that for community things – like Office and Choir and formal occasions – we would wear our habit, but that when we were off-duty, or on holiday, or when it was just more suitable, we would wear our own clothes.

We were given a clothes allowance each, and we went out and bought clothes, most of them from Oxfam. We had an original, totally impractical vision of a sort of community boutique, where you'd have clothes rails and hang things up and people could share. Well, you've already seen enough of us to know that we're dramatically different shapes, and it just didn't work.

I can't remember how much the allowance is now: £100 a year, or something. But it's got to include things like shoes, and tights, and all those things, so it doesn't stretch far. And then there's £7 a month pocket-money for other things like postage stamps for personal letters, but then I have such a massive correspondence that the community pays for my postage. The trouble is, I'm always an exception! Oh, writing materials, hobbies, chemist things, they have to come out of it too. So as you can see, poverty's changed from the days where we had practically nothing of our own.

The obedience I haven't found difficult because as I mentioned I am a person who found it quite easy to conform, and the obedience never really crossed my conscience. There was nothing that made me say, 'I can't do this, I risk my integrity if I do this.'

However, the chastity bit . . . Well, I suppose if at any stage I've questioned it, chastity would probably have been the most difficult, in the sense that I do enter into very deep relationships, and it's quite hard sometimes to draw a line as to what is appropriate and what is not. But I suppose in another way, chastity's the vow I value the most because it does safeguard the central relationship with God. And I believe it does render you available to respond as and when God asks you, whatever he asks of you. You don't immediately have to consider husband and children and home and all those things.

We'll be talking about this later, won't we, that now I'm in quite a strange position of being actively mum to somebody, and although I adore him, I feel quite keenly that I'm not totally available for some of the people I care for, because Kojo has prior demands. And that's not easy. But then you have to think, I didn't go out looking for a baby, it all just happened, and I don't believe that was coincidence, I believe that was part of God's plan.

I suppose one of the things that has become clearer to me over the years, however, is that vows within the religious life as a whole are a means to an end, and not an end in themselves. They are a way of living out the gospel, and we try to keep hold of that, because if they ever become ends in themselves then they're just stifling and sick. The whole thing is about freedom; freedom to respond to God's call. God is always a step ahead, taking the initiative, God inviting, God calling, God pulling, God nudging, and it's simply ours to respond – or not. We have the choice.

I'm also absolutely convinced that one of our roles as nuns is a pioneering role, and I think that all too often religious communities have become passengers rather than pioneers, and that's a death sentence. We have to have the courage to step out of ways of life once they're no longer immediately relevant, and to be able to do that takes courage. And it's nothing to do with age, I've discovered; some of our oldest Sisters in community are the most courageous about abandoning old ways and accepting new. But we should all be at the forefront of the Church, pushing out the frontiers.

After all, Jesus's own life was fairly political, wasn't it? And I mean, I am the *least* political animal that you could dream up, by temperament, but I get extremely angry about social issues, and that involves politics. I'm instinctively the kind of person who prefers to do hands-on stuff with the actual people who are suffering as a result of political injustice, but I recognise that it's no good just doing that, I've got to do my share of nagging in the appropriate quarters to get things changed. You can't just be doing first aid and mopping up, which is of course something I've learnt since I came here.

I promised I'd talk about Helen House, didn't I. I talk about it so much, you must stop me if I go on.

In 1977 I was elected as Mother of the community, and in August 1978 a woman phoned me and said her little girl was critically ill in the Radcliffe Infirmary, and somebody had given her my name and telephone number: she desperately needed to talk to somebody outside the immediate family and the hospital, and was there any chance of meeting? So I went to the Radcliffe and she said, 'Please can we go somewhere else?' We came back to this room, actually, which looked a bit different in those days, and she told me that Helen was their only child, she'd been normal, happy, intelligent, lively – all the things that parents dream of – until a few weeks previously, and then she'd become a bit unwell, and over the next weeks, increasingly unwell. Then one day she had a severe epileptic fit, and her parents rushed her to casualty, and a few hours later investigations showed that she'd got a massive brain tumour. She had surgery immediately, her parents being told that if she didn't she'd probably not survive twenty-four hours.

I met her and her parents about ten days later. Helen was still profoundly unconscious, desperately ill, and when I saw her I thought she'd only survive a few hours, she looked so far gone. But she didn't die. She had six months in hospital, and everything possible was done to try to promote her recovery.

It was a whole new learning experience for me, because I was on the wrong side of the medical fence, as it were, and felt as de-skilled and inarticulate and at the mercy of the professionals as any other relative, friend or patient is prone to feel. Also, as the weeks slipped by, and Helen didn't respond and didn't respond, I was very conscious of the effect it was having on the members of the ward team. Some simply ceased to be able to have eye contact with the parents, and sometimes the ward round would pass by the end of the cot – the sort of thing which is obviously not deliberate, it's busy people in a busy world, facing a very painful, difficult situation.

Five months after Helen's operation, her mother had another baby, and I acted that week as a kind of surrogate mother to Helen. Then, six months post-operatively, Helen had more brain scans, and her parents were told that she had severe, irreversible brain damage, and there was nothing that could be done for her. They decided then and there to take her home, and she's still there.

Actually, she's in Helen House for the day today. She's fifteen now, and totally helpless: no voluntary movement, no means of communication, minimal awareness, really, and hasn't smiled from the day of her operation. She hears, she responds to music, sudden sounds: we don't think she sees very much. Anyway, her parents took her home, and they had many, many sleepless nights. You can imagine the anxiety and the grief, terrible, terrible long drawn-out grief, which couldn't be resolved in one sense, because she'd neither died nor recovered.

I visited them often at home, and one day I plucked up enough courage to ask them if they would lend her to me sometimes, so that they could have a bit of a breather. And that was how it began. We used to put up her cot in this room, and she'd come and stay with me for a few nights at a time, five, six times a year. It wasn't much, but her parents said that knowing there was someone who also loved her and could look after her made it possible for them to cope with the intervening weeks and months.

Once when she was staying here, I began to think: if this is helpful to one family, what about other families in a similar plight, especially in a culture where the extended family's almost ceased to exist? And that's really the concept of Helen House: the extended family. Helen's family and I thought maybe we could extend that friendship to other gravely ill children and their families, and that's all it is, really. We've never had a committee. We had a little working party, and the most important people on that were Helen's parents, a couple of doctors, couple of nurses, and Helen's physio. There were only about ten of us, and we just plotted it with the architect, who is a domestic rather than a hospital architect, because we wanted it to be more like home than hospital. Helen's parents insisted that we shouldn't be able to take more than eight children at a time, because otherwise it would become institutional, so eight it is – plus any bits and pieces of their families that choose to come.

My first idea for Helen House was in February 1980, and obviously I put it to the community first. One by one they said, 'Yes, good idea, go on,' and the place opened in November 1982, so it was incredibly fast. In those two years we were given a million pounds. Helen's parents and I produced a leaflet and circulated it to a couple of hundred of our friends and contacts, and it just snowballed from there. Five-year-olds having recorder recitals; the RAF Chaplains adopting us for their Charity of the Year; OAPs giving us their £10 Christmas Bonus. It crossed all the barriers of age and background and politics and religion and so on in the most astonishing way. I visit prisons too, and there was a lot of support from people in prisons.

So from August 1980, I just got caught up in a whirlwind of activity, because there was all the planning to do, the responding to invitations to go and talk, the negotiations with professionals, assembling a team together. The architect was *inspired* – it's built in the grounds as you know, we had a spare bit of land – and the community was incredibly supportive and loving and tolerant of a Mother who was hardly ever there. I mean, I was never in one spot for two consecutive minutes. I was *always* moving. Always on the go.

Now I'm not nearly as involved as I was, because all sorts of other things have come into my life, but when I'm at home I still spend a little bit of every day there, and I still do a lot of public speaking about Helen House, because I feel there's a sense in which the families have commissioned me to go out and tell people what it's like to be in their shoes. And part of what I say is: 'We must recognise that the families themselves are the experts. They're the ones that we can learn from, they're the ones who can help us to serve other families better.'

There are lots of things I could say to you about it, but one of the most thrilling things is that although it was my baby, others caught the vision and made it their own, expanded it, gave it more life. Now the baby's grown up and is independent, it doesn't need me in the same way. It's very thrilling to me, it's a sign that it worked.

I think part of my motivation for the whole thing was that I had glimpsed a degree of pain which I couldn't actually tolerate as an onlooker. I think this is partly what has motivated me through a lot of my life, actually. It's a ridiculous example, but as a small child I was taken to a concert in the Festival Hall. In those days, those huge plate glass doors didn't have any markings on them, and I watched a woman walk straight into one of the doors and smash her face in. I must have been about nine, I suppose, and I fainted because I was a small onlooker who couldn't be involved. In the same way, when I've come upon road accidents or something, if there's been something I could do, I'd get on and do it. If I just looked at it, then I'd black out. If I felt I could do something, then the pain was bearable. I'm old enough now to realise that I can't save the world all by myself, but I find it very, very hard to look at pain and not be involved in it.

I also think that at the centre of any tragedy, there is a need for, well, a *friend*, basically. Somebody who is going to listen twice as often as they speak, and be there for as long as they're welcome. Somebody who'll do the shopping, or make cups of tea, or just pop by. That doesn't need training or qualifications, it just needs the courage to be yourself, and to allow the other person in the middle of the tragedy to be themselves too. And it's something I think we're in grave danger of losing sight of in our society where we're so geared to skills and specialists and so on. And also, people are so frightened of other people's grief. You know, six weeks after a major bereavement, or a divorce, or splitting up from someone, you're expected to be showing some signs of normality again. And that's ridiculous, but it's a very common attitude, and it leaves the grieving person, as you well know, feeling that they're abnormal, that they're out of step with the rest of humanity.

I remember quite soon after Helen House opened having a phone call one evening from somebody I scarcely knew. They said they were ringing for neighbours of theirs whose daughter had tragically died a few weeks back, and they'd asked instead of flowers that the money should come to Helen House. They all wanted to bring it round that evening. I said I would be very pleased to welcome them. Then the chap said, before he hung up, 'By the way, I ought to tell you their daughter was murdered.' So I thought, oh no, who the heck else is here to handle this better than I can? And fortunately, before they got here, I pulled myself together sufficiently to think: well, when these parents walk in they will actually have two legs, two arms and a head apiece, and they will probably just want to speak about the daughter that they've loved. All they will actually want is for me to respond as a fellow human being, not as some person who's skilled in handling people who are bereaved through murder.

And it was exactly like that. They stayed a couple of hours, and they had photos of their daughter, and they talked a lot about her. They talked about the crime, and about the boyfriend who'd killed her, and so on. And it just proved to me that there is no suffering so extreme that an offering of human friendship and compassion is not the most appropriate thing. And I find that very reassuring actually, because we've all got it.

The incarnation has become very central to my faith since Helen House began. There's a lovely Michel Quoist sentence: 'He fell, for a moment he staggered, then fell, God in the dust.' That sort of thinking has been important for me. But I think most important of all, hospice has a lot to do with the word 'companion', which is *companis* – to share bread with. The disciples didn't recognise Jesus until he broke bread, and somewhere in that story there's something that rings lots of bells for me, that in the breaking of this very basic substance they knew him. So companionship's about shared cups of tea and things, I'm sure, and shared human experiences and feelings and doubts.

What about prayer? Well, I pray for people in Helen House, but no, I don't pray specifically for a child to be cured. I just pray: Your will be done. Now, I don't in any way mean to diminish the impact of a child's death, because every time it happens it feels like outrage, and the grief, the immensity of grief, is unspeakable. But ultimately, I don't believe death is an end, I believe death is a beginning and an opening out into the fullness of life, and that if our Christian faith means anything to us at all, then we cannot see death as an end.

With death there is the pain of loss, the pain of separation, and there is the promise of eternal life, and the two things can't be separated, as I understand it. And I've yet to meet anybody who comes to Helen House, who hasn't believed that there's something beyond, something bigger than life. I think it's instinctive, it's a gut thing, if we'll only allow it to surface; that this life is small, and our understanding very limited, and there's got to be something beyond, because otherwise the whole of life becomes very meaningless, very pointless.

You know, talking to you about all this takes me back to my nursing daydream of working with *Save The Children Fund*, and doing big things in faraway places. But I don't think God measures things like that. There's a nice card one of our Sisters did out in calligraphy, about how love is giving and giving and giving, and it is, isn't it? I don't think it matters in God's terms whether our energy, our love, is spent on a very tiny number of people or mass support to disaster areas. What *matters* is that we're doing what God is asking of us in the right place at the right time.

Going back, though, to what effect Helen House has had on my faith: I think a lot of people are either bored by the Church, or scared off by the Church, but when it comes to a crisis in their lives, they look to those who are part of the Church as a kind of bridge. Perhaps that sounds arrogant. It's not meant to. It's just part of how I see my role. Certainly there's a lot about the Church I find hard to accept; its irrelevance to real life situations, its ecclesiastical politicking, its sheer unprofessionalism, very often. They're the kinds of things that get me angry. I don't think the Church should be about success or failure, either, because after all, in the world's terms Jesus was a pretty dismal failure. But it is quite possible within religious life to be lulled into some kind of irrelevant complacency. There are so many people who, to use a cliché, are marginalised in our society. Whether it's through grief or old age, homelessness, sickness, loneliness, they somehow feel that they have been excluded from the circle of human fellowship. And that's where religious communities should be – saying, 'Come into the circle of human fellowship, it's big enough for you too.'

Now Mary, I *hate* to say it, but I'm going to have to go and collect Kojo.

Kojo. Ah, yes! We must talk about him today.

Well, I've had him nearly three years. It was 1988, so I wasn't yet into my final year as Mother. I stopped being Mother here in 1989. After Helen House, I just knew that my creative energy was at a pretty low ebb, and that's the first thing that goes if you're tired, isn't it? I also felt that I'd been a very odd kind of Superior, really. I was away quite a lot, and we needed somebody who would redress the balance, who would focus on the internal affairs. I'm not good at that.

In 1988 I went to Ghana, to St Nicholas' College, Cape Coast, to speak at a clergy conference on the subject of healing. If I'd known what I was going to get into when I went! When you're in a witch-doctor culture, you're in deep water when you start talking about healing, I can assure you! But in a larger sense, it was an experience I wouldn't have missed for the world.

It was my first visit to Africa and it was absolutely marvellous. It's a very, very poor country, but the happiness and the generosity, the general joie de vivre was *incredibly* impressive. There were two of us leading the conference: myself, and a very radical member of the ANC, Michael Lapsley. He's just had both hands blown off and lost an eye in a letter bomb because of his ANC involvement.

Michael talked about healing of the nations, and I talked about healing of the individual. It was a lovely experience – all very random, nobody quite knew which day it was going to begin, let alone what time or anything like that. Then the second Sunday I was there, somebody said would I like to come and preach in the prison, so I said, 'Yes, I'd *love* to,' because prison is one of my great interests.

The prison was in an old castle, and in the centre of the prison was a courtyard. In the centre of the courtyard was this incredible structure, St Paul's Church, which was literally a roof on poles, with an altar and so on, and everybody in the prison went to it every Sunday. I preached there, and then there was a great hand-shaking ceremony; everybody wanted a blessing or a handshake. And in fact, the theme which I preached was: Jesus is Here; this is where he feels comfortable and at home, because it was the kind of place where he would have felt at home. It was so friendly.

Afterwards, one of the theological students said to me: 'Now would you like to come and see the hospital?' So I said, 'Oh, I'd love to,' because here were two of my biggest interests in life, you know, prison and hospital. So we went and looked around, and the conditions in the prison had been relatively okay, but the conditions in the hospital were much worse.

In hospital you could see the vestiges of where there had been useful equipment and so on, but it was all either stolen or destroyed, and the stench was awful and the conditions were ghastly and people were just sitting or wandering around aim-lessly, and other people were groaning with pain. It was just mind-boggling. I nearly did one of my black-outs.

We walked around the hospital, and then we got to the place where the children were, and everybody had an adult relative with them because that's law; you have to have an adult relative with you to supply your food and your daily needs, and they sleep on a mat beside you. Except for one, this minute individual lying alone. So I said, 'What about him?' He was grinning, he held up his hands to me, and they said, 'Oh, he was abandoned, he's been here several months,' and I said, 'Several *months*!' I thought he was a few weeks old. They said, 'His mother was traced, he's ten months old, but he only weighs four kilos,' which is like eight and a bit pounds. So I said, 'May I pick him up?' and they said 'Yes,' and I picked him up and he gurgled at me, grinned at me and he was just super, my heart went out to him.

I said: 'What will happen to him?' They said, 'Don't know. He's been abandoned, and his mother won't accept him.' So I thought, well the least I can do is leave a traveller's cheque for his food for the next few weeks, because there was nobody to pay for food, and he would just get what happened to be around, which wasn't very much. So I did that, and when I went back to the college I said to Ralph Martin, who was the rector, 'Oh Ralph, I lost my heart there, the little scrap.'

The next day a message came from the hospital, saying the doctor had not been there and she'd love to meet me. Well, I was due to fly home two days later, and in the meantime the programme was packed. But I went to see the doctor, and on my way I went to find the little boy, and discovered that the ward where he'd been – 'ward' is a euphemism – was closed down because there'd been an outbreak of cholera. Eventually we found him, and by now he wasn't in a cot, he was just on a soiled cloth on the concrete floor, and he was grey with gastro-enteritis – and I *mean* grey, he didn't even open his eyes. And again I picked him up, but he was too weak to respond at all, and I thought: 'This child isn't going to survive.'

I put him down and found the doctor, and I said, 'Tell me the story of the little boy,' and she did. I don't talk about this very much now because I don't really want Kojo to have his story made too public, but he'd been found abandoned and in a really pitiful state. He was taken to the hospital, and then they tried to rehabilitate him in the village, but the family was so ashamed of what the mother had done that they wouldn't own him. So he stayed in the hospital.

So I said to the doctor, 'What will be the outcome?' The doctor said, 'Well, we've tried all sorts of things, but he's picking up every infection, he'll probably die.' So I took a deep breath and said, 'This is probably a really stupid idea, and it's against anything I've ever believed right, but if he's going to die, then can I have him?' And she said, 'Yes, I'll fix it for you.' I said, 'Well, I'm going home the day after tomorrow,' so she said, 'It's all right. We'll cable you when to meet the plane. You leave money for his fare and we'll arrange it.'

So I went back to the college and I said to Ralph, 'Ralph, listen to this. I must be out of my mind,' and bless his heart, he said, 'You're not out of your mind. That's one of the best things you've ever done.'

Anyway, there was no telephone, there was no way of getting in touch with the community, so I flew home and the Sisters said to me, 'Tell us about the trip,' and so on. And I told them with great enthusiasm about it all, and I said, 'But there's just one thing: we're expecting a baby!'

And sure enough, two and half weeks later, the cable came: 'Meet such and such a flight at Heathrow, on Saturday the 2nd of July.' I was already preaching at somebody's wedding that day, but the flight was due in at nine, and the church wasn't too far away, so I went to Heathrow and collected the bundle. My parents live only twenty minutes from the airport, so I delivered one black baby into their arms, went and preached at the wedding, and came back again!

My original idea was that if we could build him up so that he would survive, then we could work towards fostering – preferably by a West African family, either back in Ghana or here. Adoption was out, because the family back in Ghana have thumb-marked a form agreeing that I should be his legal guardian for the time being, but not agreeing to adoption by anyone. However, quite a lot of things have happened. One of them was that I hadn't taken account of the fact that even a tiny child is going to put an immense amount of energy from *his* side into bonding, so that within two days I was feeling this *incredibly* strong energy from him. I had naïvely thought, if I'd thought about it at all, that it would be the adult who would start building the relationship, and it's not actually, it's the child. I've talked to quite a lot of parents since, and they have confirmed what I experienced. It's amazing.

Kojo responded very fast indeed to good food and love, and his chart for the mother and baby clinic that I used to take him to is dramatic. The doctor said he'd put it on his wall, because Kojo didn't feature at all on the graph to begin with, he was so grossly underweight and undersized for his age, and now he has more than caught up. He is quite a big boy for three and three-quarters, and highly intelligent – full of effervescent, strong-willed personality.

The community most generously owned my decision to bring him back. It has not been easy for individuals, or indeed for the whole community, to know whether at any stage we have done the right thing. But having accepted it, they were prepared to stay with it, and we are now actively looking at two main issues, really. What, objectively speaking, are the most important things in a child's development? What is the ethos of this community and what is its threshold, as it were, as far as normality and silence levels and all that sort of thing is concerned? And how, if at all, are the two things compatible?

What about Kojo? Well, as far as I'm concerned – sorry, as far as *he* is concerned – I am mum. I mean, I am working on it because he must know the story, but you've got to do it in easy stages I think. He knows that his daddy is in Ghana.

His mum? Well no, he doesn't know about that, not yet, because that would be too confusing. After all, he's got two mums, hasn't he? As far as he's concerned, I'm his mum. I never intended that he should call me 'mum,' but because everybody else calls their main care-giver 'mum,' he does too. He's never called me Frances, although all the kids in Helen House call me Frances quite happily. But he never would. It's quite a difficult word to say actually: Frances.

Anyway. It was mama, and then it became mummy, and then it became mum, and I didn't actively try to stop it because a child does need to label their main care-giver something. I laughed to begin with, actually. And his friends at nursery school are very accepting of me. I normally go in ordinary clothes, but like yesterday we ran a bit late, and I went in my habit, and the children really don't bother, because some of the mums go in nurses' uniforms to pick up their children. They're not fussed at that age. They will be in a couple of years' time, I think, but by then I hope I will have given Kojo sufficient a) security and b) knowledge of his own situation to be able to stand up to other people's questions, teasing, and worse, possibly. But he is a strong personality. He is a survivor.

Without doubt it's an extraordinary situation. But then you have to look at an imperfect situation within an imperfect world, and what are the priorities? We talked with a child psychiatrist a couple of weeks back, and what he said was: 'The top priority is continuity of the main care-giver in the early part of a child's life.' Kojo's already had one change, and he's amazingly unscarred by that experience. But there will be scars there, because you can't have a very chequered career for the first eleven months of your life without being scarred – you cannot.

By the way, do you get the *Independent* on Saturdays? Because there was a fabulous article a while back, and it really chimed in with where I was at with Kojo, because it was talking about bringing up small children, and how we in the West put a child into a cot with a cuddly toy as a human substitute, whereas in almost every other culture the child will be cuddled up to members of the family. And Kojo, when I started putting him in a cot, he didn't sleep. So what did I do? I took him into bed with me. And he still starts in his own bed, but he doesn't stay there very long, he cuddles in and he sleeps without any doubt much better close to me. Well, once I might have worried about that, but I think there are huge advantages to being in your middle forties when you start parenting, because you have the courage of your convictions.

I do find the future very difficult to think about, if I'm honest. I think that Kojo has started with very big disadvantages. But then when I talk to my closest, most respected friends, they just say to me: 'What's your problem? What's the matter? Why are you questioning it?' After all, he's quite a secure little chap. I mean, he has his days, but what three-year-old doesn't? He's very different from me: he could never have been my natural child, because he's so extrovert, so brave, so strong-willed. Gosh, there is battle after battle after battle. And of course that's where you feel being a single parent, because you think: 'If only there was a partner to share this with.' I mean I don't want to be married now, there's no way, but if there was a partner to share in the upbringing of a child, in an ideal world it would be very much better. Yet when I think about it I realise that many of my friends have far from ideal marriages, and actually there is conflict over child upbringing.

So as far as my situation is concerned, I personally think that being a nun and a mother are easily married, but you have to explode people's myths about it – without necessarily being sensationalist. People do very often put nuns on a pedestal, or 'somewhere over there' where they don't need to think about them, because as far as many people are concerned, nuns are not really part of society, they're just on the edge, if not outside. They think we're a load of nutters, that we're people who have either had broken affairs or don't like the idea of a sexual relationship or have got some kind of religious mania. There are all sorts of ideas, aren't there, about why people become nuns. And I think there's quite a narrow dividing line between making it clear that it is possible to be both a woman and a nun, and cheapening the whole thing. You have to be quite careful not to cheapen it.

Reporters have sometimes tried to cheapen it with me – you know, my 'cornflower-blue eyes' and all that stuff, very Sound of Musicky. It's partly why I have lain very low about Kojo, I mean I don't particularly want the press getting hold of that, and they've tried from time to time, but I've refused to speak about it. I mean, can't you imagine? Here I am, mother-substitute, experiencing things in common with many other mothers, from inside rather than as an observer. And while that is enriching for me, it is threatening to many others.

Oh sorry, not more disturbances!

Hello Barry. No, come in, it's okay. Have the carpet men been? No? Well, can't we put a bomb behind them? Hang on, I'll phone them. *Sorry* Mary.

Hello? Mike? Your lovely carpet men came last Friday and did a super job and said they'd come back on Tuesday and we haven't had sight nor sound since then. Right, okay. Lovely.

They're coming tomorrow, Barry. What colour for the walls? Oh I think the green, don't you? Oh, hello Barbara. Barry was just saying what colour for the walls and I said pale green. White for the bathroom, yes. Lovely, super, fine.

*

133

Sorry about that. I do quite a lot when we're converting something for a different use or whatever. I'm interested in all that sort of thing, and I loved being involved in all the interior design and furnishing of Helen House, it got rid of all my pent up home-making instincts! But the building trade drives me absolutely bananas, because they are always so optimistic about when they are going to get finished, and there's always a complication some-where along the line.

But Kojo, yes. My conscience says to me: I did not go out looking for a child. It's been quite hard in some ways to accept the role, but I have been convinced that it was actually what God was asking of me at the time. I could be accused of kidding myself. I mean, for goodness' sake, he's an attractive, loving, mischievous little brat, and I would find separation *excruciating*, but I recognise that there might be a time when there has to be at least a partial separation. In the meantime, the community is trying to work out what to do, because we can't go on with him living here and interrupting all sorts of things.

Over the years, one of the things I have found interesting, and it isn't just with the Kojo issue, is the far greater degree of indepen-dence that men have in religious communities than women. For example, I suppose of all my contemporary Superiors, I was prob-ably the one who was away most from my own community, and yet that was certainly no more than some of the men Superiors. The men's communities would accept that as the norm, whereas the women's would not. I'm not saying I want to be on detached service, because I don't, but it's interesting to see how the whole tradition has grown up differently within the communities. Many of the members of the men's communities have been priests, and have continued to have their ministry and parishes, whereas nuns, just like other women, have been expected to stay at home.

It's not that I have an axe to grind about ordination, because I don't. I do not feel called to ordination myself, but I do feel that it is *grossly* unjust that there is not the opportunity for those women who *do* feel called to ordination to be ordained as priests. I mean I *cannot* discover any valid argument against it, and I get pretty angry about some of the arguments that are used, and some of the attitudes. I *abhor* the vitriol that's around, I find it very distasteful, and when I come up against it I simply say, quite straightforwardly, that I cannot see any valid argument against the ordination of women, and I just think it's prejudice, actually, if we're honest. After all, at the beginning of the century, there was almost as much argument against women doctors, wasn't there? And we all accept women doctors now. Nobody in their senses would claim that they don't have the right to practise. Likewise, it's surely a person's right to respond to a religious vocation.

As a nun, I have met some revulsion, from men, though it's not something that I have seen as very difficult to handle, because it's very minimal – lads travelling on the underground who love to go about saying things like – what's the phrase? – 'Ain't got nun, don't want nun, can't have nun.' I suppose we're seen as an affront to their masculinity, and they don't like it.

Yes, my parents too. They hated it, but by the time that I was elected Superior they began to thaw. My brother got married around that time and I was allowed to go to the wedding, and that was the first time I'd been seen in public with my family and it was hard. Then, of course, the ideas for Helen House began, and that really did do it. My mother could identify with it, with my brother having been so ill, and she became my greatest supporter, and my father along with her. My mother typically energetically, my father just solid behind me, very proud.

There was never any apology. There was a sort of, 'You do understand, don't you, it was that we were so distressed to see you turn your back on your gifts and skills,' which of course, ultimately, I haven't. So I don't feel any bitterness or anger towards them. Some of my friends do: they say, 'Why don't you have it out with them?' But there's no point, life's much too short. I can see very clearly why they behaved as they did. Our community, twenty-five years ago, was *archaic*. It was very closed-off from the world, the Vatican II renewal hadn't begun. And for parents who cared about the well-being of their daughter it must have been very hard. All sorts of silly little things upset them, like the Victorian underwear we had to wear; no bra, and airtex vests with sleeves and bloomers! I mean, to have a twenty-three year old daughter who'd enjoyed clothes, the contrast must have been awful.

But now they are immensely supportive and very proud, quite embarrassingly so, sometimes. Now they'd be the first to throw up their hands in horror if I came out!

So how do I see my future? It's always my most difficult question to answer, that one, because, by nature, I don't look ahead. But one of the themes I've been working over recently is that each individual's life is like a kind of divine jigsaw puzzle. Unfortunately, we have to work at it face down, and we can't see what the final result is going to be. But nevertheless, the pieces are all there: some are already fitted together, and some are in a pile still waiting to be fitted. After all, you aren't ever complete while you're alive; you go on becoming, don't you? Although I suppose ultimately the person will be whole, the jigsaw will be whole.

So I can look back at my own life, and see the security of my grandfather's home; I can see the adaptation when my father came home from the war; I can see my early days of unhappy schooling; my happy times with my family; the birth of my brother and his illness; failure at school, and then my dream come true when I started nursing. I can see meeting that priest and being led ultimately into religious life, and all that's happened since then – all those different bits of jigsaw, with the usual monotonous bits in between, of vast expanses of sea, or the foliage of trees, or grey skies – all the encounters that seem to be chance encounters and so on, they're all part of the jigsaw. They all fit together.

Recently, though, one or two friends have said to me: 'You ought to leave and make a proper home for Kojo,' and there is nothing in me that responds to that, nothing at all. Because it's like saying to me: you've got a very, very good marriage, and you've got a child, but now you've got to choose between your marriage or your child. And other people could come back at me and say: 'All you want is to have your cake and eat it,' but I am sufficiently convinced that God's hand was in all this to believe that it'll go on being in all this. I'm in a soil that nourishes me, and anyway I believe there are phases in people's lives. I mean, this is a very active phase for me, but I don't believe that I shall always be skidding around. I hope I won't be. I hope one day I'll be able to go back to just being an ordinary Sister.

Yes, I do. Honestly. I think.

You know that lovely title of C. S. Lewis's autobiography, *Surprised By Joy*? Well, there's a sort of constant being surprised by joy that comes with the willingness to change. And although I've sometimes feared over the years that Helen House and Kojo and all the other things I get caught up in might have taken away from what I believe to be my vocation, I have known myself that the heart of the community comes first. The other things may be much more open to public acclaim, or emotionally, emotively appealing, but without the community, without coming into religious life, they would never have happened. And that's what counts.

(Six months later, Frances and Kojo moved into a house belonging to the community, across the road from the convent. They now share it with Kojo's best friend from nursery school, and her mother.)

LAVINIA BYRNE

Institute of The Blessed Virgin Mary, Hampstead, London
ROMAN CATHOLIC: APOSTOLIC

Age: 44
Nationality: French/Irish
Age at entry to community: 17
Number of years in community: 27
Previous employment: None
Present employment: Writer and broadcaster/Associate Secretary
for the Community of Men and Women in the Church, The
Council of Churches for Britain and Ireland.
Dress: Ordinary

---

*Lavinia presents herself immaculately. I wrote to her after reading
her third book,* Women Before God, *and when she replied, I was
struck by the beauty of her Italic writing. When we met, I noted
with interest the care with which she dressed and spoke. The overall
effect was disconcerting.*

*Lavinia's community is part of a well-known teaching order,
although the Sisters who comprise it do an enormous variety of
jobs. Lavinia works primarily as a writer and broadcaster, and she
and I met not at her convent in Hampstead, but in the central
London offices of the* Institute of Spirituality, *where she wrote her
books and worked on a Catholic journal,* The Way. *The offices are
part of a Jesuit training college, and the place contains a large
assortment of religious persuasions and professions. On the first day
of the interviews, Lavinia decided to put my 'nose for nuns' to the
test. Three plain-clothes women walked past, and I was nudged:
'So what do you think? Is she or isn't she?'*

*Lavinia was very supportive of me in the critical early stages of
my work on* Unveiled. *She lent me articles to read, suggested
people I should contact, and told me not to work for long hours
at a word processor unless I wanted myopia and a bad back. She
also gave me special recipes to help combat PMT, and showed me*

how to work her expensive portable computer, an item of which I was deeply jealous because, compared with mine, it was about the size of a large sandwich.

Lavinia was stimulating company. She has a quick mind, a lightning wit, and she made me laugh. However, she was extremely tricky to interview. Her volubility kept unwelcome questions at bay: as soon as the tape recorder was switched on, she disappeared behind an impressive verbal shield. I was armed with only my usual interview technique (mostly silence), so Lavinia dodged many of my questions with little difficulty. Once, in an attempt to break through her defences, I renounced silence in favour of the sledge-hammer approach. I should have known better: it was a counter-productive move which did not bring out the best in either of us.

On our last working day together, Lavinia heard that she had been appointed to her present job (in the Council of Churches for Britain and Ireland). I wanted to buy her a present, and I told her it wasn't allowed to be sensible: she chose some earrings from Ratners and a Bloody Mary in the local pub.

Lavinia Byrne

I cannot remember a time when I haven't been surrounded by Roman Catholic culture. The entire fabric of our lives was governed by the fact that we began the day by saying morning prayers, we had altars in our bedrooms, we said night prayers together, we said grace before meals. Every single time we went shopping, we stopped off at the church. We would stay late after mass and light candles. I remember as a child wanting to be a priest, and endlessly playing a game called 'altar boys' in front of the mirror in my bedroom. I remember preparing for my first holy communion when I was seven, and I took it extremely seriously.

I was very pious and devout, and I suppose my earliest religious memories are of listening to Dame Clara Butt singing Toplady's 'Rock of Ages, Cleft for me, Let me hide myself in thee.' I was tall enough to reach the 78 records and put this on, and Dame Clara Butt's magisterial voice was quite wonderful, booming out Rock of Ages. It made me feel incredibly pious, and I can see now that I was early affected by some of the scriptural images that are used to describe God, the ones that are non-gender specific like 'rock', and I find it not inconsequential that it was a big, powerful woman's voice beaming this sound to me.

I was born into the heart of the Catholic ghetto, to an Irish/French Roman Catholic family. My father was a steel manufacturer, and my mother didn't go out to work. My parents lived in Edgbaston and we used to go to church at the Oratory in Birmingham. My grandfather was the Catholic doctor to the Oratory parish, which meant he looked after the bishop and the nuns at the convent, and the Oratorian Fathers, and Tolkien, the novelist, who lived in the parish. And then the other side of the railway track, he looked after the Irish immigrant community. He was very proud of his faith.

Although I was one of a family of four, a lot of my childhood memories are of being alone. My sister went to boarding school when I was one, my eldest brother when I was three, and my next brother when I was five. I can't remember very much about my childhood in Birmingham. We had Austrian au pair girls who brushed my hair a lot. I had very curly hair; there are amazing photographs of me with my hair tied up, or curled up, or whatever. But my real memories began when we moved to Somerset, just outside Wells, when I was eight. I loved animals, and there I had animals; I had a pet cow called Chloe, and a pony, and lots of chickens, and I used to sell my eggs to the Somerset Milk Marketing Board and put the money in the bank.

My mother wanted to be an actress. When she was young I believe there was only one person she was allowed to bring home from the Birmingham Repertory Company where she hung out – and he was allowed because he was a vicar's son, and that was considered suitable. His name was Laurence Olivier, and that's a nice irony, really.

Do you know, my mother is the most *amazing* cook. She trained to be a professional cook before she married. Recently, I found her cookery certificates, and had them framed for her, and one of them says that she did six hundred hours' practical work and passed with distinction. As an ordeal, it's unbelievable, isn't it? But she did very fine cooking, dressing stuff and making sugar animals. Food was always the centre of family life, and my mother as cook inserted herself into a central position in the family because she made the food and brought us together at table to eat it. Eating was a very religious act, a very serious act, and that's where she officiated.

My father. Well, my father was very proud of the fact that he'd been so happy at his Catholic school, and he sent both his sons to the same one. He used to go on an old boys' retreat there every Easter. And I remember when he realised that I'd given up making the sign of the cross in church, he got hold of a sixpenny copy of what was called a *Simple Prayer Book*, which had the Order of Mass in it, and he went through it marking in red where I had to make the sign of the cross, and in green where I had to kneel down. It was done to help me to pray better. In retrospect it's rather touching.

The other thing I remember is that he had a brilliant system for giving out pocket money. He got his secretary to make us things that looked like cheque books, and they were called 'pocket-money books'. They said, 'B. J. Byrne owes', and then the child's name – in my case, L. M. Byrne – and then the amount. There were fifty-two of these bits of paper in your pocket-money book, and they were each date-stamped. It gave you a total feeling of security. When I went away to boarding school I remember knowing that if I saved up I could present four of these and get a ten shilling note, which was untold riches. I also remember once, how he called me to his office and read me an incredible story from the *Financial Times*, about bears and bulls; he obviously took this as a very serious duty, telling me when you should buy and sell shares.

I'm never very sure exactly what my father did. I know that they sold up when British Steel came in. He went to 'the works,' and that was it. I had no curiosity about it. I think he would have liked to have been an architect; he loved drawing and he was extremely good at it. I don't think he liked going out to work. He retired when he was fifty, stopped as soon as he was able to. He liked gardening, and he liked bee-keeping. I used to help him keep the bees when I was little. When we moved to Somerset he did things like cut the grass with a scythe, out in the field. He went very rural. Then unfortunately he caught brucellosis from Chloe, my cow, and that was bad because it meant his idyllic days were slightly curtailed. Brucellosis is not very nice. It's undulating fever. You get temperatures that come and go, and then you start hallucinating.

My father died about ten years ago, and for all sorts of reasons I think I'm closest to my mother. And there are age gaps between us, but I get on well with all my brothers and sisters. I suppose I was closest to my younger brother before I entered here, and we played a lot together when we were little. I was quite a tomboy, I had a gun from about my eleventh birthday, and I enjoyed shooting. My father and my younger brother taught me to shoot. Both my brothers were also extremely musical. My elder brother plays the bassoon and the contra-bassoon, and my younger brother plays the French horn, so my childhood is dominated by memories of them practising Mozart's concertos; all those tunes just echo round my childhood.

I was totally extrovert, and I had friends at all my schools. At the age of eleven I went to St Mary's Convent, Shaftesbury, in Dorset, which was a wonderfully happy school, right in the middle of the country. You could walk for miles and miles without crossing a major road. It was a very Catholic school, it was run by members of my present community, and I realise now that the Sisters who taught me were probably all younger than I am now, and they were *amazingly* attractive. They were fun, they laughed a lot, they liked each other. They were intelligent, they were gifted, they were happy, they were devout. There are many natural causes for any religious vocation, and I'm sure one of the natural causes for me was the sense that I would like to be like these women.

When I went to day school in Birmingham with the Holy Child Jesus Sisters, we had to curtsey every time we walked past a picture of their founder, Mother Cornelia Connolly. I suppose that inspired a lot of respect for nuns in me, because I was told she was important and wonderful. I also thought God lived in the Birmingham Oratory, and I was convinced Jesus lived in the tabernacle. I used to look up at the ceiling sometimes and wonder if my soul was as black as it was, because like all Catholic children I was guilt-ridden.

I remember praying, though, in all sorts of different places as a little child, quite naturally and spontaneously. I loved praying. I've got my first prayer book, which I wrote for my first communion in 1954, when I was seven. When I was about fourteen I wrote myself another prayer book. I cringe a bit when I look at it now, because I've picked up the idiom of hymns, but I loved hymns when I was a child. I used to stand up on my seat when my family went up to communion, and turn round and belt out 'Soul of my Saviour,' facing the back of the church. I must have looked like a little angel because of my curly hair. My other favourite hymn was Cardinal Newman's 'Lead kindly light.' Extraordinary! Think of me, aged six, seven, eight, belting out this stuff from the hymn about, 'Pride ruled my will. . .' Oh I was very, very devout. I also collected holy pictures, and said novenas – prayers that you repeat daily for nine successive days. I remember having a cousin of mine to stay, and tormenting her by making her say novenas that carried indulgences, which are not fashionable nowadays.

So I was nourished by hymns, prayers, statues. We had the Sacred Heart statue in our house, and lots of rosaries, but it was all totally spontaneous and natural, it was not contrived at all. There was guilt too. Everything I heard in church conspired to make me believe that God punished bad children. I think I used to feel I should go to confession because I told lies to escape facing up to unpleasant truths, or because I'd been committing indiscretions with my boyfriends, but I didn't feel guilty for just *being*. I was frightened of the God I heard about in church, of the God who was behind the catechism, the apostles' creed, the Ten Commandments. I never went hell for leather to win the catechism prize at school, but I was very interested in theology, and in the sixth form I used to borrow works of theology. It was the early days of the Second Vatican Council, and I really enjoyed being stretched and pulled by all of that.

Until I was in Lower Five we had all our lessons in Nissen huts that were left behind by the American Air Force. One of the Sisters would get up at about four o'clock in the morning and come down and put on paraffin lamps to heat the classrooms, so my memory of school is this incredible smell of paraffin lamps, which was added to at 11 o'clock, because for break on a good day we had dripping sandwiches, and if you were lucky enough to sit next to the radiator you'd put your dripping sandwich on it, and occasionally it would fall down into it; so put together the smell of paraffin and dripping sandwiches burning, and I am back in one of these chilly Nissen huts, learning how to conjugate Latin verbs.

Apart from school, the most important single influence for me during those years was going regularly to stay with my grand-mother in France. We'd spend the Easter holidays and summer holidays there, playing on the beach. I've been to that beach now for thirty odd years because I still go back to that part of France. We used to go mussel hunting, or we would build sand castles, or go sailing or swimming. Often we'd just play on the beach for hours. We became very friendly with a boy from a French family who used to play with us on the beach. Then one day this boy, Phillipe, arrived at the front door, carrying a visiting card. It invited us to tea – 'Cinq heures, le goûter' – so on the day in question we bundled into the car and set off to this address. When we got there, we found it was the most lovely French château, and a butler in full uniform was waiting outside to show us in. The women were wearing silk dresses. Whisky was offered as well as tea. This was the beginning of an entry into another world, a side of France that unless you're invited into, you don't even know it exists. This family have remained very close friends right up to this day, and I still visit them. My life is littered with images of that beach and that home in the north of France.

Ah now, boyfriends! I had lots of boyfriends. Ask me their names now, and my mind absolutely blanks over, but I can assure you that they were numerous. We had lots of friends who were boys, as well. There was a harmonium on the top floor of the house that my parents picked up for a fiver in a rubbish tip or an antique place, and we used to go up and play the harmonium, which was a lot of fun. The house was quite big, so it was possible to escape from grown-ups, and to practise the kind of adolescent explorations which would throw nice Catholic children into paroxysms of guilt, because you knew what you *couldn't* do better than you knew what you *could* do. So life consisted in experiment with what one *could* do. Certainly by the time I entered I had somebody who would have made a very attractive alternative to the convent had I been willing to consider him, but I wasn't. I was absolutely certain of what I wanted to do, and I knew I had to do it.

I don't think I ever woke up one morning and thought, oh gosh – I'm going to be a nun. I just knew it from the inside outwards, and it wasn't as though I chose it. It chose me. I believe religious vocations use natural means to communicate themselves, and as I said, at that time nuns were the most attractive role models I saw. I didn't want to be any of the people who were rolled out for our edification when I was in sixth form, almoners or nurses, who gave us careers talks. I just did not want to be like that. Becoming a nun was also about finding a focus for my devotion. It was about belonging to God in what was those days called 'a very special way.'

The presence of God in the eucharist was taken very seriously by church teaching in my childhood, and that had an enormous influence on me. There was one place where I was certain I was in the presence of our Lord, and that was kneeling praying before the tabernacle. I remember, in 1959, at the beginning of Christian Unity week, our parish priest said we should go to mass every day and pray for Christian unity. So I went to mass on my bicycle every day, and on the fourth day the nuns were beginning to notice. One of them asked me why I was doing it, and I said to pray for Christian unity, because we were told to. After that I was made to testify in class, and I think it was a sort of break-through for me. We went to mass anyway three times a week, when I was a child at school. We lined up in the assembly hall and put on white veils, and filed into the chapel, in line. The chapel was always there, and you could slip into it and hide from the rest of life. When you're very extroverted, as I am, you need periods of quiet, otherwise you just go into orbit. I suppose in chapel I was getting out of orbit.

I hope I'm not making it sound as though I was a goody-goody, because I was healthily naughty. Nevertheless, from the age of fourteen I knew I wanted to be a nun, and my whole life was shaping up in that direction. When I was in the Lower Sixth, I saw the Provincial Superior of our congregation, and she made encouraging noises when I said I'd like to enter. She told me to go to mass every day, and to pray a lot, which I did, and the feeling developed rather than going away. I wrote and told my parents and they wrote back a marvellous, Catholic-parent answer saying, if this is what God wants, of course you must do it. But when, in the event, I said I'd be entering when I left school, they very much wanted me to go to finishing school or do a degree or travel first – and I didn't.

I finished my 'A' Levels in July 1964, and entered the convent in the November. It's very difficult to recapture the innocence of the early sixties, when it was possible to drive all over Somerset in open cars with petrol at three shillings and sevenpence a gallon, and to go to Weston-Super-Mare for the afternoon, or to go out for walks in the country, or to go out with a gun, or to go out to parties. It was a very carefree time, so the transition from that to the very formal and controlled atmosphere of a religious noviceship was a curious one. Though my parents were reluctant to see me doing this as I was so young, through sheer stubbornness and pig-headedness I succeeded in doing what I wanted to do. However, when you enter a convent, the understanding is that you're in training, and in our case the first eight and a half years are a time of probation. You don't enter and just say farewell to every other opening. Yet from the moment I left home, I was committed to it, and went for it, hammer and tongs. I genuinely had the inkling that the best way in which I could be human and holy was through the life of consecration represented by the religious life. I also had an inkling that if I were to marry and settle down in rural Somerset I would quite likely become extremely bored. What I was doing instead was going into a way of life that would commit me to process and to human growth, a way of life where the community said, 'Look, we're going to spend the first eight and a half years training you.' This is an immense privilege. What young woman of seventeen has the prospect of eight and a half years of training put in front of her as a real possibility?

I've heard it said that a religious vocation is ninety per cent idealism and ten per cent realism, and I recognise that formula. The idealism and the sense of purpose give you the energy to set out on this journey. And also, the confidence that you're not journeying alone, that you're doing something you believe God desires for you, means that you will be offered the grace – whatever that means – to undertake the next step of the journey. I was quite hard-headed about it, but I think resolve is essential, there's plenty of sanction in scripture for it: 'Leave your family and follow me. Put your hand to the plough and don't turn back.' Those kind of texts were very supportive and sustaining at the time, though in many ways I was in a state of shock, because it is an immense step to leave home and go to something unknown. But the sense of call was all-pervasive; I didn't hear 'a voice', and I cannot name 'an occasion', but I had a clear sense that this was what God wanted me to do.

Taking the vows didn't emerge as an issue, really. With hindsight I can see that the vows commit all that I am, all that I have and all that I do, to God. All that I am, meaning celibacy; all that I have, meaning poverty; and all that I do, meaning obedience. Well, I am and have and do all the time, and it's always I who am the subject of these verbs. It's the giving of one's whole self which matters. However, all my high idealism took some battering over the years, because I had to grow up. I had to realise that the person I call 'I', who is the subject of each of these verbs, is a person who is capable of doubt. I am capable of uncertainty; I am capable of being exhausted; I am capable of making mistakes.

But I am convinced that the 'I' who left Somerset in 1964 was doing it with total generosity, and with a curious depth of understanding. There's a very powerful image that I have. The Somerset levels are all reclaimed land, and recently I realised that in a curious way I was claimed – just as that land was once claimed. Sometimes I've scurried around looking for the treasure in the religious life, whereas the treasure was the transaction. I sold everything. I gave away everything. And now everything belongs to me. Everything.

The training had three elements to it. The first two were informal. When I entered the convent, there were sixteen of us in the novitiate, an extremely attractive, intelligent group of young women who were immense fun to be with. We supported each other through friendship and through what Christian feminism has now taught me to call bonding. We became really good friends, and emotionally it was a very enriching period.

The second informal influence was the people with whom we worked in the community, particularly what used to be called 'Lay Sisters', the people who did domestic work. The system was positively feudal in the sense that they, and we – the Novices – were put in to do the domestic work in order to enable a large girls' Catholic boarding school to operate with practically no official domestic staff. Later, we were all replaced by a washing-up machine, and then eventually by a cleaning firm.

The formal training was instruction on the history of religious life, on theology, and on the rule of the life. That was supplemented by the sort of domestic work that I've just described. Very occasionally it flashed through my mind that if I hadn't entered I might have been with some of my peers from school and having rather an interesting time at university; instead, I was washing floors, or plates, or glasses. Sometimes when the children came in for tea at five to four, we would just be finishing the washing-up of their lunch, and the temptation to barricade the refectory door and say, 'Don't you come near any of this, because we're only going to have to wash it up again after you've finished,' was really strong.

It was incredibly tiring, and physically hard, and it prepared one for any eventuality. It also removed any sense of hierarchy of tasks. Now I have no problem with cooking or cleaning. I realise this is rather a privileged comment because I don't do that much of it, but nevertheless, I value the opportunity. I love cooking. One of my jobs as a Novice was as carver. This meant that you arrived at the kitchen wearing a white overall at eleven o'clock each morning, and the head cook gave you the task for the day, which was either to carve meat, or to dish up the meat for the children and the Sisters' lunch. The first day I appeared, there were seventeen legs of lamb ready to be carved, and by the time you'd carved that number – well, basically you knew how to use a knife. To this day, I cannot bear seeing meat being badly carved. Put a knife in my hand and I can fillet or carve anything.

The time came for me to go to university, and I was sent to read French and Spanish at Queen Mary College in London. We're talking now about 1967, and the change from the noviceship was quite breathtaking, because from living in an extremely closed set of circumstances, I found myself wandering up and down the Mile End Road in a full-length black habit, and attending a college where there were 2,000 students – 700 of whom were engineers, recognisable because they all had mole wrenches in their back pockets. The people who were at the college did not come from privileged convent backgrounds, and very few of them had been to boarding school, so university was an extremely important time for me. It was a time of change and growth.

I was two or three years older than most of my contemporaries, and I found that quite interesting. I used to scurry home when college was over, although I did join the college orchestra because I played the violin, and I enjoyed the kind of social life that centred around the chaplaincy. I had a lot of friends, and really enjoyed my time there. I can't stress enough what an exciting time that was to be at university and to be reading French. I went to France in June 1968, after the May riots, and wandered all over Paris seeing slogans saying, 'Beware – walls have ears': the feeling of excitement that was bubbling around *ideas* had a profound influence on me.

After I finished at university I was trained to be a teacher, and for that I went to the Department of Education at Cambridge, and lived at our convent in Cambridge. It was an immense privilege being in such a beautiful atmosphere after London's East End. Also during that period, I began to study for the Westminster Diploma in Theology, a part-time diploma which I did for the following four years. You have to remember that at this time the Second Vatican Council was beginning to make radical demands of religious Sisters. Our entire way of life was crumbling and changing. The religious community I had joined was undergoing immense transition, and to be part of that cauldron of bubbling ideas, and to see them changing the very way we lived, was immensely exciting.

The noviceship was extremely demanding. Poverty, chastity and obedience – and that's the order that they were listed in at that time – ensured that our lives made total sense, from the moment we got up in the morning to the moment we hit the hay in the evening. As long as you were totally committed, you did okay, so during my noviceship years I tried to keep my head down and get on with it. I think at the time that the way I was looking at God began to be rather negative. I began to have the feeling that God was like a sledgehammer, and that if I stuck my head up between the floorboards, I'd get into trouble; I would be trampled on in some way, I'd be hurt. Therefore, I chose to keep my head down.

I was frightened of the opportunity for growth that was being given to me, I think, the opportunity for discovering more about myself. And if there was a certain immaturity in me at that age, it was, I believe, because I sheltered behind idealism. By adhering very closely to the ideals I could ignore my fears and my reservations about the training process.

Nowadays, in a changed climate, when first formation is so personal, and is also highly therapeutic, young people who enter the religious life are given the opportunity to work on their own personal agenda. Whereas the sustaining image behind the formation that I received was one of perfection, and it was very easy to hide behind getting the externals right. The other element of our noviceship training was that it was highly competitive. Whatever task we did, we did as a race.

So in a sense I lived out of my shadow. I went around pretending to be an introvert because it was the best way to survive. But personality is so strong, and God's grace is so abundant, that eventually the extrovert self emerges, and says, 'Now, pay attention to me.' I realise now that the levels of silence, and the monastic practices that were expected of us, were extremely oppressive to me.

Apart from all that, I have to confess to being totally boring: I have not really doubted the existence of God or my own sense of vocation at any time during my life. What has happened is that these have changed naturally. My understanding of the religious life has changed profoundly from when I was a young nun. It had to, because God is good, and life and reality come hammering on the door of one's false idealism, and say, 'Look, who are you, really? Do you want to live your life like this, or do you want to try to become something that is more human and more authentic?' I remember as a Postulant, the Novice Mistress, who was a good woman, sat us down and said, 'Now I'm going to teach you how to pray.' And I felt *outraged*. I felt the fact that I'd been praying since I could remember was being ignored. The way we prayed as Novices was through the scriptures, so I said all the right prayers, said the Divine Office, said the rosary, said the litany of the saints. I can look at that experience dispassionately now, but I could never return to it. It was a task-orientated way of praying, and I did every damn thing.

I look back at myself with a certain amount of horror, because I was obviously such a late developer that it took me to the age of thirty-plus to take on board what my training had probably been trying to give me all along the line. But the image that I have of my growth is a natural one. It's like a snake shedding her skin, rather than a cataclysmic or apocalyptic one. And although it's quite painful shedding one's skin, it's an organic image. It's not as painful as – well, as being blown apart.

I get the feeling that behind your questions about doubt, there may be one about trial and about failure, and I think that my failures have been enormously instructive to me. Loss of confidence in my own willpower – the fact that willpower alone is not enough – was very important in breaking the perfectionist mode, because if you can't trust your own resources, then you have to turn to God and say, well, what next? So loss of confidence made me put the brakes on, and other experiences also forced me into looking at myself. A very fundamental experience for me was of the love and friendship I was offered inside the community. It was sometimes misconstrued by me, because someone who so obviously needs affection is a bit of a liability, and the bit of me that I was neglecting was going around craving attention. But the people who loved me into life did me an enormous service. I learned that I was responsible for some of the vulnerable, sad, sorrowful parts of myself.

It wasn't that anything in particular was wrong. I think I was just experiencing the natural sadness and vulnerability that go with being in one's twenties and thirties, and that go with a sense of loss, which for many religious is quite unacknowledged, of one's femininity and its legitimate expression in marriage and in having children. Physically and spiritually and psychologically there are parts of me which are still in mourning for that; and for the avenues and opportunities for tenderness that are represented by marriage and having children. I'm not pretending that all my friends who are married, who are my age, are all deeply tender people, or that they're totally sexually fulfilled, because that would be naïve as well. But I am aware that they have chosen a way of life that renders that possible, or probable even. Whereas the kind of nun I was busy being, and the kind of nun who was externalised in the clothes that we wore, and the way of life that we followed, was cut off from the expressions of being a woman that were accessible to my married friends.

I'm not saying I wish I'd got married. It's just that my inner self was mourning these things, and once we stopped, as a community, being motivated by a model of perfection, and at the time of Vatican II, when we had to find another model, I was able to grow. We found something more holistic, more human, something which offers people the opportunity for personal, rather than merely collective, growth, and we were lucky because our community has grown tremendously through that experience.

However, some communities fell apart with Vatican II. Active apostolic religious communities, such as my own, can fall apart for two reasons. Either people get stuck indoors too much, and start building community as though that was our purpose, which it isn't; or they're out too much, so that to talk of community becomes a farce, because you can't make community with people you never see. It is difficult getting the balance right, and the things that used to keep religious communities together have now been replaced by a very serious regard for community meals; they are a real place of exchange and celebration. In my community, there are also more community meetings, or faith sharing, where people actually say what's going on, what they're feeling like. Someone could be feeling atrocious but at least you know it, and if you know what people are feeling, then there's a chance that you're really talking to each other at a deep level, not just exchanging platitudes about the weather or the Royal Family.

This is important because the kind of relationship that is represented by religious communities is a relationship of adults who choose to live together, and it demands a lot of respect and space for people. It's extremely difficult to live alongside people, but the monastic system has built in a great number of securities – silence, for example – which enable people to live together without getting on each other's nerves. In the community in which I live in north London, we range in age from ninety-one to late twenties, and I find an enormous amount of respect and acceptance in that community. An enormous amount of friendship too.

Do you know, I had my silver jubilee last year, to celebrate twenty-five years of life in the community, and I found it so very affirming to receive gifts and tokens of love and affection from people, and to come together for a jubilee celebration, with a big mass. I felt like a million dollars! I was given sixteen bars of soap, seven sponge bags, about thirteen different sets of letter writing equipment, and endless sundries, because people in orders such as my own have spending money nowadays, which we're given each month, and which doesn't all go on cups of coffee and visits to the dry cleaners. Some of it is available for presents.

How much? Well, I think it's gone up to £45 recently. We're quite likely, actually, to go on a sliding scale soon, depending on people's needs. In which case I'll take a jump – up. The useful thing about having a personal budget is that you have to make choices. You can no longer go along to the Superior and say, 'Please may I have a new pair of shoes,' and expect to be given them instantly. You have to save up for a pair of shoes, and you'll be rather careful of them because you only have limited financial resources.

Having money breeds a far greater sense of responsibility, because you're facing the same kind of choices and decisions that other people face who are not vowed to poverty. You know the old tag: somebody is supposed to have said to a monk, 'You make the vow of poverty, but I and my wife and ten children live it,' and there's a certain wisdom in that. Nowadays, where priests and religious have access to money, they are forced to live their vow of poverty in a way they could escape before. Poverty, it seems to me, commits one to share what one has. But it's not the same as penury. After all, we're fighting poverty all over the world.

As far as dress is concerned, we're rather fortunate in my community in that we're recommended to wear our clothes in a way that's dignified. Some orders have rules about neck or hemlines. But to my mind, a vow of poverty is not an excuse for going round looking like a failed Oxfam victim. I believe that what every adult Christian woman is being asked to do is to present herself to the world as somebody whom God loves, not somebody who's crept out from the last pages of the Book of Job.

Did you know that Job's daughter is named in the final chapter of the Book of Job; her name is Mascara, and nuns in the United States wear mascara and other forms of make-up. In our culture, in Europe, that's not particularly acceptable. My jewellery? Well, earrings are a sign of being baptised in many Catholic countries.

These are all questions about externals, and they are terribly important, because lack of self-regard and self-esteem does demonstrate itself in how people appear. If you see a nun who's looking very down-at-heel, she's making a statement about how she feels about herself.

The great buzz-word among Christians nowadays is 'frugality,' and the witness of a simple life-style, of shared food, shared hospitality, shared resources, seems to me very important. And this doesn't mean a boring, banal existence. You know, the inside of your room is not supposed to look like the inside of a prison cell. You can make a statement about your taste and what you find important when you start having some kind of influence on your own environment, your own bedroom, for instance – or your office, if you're fortunate enough to have one.

We live in a world of emotional poverty. We live in a world where we know people can murder six million Jews; we live in a world where people can drop an atom bomb on Hiroshima or Nagasaki. We've witnessed poverty, famine; we see it on our television screens. In a world such as our own, the theme of self-abnegation as the basis for Christian asceticism seems to have changed so much. Our world is now a place which we're asked to inhabit. Nowadays, asceticism seems to be about being responsible material creatures. It's no longer good enough merely to say, 'That is the material world and I turn my back on it.' I think that if the religious life has any witness value at all nowadays, it's in showing people that there are moral choices around. So let's see if we religious can model some possible answers. After all, the religious spirit is not about ugliness.

If the religious life is supposed to be offering some kind of witness, and I believe it is; if it's supposed to have a prophetic element to it, and again, I believe it is, then it has to grapple with the questions which are alive for adult Christian people nowadays. So it has to be conscious of the Women's Movement; it has to be conscious of questions around power and authority; Green Christianity; social justice; a commitment to making our world a better place. And if you take those seriously then you have an agenda to last you a lifetime. As soon as you start inhabiting the world in the way I'm describing, you have to start facing emotional, physical and sexual choices, which I fondly imagine – I might be quite wrong – were not around for earlier generations of religious women.

You and I have been talking about clothes and dress, but there is a subtext to that whole discussion as well. It's interesting that many religious women have begun to allude to the fact that they're women, now that they no longer wear the habit. I find it entertaining to think that a film like *Nuns On The Run* could allow two men to dress up as nuns and look totally convincing. It's extraordinary really. And Sisters who've started wearing ordinary clothes, and started mixing on a one to one basis with male and female colleagues, where they are as open to sexual harassment or sexual desire as their lay women colleagues, really are facing questions about what it is to be an adult woman. Nuns have stopped holding the moral highground too. You will find nuns now actively working, politically, on behalf of women who are the victims of domestic violence, or sex abuse, or sexual harassment in the workplace, and not seeing it as something rather distressing, but as part of the ordinary transaction and currency of everyday life.

All this is begging the question slightly because I appreciate that what you're also asking is: what happens when you find you're falling in love with somebody? And the answer is; the same thing as happens to anybody, really. If you're falling in love with someone you have to decide how you're going to give appropriate expression to what you feel, and how you're going to do this in a way that neither damages your relationship with that person nor goes against what you have vowed. So it's not always about cut and run, either. Some of the most attractive nun and priest friends I have are people who have fallen in love and who have faced very painful or costly choices, and have done so with courage, because they really have tried to grow through that experience. Emotional risk is part of being human.

But myths about nuns abound, and these myths make it extremely difficult for nuns to be real, because they get idealised, or patronised, or sentimentalised. If you walk around in a habit in London nowadays, people talk to you as though you're a child;

they clear their throats and speak up. On the other hand, I don't like getting into the game where one says, 'I'm a nun,' just to wind people up or shock them. Equally, I'm not going to allow them to treat me as though I cease existing at the neck, as though I have no needs, no loving heart, no real sense of being human, because that's doing them, as well as nuns, a great disservice.

When I wrote *Women Before God*, I put in a chapter about nuns, and people's perceptions of nuns, and one of the things I said was that I believe that what men in particular feel about nuns they actually feel about a great number of women, only they never own up to it. So if they patronise nuns, they're going to be patronising towards other women. If they sentimentalise nuns, they're afraid of getting close to other women. If they ridicule them, they'll ridicule other women as well. There is also a sexual agenda around because a nun is someone who's saying, 'I can construct my life without men. I don't need to be married in order to say I'm a human being. I'm not putting sexual gratification at the top of my list. Therefore, that bit of you is not going to be greeted by me because I'm just not interested in it – or I'm certainly not interested in it today.' And I assume that is threatening.

Therefore, many people latch on to nuns as freaks, rather than seeing that the religious life has been good for women because it has offered them an alternative. From its origins in the fourth century it has enabled women to break the chain whereby from being their father's possession and walking up the aisle on their father's arm, they become the possession of their husbands, and walk down the aisle on their husband's arm. Institutionalised patriarchy. And the religious life has said: 'It's all right not to be married. It's all right to be your own woman.' But because it's not the norm, in the sense that marriage is the norm, religious women take a lot of stick. I was once teaching a group of sixth formers for a friend of mine, and the famous question of, 'Do you have to be a virgin to join a convent?' came up. My friend said in a small voice from the side, 'Is that before, during, or after?' which ridicules the question, and treats it as it deserves to be treated.

Yet it seems to me right that religion and sex are very close to each other, because they're both sources of energy. So is money.

In today's world it seems that we're all struggling to become more natural, closer to our animal roots, closer to all that makes us human. The temptation has been to become mechanistic, so in today's world, religion has to offer a different form of sexual message, and it's one which says, 'Take seriously the perspective of women on these questions. Take seriously their contribution to understanding questions like birth control, or abortion, or bringing up a family.' But in a pre-mechanical world, people were struggling to be free of the flesh, because their bodies tied them down.

I believe the Church is right to try to offer guidelines to help people live well in their bodies; just as it has the right, and indeed, the duty, to proclaim a social gospel, to say that how we treat each other really matters. What I'm suggesting, however, is that the Church listens to the contribution women have to make to this debate. Women have an even greater investment in the questions than anybody else, because many of the processes we're talking about actually happen inside women; if sex and money and religion are about power, then we must listen to what women are saying about how power should be used.

Consequently, when you're groping your way towards seeing what it means to be an adult woman, you're saying something about God, in whose image you're made, and the normative metaphors you use for God begin to change as well. They've changed for me, completely. God remains the God of my childhood, and of Toplady's hymn, 'Rock of Ages', but the rock-like presence of God is now much more diffuse. It is not simply God the Father who sits in heaven, it's Father and Mother and Parent and Lover and Friend and Presence – above all Presence.

And you know, the Church is going to be overcome by events. It's going to realise that the meaning of the word 'man' has actually changed over the past ten years. Man no longer means 'men and women'; it means 'the chaps'. And the fact that the impetus is coming from outside the Church is going to make for fascinating consequences. Within the Church, we're going to be faced with the question: do we really exist to serve people, and to attend to them in their needs? Or do we exist to impose ideologies? Language is so important because not only does it enable us to say things, but it controls how we think. If we're constantly calling God 'Eternal Father', or 'Lord and Master', then we're limiting the divine activity in the world, we're limiting the ways God can be for us.

Nowadays, there are women saying, 'I no longer want to go to church because I feel ignored when I get there.' Or: 'My name is never mentioned, my gender is never alluded to. Not only that: not only is it about my naming and my nouns, but it's also about my verbs. My preferred verbs are not the verbs I hear in church, so my whole way of being in the world is being negated by the Church.' And it's not just radical feminists who are putting out a new party line, it's ordinary women who are speaking with real authority about this now. So the Church requires a form of evangelisation that takes account of the bad experience of many women. It needs positive discrimination in favour of women.

When I think of my own journey, the journey away from the traditional values represented by the Birmingham Oratory: if somebody as middle of the road as me has been led by circumstances to start using radical language, then there is movement afoot. I don't think the religious life in twenty years' time is going to bear a shred of resemblance to the religious life as it's lived now, and I don't think the Church will either.

So there's been a natural progression in my thinking, which is partly why I want to see women ordained. Not to the priesthood as presently constituted, because I think that just puts them in a place of pain and inferiority in *all* the churches. I met somebody the other day who's at a large Free Church training college, and in her bible group one of the fellow students calls them all 'Brothers', and when she objected she was told: 'If you're training for ministry, then you've got to be prepared to get used to this.' So women's problems don't come to a halt as soon as they become ordained. But if priesthood is re-conceived and re-imaged, I think that it will attract a particularly joyful and energised group of women and men.

I've had at least three vocations to the priesthood myself. The first was when I was a child, and it came to me as an acute disappointment to realise that I couldn't be. I was baffled by that, simply on grounds of gender. I had a vocation to the priesthood about ten years ago when I looked into a sanctuary and suddenly saw how glamorous it was to be the principal actor in this drama. I adore theatre, and the embroidery looked so lovely, let alone the sacred character of the action! Then about four years ago, when a friend of mine was being ordained overseas, suddenly all the old longings came back. But at present I don't have a vocation to the priesthood, and until the priesthood is imaged quite differently I don't think I'm going to.

Since I left teaching in 1980, I've done a lot of youth and retreat work with adults. And since I've worked here, at the Institute of Spirituality, I've helped run training courses for Spiritual Directors, I've taught a course for Anglican women deacons. I've done endless workshops with women all over the country, and I've written four books about women and spirituality. I began experiencing a call towards all this sort of work when I began writing the story of our founder, Mary Ward, in 1984, for the four hundredth anniversary of her birth, and when a job presented itself here I applied for it, and was appointed for it.

Anyway, what I notice happening is that some of the tasks which I once understood to be priestly are increasingly coming women's way. In the field of spirituality and retreat direction in particular, you are ministering to people's spiritual growth. You have the cure of souls, and you find yourself hearing confessions until you're blue in the face. And I find that enormously exciting.

There are so many images of priests around: the president of the Eucharist, the person who has the cure of souls, the person who in a very pagan sense slays the victims, and therefore has to be a man because a man's got nice muscly arms. And none of these really does justice to the understanding that Jesus was and is the only priest. Everybody else is a priest *analagously*, and that if we explored what that means we'd see priesthood very differently. The present-day debate about the ordination of priests is to my mind as much as anything a debate about the forces of revelation in the Church, and where teaching authority lies. This is particularly the case in the Anglican Church, where people ask 'Is it Synod that legislates for us? Is it the bishops? Is it the Lambeth Conference? Is it parliament? What lines of communication are open between the traditional scriptural sources of revelation and the tradition? And whose tradition is it anyway? – The chaps'.

Whereas I understand Roman Catholicism to be a religion of the incarnation; a religion which says that all life is sacramental, and all life gives us access to God. I love the Roman Catholic Church even when I feel most enraged by it, though I hate going into a Roman Catholic church where all you see are Catholic Truth Society leaflets, or booklets about abortion and contraception, because it merely confirms the popular stereotype of the Roman Catholic Church as obsessed with sex.

It's very easy to parody or over-simplify the Roman Catholic position on sexual morality, but as I see it, there are three strands around at the moment. The first is the conservative strand, the position held by the Vatican, where the contraceptive mentality is condemned, and all forms of birth control which don't rely on natural infertility are also condemned. Then there's the liberal view which is held by many Roman Catholic lay people. They say, 'We hear what the Pope has said, but our needs are such that we will practise contraception,' and in enlightened liberal families such contraception is talked about. The liberal view is all very well, but it's just so easy to hold if you're in a position to make those kinds of choices.

Latterly, in the 1980s and the nineties, we've seen the emergence of as third strand, and that's one which says that all contraception is really targeted at women. I think it's highly intrusive: it's assuming that all women want is sexual activity with men, when in fact there are other questions which must be addressed. One of these is about economic control. It's only when you're rich that you can choose not to have children, and this is particularly true in the Third World. Only when we've raised their standard of living will we have the right to say, 'Now, would you reconsider the question of the number of children you have.' Similarly, women in Europe and America and elsewhere are saying. 'I refuse to be defined simply in terms of my reproductive capacity, but if you *do* want to talk about my reproductive capacity, *don't* try telling me that a fertile womb is an image of destruction, because that is doing terrible things for women. It's saying women are triggers, and pull the trigger, have a baby, and the world is destroyed.' And when you listen to the imagery and the language – things like 'population *explosion*' – it's all very contentious. So I think there's a crying need for the Roman Catholic Church to consult women when preparing doctrinal statements about questions to do with care and nurture and creativity, because if you ask women you get a totally new perspective on these questions.

Have I ever wanted children? Well I suppose at some stage in my mid-thirties I looked around at other women with children and thought it would be quite nice to have another little me, to see myself replicated in another generation. But to be absolutely honest, I haven't terribly wanted children. I love children from about the age of fourteen upwards, but before then they just wear me out, they've got too much energy and they're highly intrusive.

People assume that you want children, though. Very often, my contemporaries, my friends, would say, 'Would you like to hold my baby?' and it's very difficult to say, 'No, as a matter of fact I wouldn't like to hold your baby.' I find babies frightening: I'm always afraid their heads are going to drop off. I've never changed a baby's nappy, and I wouldn't know where to start. So people needn't assume that I'm quivering with maternal anxiety. I'm not.

I think that the religious life is moving in new directions. I'm confident that in the area of retreat work, in particular, or through writing and broadcasting, or through counselling, or working with alcoholics or prisoners, or the dying – all the kinds of activities people in my province are engaged in at the moment – the focus has changed. It's still educative, but 'educative' doesn't mean brain-damaging people and trying to get inside their heads and tinker with them. It means enlarging the field of choices for them, so that they hear the voice of God within, rather than believe that the only source of authority lies outside them, and is inescapably contained in pronouncements which are prepared by men in the Church.

Education in the *specific* sense is an absolute landmine. You wanted to know how we can justify our private schools, didn't you? Well, in common with many 'teaching nuns', my community has run very successful, very prestigious boarding schools and superb grammar schools in this country. We do try to address the question of how these schools can have places which are available to people who don't come from privileged backgrounds, but it's very difficult. Again, it's so easy to adopt the moral highground, to say that we should not be contaminating ourselves by teaching in prestigious schools, that we should be all working in very deprived and depressed schools. Well, some of our Sisters are, but there are some others who are doing admirable jobs in the big boarding schools. And I don't want to stand in judgment over either. I can't say mine is the moral highground.

Some of our ex-pupils are now in political life, and the kind of influence represented by access to somebody like that is worth a hundred protesters walking up and down the street, waving banners, because when they come to visit, you can say over supper, 'Look, have you ever thought of such and such?' I could reel off a name of prestigious past pupils, and if you can call these people up on the telephone, then you can exercise political authority. That's a privileged position to be in, I realise. . . No, I do have a problem with it, I have an enormous problem with it. People just feel differently about taking advantage of it.

In this, as in every other matter, it's very difficult to respect difference – particularly when you're living on top of each other. But, you know, there are two things I've done over the last five years which have helped me to be more accepting of difference. One is called *The Myers-Briggs Personality Type Indicator*. It's one of these personality assessment tests, based on Jung's understanding of typology, and it can really help you to respect other people. People who used to threaten me desperately because they were so different, now enchant me, and I've found that very liberating.

The second is much more fanciful, but has saved me an enormous amount of money, and enabled me to enjoy externals, and that is *Colour Me Beautiful*. When I worked with Anglican women deacons, I advised them all to do *Colour Me Beautiful*. It's the colour testing where you discover if your skin and hair colouring suggest that you should wear colours described loosely as spring, summer, autumn and winter. And since I discovered that I am a spring, with a wing into winter, I have been able to walk into shops and know exactly what I should and should not buy – and

I've saved a fortune. I've got the pattern book out there. I don't know what you would be; you could be what's called a summer. You're not a winter. A winter wears beautiful, bright, bright green – jade green, shocking pink, turquoise, black, white. No, you're definitely not a winter, you can't wear strong colours. Though you look good in black I suppose, with your blonde hair. So *Colour Me Beautiful* and *Myers-Briggs* between them have been wonderful.

Does anything worry me?

Death doesn't worry me. What frightens me far more is the thought of decaying and growing old, and getting Alzheimer's, or getting crotchety and becoming deaf and blind and batty. Death itself is wonderful: I love the Salvation Army expression, 'Called to Glory'. I think Mrs General Booth was an absolute marvel. She wrote a book about women and ministry at the end of the nineteenth century, which was totally triumphalistic. That idea of being called to glory, that's how I see death, going through to the next stage.

I'm forty-three, and in January I'm beginning a new job. But I don't have any mega project I need to achieve before I die. I have done my best and if I were knocked off my moped tomorrow – well, I've been praying, 'Into my hands, oh Lord, I commend my spirit', ever since I can remember, and if I was taken at my word that would be fair enough.

Do you know, I live just down the hill from the cemetery in Hampstead where Evelyn Underhill is buried, and her tombstone says: 'Evelyn, daughter of Sir Somebody Somebody, wife of Somebody Underhill,' or whatever his name was, and I feel, good Lord, here was this woman who wrote seventy books on mysticism, who was regarded as a world leader in the field at the time, and on her tombstone she ends up as the daughter of her father and the wife of her husband. So there are undoubtedly ironies around one's death, terrible ironies.

Perhaps I feel so confident about death because my grandmother was ninety-seven when she died, and my mother is eighty-one and going strong. I belong to a family of very strong women: we last far longer than the men. But also, if you have been living a consecrated life with whatever degree of success or failure, you have received immensely reassuring messages all along the line about how your life has meaning, and how it has value, and therefore to lay down a life that has meaning and value is not difficult.

When I was a child I learnt Italian, and I loved Dante and the idea of the court of heaven, and how we'll all be there, giving glory to God. And in my mind I see it as a medieval tournament, with everybody jousting – rather like a polo match. People in the stands, having enormous fun, and then *you* arrive in the middle of this arena, and you say hello to the people who are at the heart of this court. Then once you've greeted them and been held in their embrace you go and climb in the stands and start enjoying yourself. That's how I see it. Heaven as party, where we give praise to God by being happy, and every tear is wiped away.

Yes, I do see it that way. I do. Heaven as a medieval joust. Nice food, nice drink, people happy, people praising God and wandering around finding all their ancestors, all the people they have ever loved. Reconciliation. Me meeting up with Mrs General Booth, and both of us called to glory.

RENATE

Community of The Holy Name, Derby
ANGLICAN: APOSTOLIC

Age: 67
Nationality: German (British citizen)
Age at entry to community: 39
Number of years in community: 28
Previous employment: Sculptor/Art teacher
Dress: Habit

Renate was the first contributor I met when I started work on this book, and I remember being struck by her enthusiasm for it – something which gave me great heart as I took a professional leap in the dark.

When I went to Malvern to interview her it was in the middle of a scorching summer. The atmosphere was altogether different from my one-day visit the previous winter as all but three of the community, of over fifty women, had just moved to new premises in Derby. Renate and two other Sisters were house-sitting until the new owners, who planned to turn the convent into a retirement home, arrived with the builders.

Sweet-natured, slight, with wispy white hair, smooth skin and eyes of bright steely turquoise, Renate has a manner to match her looks; soft around the edges with a firm core. When she spoke it was with a strong German accent, and the construction of her sentences was often German rather than English.

We talked for four successive mornings in the beautiful walled gardens of the vast eighteenth-century house. Renate stayed cool in a loose blue habit: I nearly passed out from the heat in a succession of silly skimpy skirts. Renate sat very still and frowned a lot as she spoke, bending over backwards to answer my questions clearly, and stopping every so often to ask me if she was doing okay.

Every day, Renate's fellow Sister, Bernie, produced gargantuan

lunches – specially prepared vegetarian dishes and puddings drip-
ping with fresh cream and strawberries – certainly the best convent
fare I've tasted. A gluttonous boyfriend had accompanied me on
the trip to Malvern and he joined us for meals, to the delight of
the Sisters. Bernie was overjoyed to meet someone who knew the
meaning of a good pudding, and confessed that if she hadn't
become a nun she would have liked to marry a farmer and have
six sons: 'Only so I could cook big lunches for them, and proper
breakfasts too; none of this muesli stuff.'

Once or twice, Renate and I tried talking on through the after-
noon, but Bernie's lunches rendered this more or less impossible.

Renate

I come from a German, Christian family. My father was a Lutheran pastor. I had a very secure, loved childhood, and I was the eldest; I had a younger sister and four younger brothers. We were a very self-sufficient, very artistic, musical family. And when I was ten, Hitler took over and everything altered, because we realised that we were despised by the official line which was practised in the country. Then we became an island.

We were a very natural Christian family. There was nothing sentimental or pious about our Christianity. It sounds very childish when I say it like this, but as a small child I would not have been a bit surprised to have seen Jesus at the bottom of the garden, where I imagined I saw fairies. It was on that level. And when you think it is nearly seventy years back, well in those years you were less sophisticated when you were eight or ten than we are now. We had a lovely old, old vicarage, big walled garden, we had everything going for us. We read, we had a marvellous place in the attic where old costumes and things were kept, we performed drama amongst ourselves; I wrote plays for Christmas and Easter. We played naked in the garden, we had a sandpit, and a swing, and a tree house . . . It was *marvellous*, because we were considered and treated completely as persons as children.

I know it sounds as if my family was years ahead with bringing up children, but I believe we were. I think it was partly because both parents came from old families where it was the natural thing to respect and nurture individuality. My sister's no longer alive, but when I meet my four brothers now, we all say the same thing: we say, 'I look back upon my childhood, oh it was lovely.'

I was very serious. Quiet. As a very small child, I had a vivid imagination. I saw things in the garden, I made poems about them, I sang, I danced. The vicarage and church were in the same grounds and to us they were our own place. My two sausage dogs used to follow me up the aisle in the Church. It's odd you know, but we were very simple, far less complicated than now.

There were certain formalities. We had a gong to call us in for meals, and there were always two gongs, the first for washing

169

your hands, and the second one for meals. You had your proper place at mealtime, and you certainly ate what was given to you.

When I was ten we moved to a much larger vicarage, and I look upon those years as the most precious time. The first ten years had been in a very poor part of the country, right up in the mountains, and I remember the winters were very long there. And, those first ten years, my father was slightly remote. We were taken to his study in the evening, to say goodnight, and we would never, never go to his study unless he wanted us there. Then we moved, and things changed. I remember vividly seeing my father sitting on the carpet playing with soft toys with my younger brother.

I thought it was absolutely wonderful to have God as a father. When my father preached he appeared in the pulpit, this little wooden nest, and I thought, 'That is God there,' and then a couple of hours later, this God would sit at the dinner table. So I related to my father on two levels. I always admired him. He was a remarkable teacher and I was terribly proud of him, because he opened an inner door to investigate and to question.

We lived in an almost feudal village; it was very much Squire and Vicarage. We had no friends in the village, friendships were really school friendships. Even so, there was a certain aloofness as far as my family was concerned. We were far too self-sufficient, because we belonged to a family who went back to 1500. There was a certain conscious separateness.

All this I accepted until I was ten, eleven. Then I began to query it. I realised that my father, and my whole home life, was ridiculed. It was poisoned deliberately by what other people were saying about us as Christians. And I remember thinking, 'Oh why can't my father be a teacher?' I began to query whether it was really worthwhile to belong to a religion if it caused so much trouble.

By the time I was a teenager, we knew that it was dangerous to be a Christian, that my father risked his life belonging to the confessing Church, and it was then that I chose . . . no, I have to alter that, then that I was *compelled* to belong to the Hitler Youth, to justify my own existence as a pastor's child. I realised later on that it was totally contrary to what my whole family stood for, but for a while I became a very enthusiastic Hitler Youth member.

I was aware that I lived in two worlds. One world was at home, where, for instance, we would have tramps in the house: they wouldn't sit at our dining table, but hand-shaking in Germany was always the custom, and we children would shake hands with them. Then, when Hitler started, no more tramps were allowed. When someone was sick in the village my mother would often take some soup and some flowers, and my sister or I would go with her. We grew up realising that the wellbeing of others concerned us and was part of our responsibility.

But at school it was different. I realised forcibly that I belonged to this 'despised class' when one of my teachers turned round to me when we were doing Jewish history in the lesson, and said 'Of course, you would know all about it.' And I was very cheeky, I said, 'I wish I *did* know more about it, because the Jews are the ancestors to our Christian belief.' And I remember he blushed and quoted a couple of hymn lines to ridicule me and Christianity.

As I said to you, when I was eleven I had joined the Hitler Youth, and I began to *enjoy* it because I felt less ridiculed. Hitler Youth was the only permitted youth organisation anyway, every Saturday afternoon. It was to start with very much like Guides; you walked, you sang, you went to camp, you learned certain signs like morse codes, and that kind of thing.

But then Hitler Youth began to give out its own kind of song-book, which was nothing but adoration for Hitler. There was a probationary period when you didn't wear a tie, and you got your tie only when you passed an examination where you had to recite Hitler's life and the wonderful person that he was. It became more and more regimented. I went to some camps with the Hitler Youth to the seaside, which was an event for us because we lived right in the middle of the country. And though you had fun, you had to have that flag up every morning and sing to it.

I don't think all the leaders were Nazis. I was for a while a local leader, and I would compare myself, certainly, to a Girl Guide leader. When the war started and the first wounded came to our village, I was the local Hitler Youth leader, and we put on entertainment for these wounded or recovering soldiers. Incredibly harmless, but looking back now – I remember my father called me and said that I was occupying myself with things against which he stood.

I really don't think I was aware of anti-Semitism. I remember seeing in our town an elderly man with the yellow star and I didn't know what it was, and I asked my mother and she said, 'It is something we do and it is very dreadful,' and I felt very uncomfortable. She didn't explain it. I wouldn't be surprised if my father kept it from her too. I can't imagine that my mother knew the existence of concentration camps, I don't think she would have survived it emotionally if she had. But the Church knew long before 1933, when Hitler took over, that things were very, very wrong.

But because we had a hospitable, open house, with interesting people, writers, actors, singers, musicians, we never queried anything. Then when I was sixteen, my father called me and my sister and said: 'From now onwards you will no longer be told the names of our guests. It will save you awkwardness at school.' I realised soon afterwards that we were having people in the house who were trying to get out of Germany.

I left school in March 1941 when I was eighteen, and Germany began to evacuate its towns because of bombing. Many of us who had just finished school were detailed to take a transport of youngsters into what is now Czechoslovakia, to teach and supervise them.

We were 'politically trained' for two weeks in Prague, and then we were put into action in a small town. I was supposed to teach history, because I loved history, but I realised then that things were very wrong indeed in the country. It was the year when Heidrich, the Protector – one could not have misused a name like that more than he did – was assassinated, and the Germans massacred a whole Czech village in retaliation.

I remember their tanks appeared in the town where I was teaching. And then in Prague one day, two of us were walking along in this marvellous medieval town, and I will never in my life forget this. We stopped in front of a shop which sold pictures, and in the shop window was nothing else but Van Gogh's Cornfield, and the window was beautifully done, with some drapery picking up a bit of the sky and the corn. And I said to my companion – we were two girls of eighteen plus – I said, 'How beautiful,' in German. And as we turned around to go away, two Czech men spat at us, and some spit landed in my face. Neither of us did anything, but inside me something cracked, because the first bit of being ashamed to belong to Germany dawned. I realised that if this kind of thing can happen, there must be something terribly wrong. And it was then that I realised that only some sort of unconditional acceptance can heal that kind of wrong; and when I started in community over twenty years later, I knew it had begun in Prague.

My teenage life, which should have been packed full of explorations, was totally conditioned by historical events. Even our boy and girl friendship life was affected. For instance, we hardly ever danced together, because dancing was too un-military by the time the war began. Life was only about becoming fit to defend your country. I did have a boyfriend, but he was much more fond of me than I was of him: I was very fond of another one who was far more good looking! We went out together, met each other after school, had ice-cream together, swam together, but that was it. Terribly harmless. It would never have dawned on us, for instance, to live together at fifteen, sixteen, seventeen. We had very good lessons in human biology at school, so we knew what was possible, but I don't think it would have dawned on me to misuse that. It was later that I saw it misused, against girls by Russian soldiers.

I managed to leave the Hitler Youth, which was quite difficult to do, because by that time it was automatic that you stayed until you were twenty-one. Then when you were twenty-one, you were expected to become a party member. But I got out, and I came home and served six months' domestic service, because the country said that girls who wanted to go to university had to be either nursery maid or housemaid for six months before they could go. After that, I had to go for six months into the Land Army. I wanted to read Archaeology, but during those troubled years, before starting an arts degree course, one had to do a course in a registered art studio, so I chose sculpting and loved it. It was a three year course, but 1944, when I'd only done a year and a half, I was called up to the Air Force Ground Staff.

It was terrible. Absolutely terrible. I had to report with other girls at the local headquarters, and when we arrived, the atmosphere was very nasty. One after another we were called into separate offices where the SS was standing around, and we were made to sign on the dotted line that out of our free will we were prepared to defend our country. Lunatic! Absolutely crazy after Stalingrad! I phoned home because you had less than twenty-four hours to leave, and my father came to see me off and said to me, 'You will see things which are terrible' – he had been a chaplain in the first world war – and 'Don't tell mama.' And I left.

I was twenty-two, twenty-three. We were put into army railway carriages. We didn't know where we were going to, but we travelled overnight because the bombing was so heavy. We had no water, nothing to drink, nothing to eat, though when we stopped at some railway place, and opened the window, a man brought us some cold coffee.

Eventually, we found ourselves in an already bombed training place for the Air Force. There were around 2,000 of us from all over the country. We were given a pair of trousers, a greatcoat, a helmet, and a gas mask. Some didn't get masks, there weren't enough. We were medically examined, and I am *completely* certain they were not doctors. We were a row of usually four or five girls, completely naked, standing in front of maybe three or four men in white coats. We were not molested, we were not raped, but you can look at a naked person and you can look at a naked person. And we knew. We felt mentally raped. Some girls cried.

We stayed there for two nights. We were given some thin porridge, because there was no food about; the beds were dirty and we didn't lie down, there was too much chaos around us.

The next night, we were put onto another train and we found ourselves in a bombing attack, although we weren't hurt. Then eventually we arrived in Essen, a practically flattened city, again into another barracks of soldiers. And there we were supposed to be trained for the Air Force. We were graded into intellectual ability, and I was put onto radar, which was fascinating, but totally useless when you have plane after plane going over.

None of us wanted to be there. We knew that Germany was at an end, and we knew that what we were supposed to defend was no longer in existence. We knew that the whole business of being a soldier was a pretence now, and then one morning something happened.

We were lined up into rows, in the hangar where we had to assemble every day, and the atmosphere was very tense. Three or four SS officers walked in, and we realised that we were supposed to take the Oath of Allegiance to Hitler, and we didn't! It was absolutely marvellous. These officers said: 'Repeat the Oath after me, and put your arm up,' and we didn't. And you can't prepare that. There were hundreds of us, and we were a very motley crowd. But there was this point of no return, and there we stood. I think the atmosphere would have gone up in smoke if you had put a match to it. The question was repeated, but of course it was hopeless, so they left, and we just hugged each other.

Then the next day we travelled to the front line, and it was terrible. I was again at the radar, and then later on the telephone lines, but it was sheer and utter nonsense. The radar was useless because the Americans simply hovered over a certain area and dropped bombs: we called it 'bomb carpets,' which it was, and it went on all day, with an interval of two, maybe three hours. And I remember trains arriving with wounded soldiers, and you saw then the human bodies which had been mutilated. Awful. It took me years and years to get over it. And one day in the trench – whether I said it aloud, I don't know – but I certainly said to myself, 'I have been brought up, and I have believed in the bottom of my heart that you, God, had something to do with love. But if this has anything to do with you, then I will have nothing to do with you.' And I didn't finish that sentence. I unconsciously realised that the bottom of my life would drop out if I denied God.

Six months later, in early 1945, we were stationed in a town which had been evacuated. It was a ghost town. Trains used to come through with the wounded, and I remember very well indeed a day when a train had been attacked, and those who were alive or could walk got out. Our unit had set up a first aid post, and we had no dressings left so we pushed sanitary towels into the wounds. And I remember the skyline, there was a tree, burned through the bombing, but the skeleton was still there. It was fairly flat country, and I will never forget seeing the figure of a soldier, without arms, walking towards that tree. Because it had only just happened to him, the pain hadn't set in, but he managed to get to our post, and we stuffed the stumps with sanitary towels.

I don't know whether he survived. For years and years, I dreaded driving round in this country, round a corner, where all of a sudden I would see a bare tree, because it brought the whole destruction back. And I eventually realised, 'Renate you are living in a cage, your freedom of acceptance is trapped by terrible events in the past,' and gradually it left me. But here at night, in the Novitiate, many a time I still cried out and couldn't get rid of it, couldn't stop seeing it.

And yet, there was one wonderful incident. It was my birthday, and in that part of the country there were big flower nurseries. They had all been destroyed, but some tulips had grown and flowered despite the bombing, and someone found out that it was my birthday and came with a great big armful of yellow tulips. I can still see her coming. There were all these flattened glasshouses with their spikes sticking out – and this wonderful bunch of light in all the misery. Ever since then, I very deliberately look for something which is good, whether beautiful or positive or good, and which doesn't give me the chance to get bitter. For years it was a struggle, but looking back, I know it was a time of tremendous shaping.

In March 1945, when the bridge at Remagen, the last important Rhine bridge, was taken, we were sent back. We were given a piece of paper and simply told, 'You can use any kind of official vehicle which you can find.' Three of us got a lift on a tank, and then there was nothing going further to the east, so we walked, but only by night, because during the daytime low-flying aircraft were bombing. It took us over a week to walk from the front in the West to the middle of Germany. When we divided up, I carried on by lorry, which in those years were heated with wood gas. I sat on the pile of wood.

Then the autobahn was bombed very badly. The road was ruined, and you had to avoid these craters, of course without light the whole time, and you crawled along, and you heard cries from the craters where other lorries had tipped over. And you didn't stop because you could be the next one in. And I remember then I prayed, probably very consciously for the first time in ages. I prayed, 'Please let me get home. I'm so near now, it's only about another hundred kilometres.' I'd written a letter home, and said goodbye, because I thought I wouldn't get out alive. I found out afterwards that it never arrived. I remember I'd put a primrose in.

I didn't pray again after that, not for a long time. I just survived. I had a rucksack I had made out of a blanket. I had taken a tin of pilchards and a loaf, and I survived on that. People gave us some water on the way. One farm was very kind and gave us some bread.

When I arrived home I had a steel helmet and a greatcoat on, and my mother didn't recognise me. It was the end of March, and my cheeks were encrusted with blood, because I had got a lift on the bonnet of a car, and the wind had made me bleed. I'm absolutely certain I smelled, because we had slept rough for about a week. But our dog recognised me. And it was only a fraction of a second later, and then my mother said, 'Oh Renate.' Oh, it was chaos: chaos in that whole country.

Yet I know that without this chaos I would not be me as I am now. I don't mean this irreverently, and I don't mean it piously, but without God pushing me to that utter limit I would not be me: because I was a very capable person, and I could have done many things, and then the choices were taken away from me. The war took them all away.

My faith had remained with me throughout my teenage years. I never visualised God, and I didn't pray automatically, but God was there. And when I was living in the village near Munich, there was a Roman Catholic church, and this, together with the shrines that were all over Bavaria then, kept that spark which had burned very brightly during my childhood flickering. But when I was a student the crucified man annoyed me, and the calmness of a Buddha appealed to me. I had a little Buddha in my room for a long time. But I realised that I needed a God who said to me: 'You can run away from me: I will wait for you. You can reject me: I will wait for you.' In the end, that was not Buddha but the Crucified. Germany was a cage, but the Christian faith reminded me that the world was bigger than this German cage.

My father once said in a sermon: 'One of my children asked me the most crucial question of the Christian life regarding the crucifixion. My child looked at a picture of the crucifixion and the question was: where was God?' And he said, 'The answer is: God is there.' I said to him afterwards, 'Which one of us was it?', and he said, 'You.' – And you remember I said to you that in the trench I nearly cursed God and couldn't – well, I realised that in the agony and in the destruction of war, God is here.

Good does not exist without evil, and you can't have dark without light, but in my own appreciation, if God hadn't allowed evil, then we would not know it, and we would almost be puppets. If good was all that existed, then I could only choose good, and it wouldn't be a proper choice. I think there is a deep wisdom in the legend that Lucifer was the angel of light. We search for the light, and it is an ongoing quest of humanity to find answers to these questions. Yet ultimately I believe we cannot find them here. In the end, I have to say, 'I believe this. It doesn't hinder my reasoning, but it is *beyond* my reasoning.' I have to be prepared all the time to accept that reason is great, but that it isn't infinite. There is a limit to reason.

I reached home at the beginning of April 1945. After a few weeks the war was over and the American Army arrived as the Occupation Force. They treated us in a humane and fair manner. From May 1945, until the Russians came in August, four concentration camp victims lived in our vicarage. These men – three Polish Jews, one Austrian Jew – had somehow managed to walk from the nearby camp, which we had thought was an ordinary prison, and collapsed on our doorstep. I will never forget the sight of them. Utter misery. Skin and bone, clothed in dirty rags. They curled up together in the beds, hardly able to sit or stand.

In August 1945 the Americans left and the Russians came to control what became East Germany. Russian occupation was terrible! The understandable hatred was vented on us. We had no rights, we were plundered, men disappeared, women and girls were misused. My sister and I spent many times in our church tower to be safe from rape by the Russian soldiers. You would only have found that room if you knew the church very well. We put sacks of wheat against the door to stop anyone getting in. Fantastic tales, but that's how we lived.

I was longing to finish the three years at the studio. I wanted a piece of paper to my name. I managed to get back secretly to West Germany to my old studio, and finished the course, and applied to art school in Munich because I wanted to get my degree in sculpting and then go to Egypt. But to be accepted at Munich I had to have a resident's permit for Bavaria, so I set out to live in Bavaria, and worked in a studio there.

Then in West Germany, in 1948, the Currency Reform came. This meant that I could no longer afford to live in the West, because the old money was worthless, and I couldn't earn my living as an artist. The studio advised us to go home. We were given a small sum of money and with this, and what I got through selling some of my jewellery on the black market, I returned to East Germany to my parents.

I realised then that I am a liability to my parents. We had ration books, and we starved. I realised that what I have planned is in ruins. I tried to find artists to work with, but they were starving themselves. Of course you had no commissions: a country which is financially and morally totally at rock bottom doesn't employ its artists. The country was in ruins.

When rationing became even more squeezed out, you only got a ration book if you had employment. Those who didn't have employment had to queue up for discretionary ration cards, and I was one of those. One day, while queuing, I was asked to work for the Communist Party as an artist, but I would have to become a Party member. Well, I wouldn't dream of it! That meant that I wouldn't get a ration book at all now, because I'd refused, and then it was whispered to me in this same queue that I was on the list for AUE, which was a uranium mine on the border between

Germany and Poland, which Hitler had started. The Russians were keen to foster a generation of youngsters who were a mixture of Russians and Germans. But you were never seen again when you were taken to AUE.

So I left East Germany that same night, for West Germany. The Russians had ripped up the railway tracks, and I walked across the torn rails, across what was in those days a no-man's-land. There was usually some man or somebody who would take you across for some spirits and money. It was always done at night, and you took your life in your hands. I was terribly frightened. But it was either that or disappear altogether.

I have not said anything about my sister yet, and I must. She was two years younger than I, and she died in January 1946, before I left for West Germany. She was one of the countless typhoid victims . . . The Russians had dirtied the water system, you see.

Her death left me completely empty. It was the most terrible winter ever: it was bitterly cold, and there was very, very little food. I felt as if the last bit of my childhood sunshine had gone. My brother was still an American prisoner of war, our house was full of refugees.

She would have been twenty-one the following May. Of course, there were no hospitals. In the next town, one of the former hotels had been made into what they called a hospital, and people were just lying on the floor on straw, and died. If you were prepared to nurse the typhoid sick, then the patient you nursed would be in a bed. So my mother went, and my sister had a bed. But she was there for less than a week.

My mother came back and she said, 'She is dead.' Then we went to see her, I will never forget this: we went on our bikes in this freezing January weather, cycled six miles to the next town, and outside the hotel was a double garage, and that double garage was stacked full of dead bodies. My sister was the only one who lay on a camp bed. All the others were in paper sacks and sometimes the legs would stick out because the sack was too short, and sometimes the head would stick out. They would be buried in a communal grave, with quick-lime in it to prevent infection spreading further. I remember on her nightie, one button was missing.

My father buried her. My parents almost froze. I remember some people in the village said they didn't love her, they didn't cry. We were well beyond crying: we cried much later on.

I stayed in West Germany until April 1950, and then I left for England. Although it sounds absolutely terrible, when I left Germany, I *hated* Germany. It had killed something in me. With the concentration camp victims in the house, I realised what Germans have done. And when I came to this country my longing was that my accent wouldn't be detected as a German accent. I was thrilled when people said, 'Do you come from Wales?', or, 'Do you come from Scotland?'

I was sent to England with a church agency, and at first I stayed with a family who had to guarantee to keep me for a year. Coming to a free country was a physical and inner shock, and it took me some months to adjust. The people who took me lived in a lovely house with beautiful grounds and I was kindly treated, but I worked as a housemaid and I did not enjoy the work. I felt diminished by what I considered to be menial work. They were earnest Christians, but to me their outlook seemed narrow, and I often felt lonely and homesick. I don't think I went to bed one night without crying.

It became clear that conditions in East Germany were not going to change, so I decided to remain in England. I moved to some friends I had made, and went out doing housework in various households. Every German girl coming to this country was in a similar position. After four years you could accept other work, providing there was no English applicant.

During those years I became an active member of the parish church and was offered work by one of the ladies, in a 'social service unit' in the shipyard. It turned out to be a fish and chip bar! My heart sank, but I worked there for about six months, and they treated me very kindly. The dockers pulled my leg, but the woman who was in charge, she was lovely. In the end I became sick with this fish, this oil smell, I just couldn't take it. I don't touch chips now!

After that, I found work in a small nylon factory. We were about twelve women and two or three men who worked the machines making nylon stockings, and I was the one who put the seams in at the back, but I wasn't quick enough at it, so I had to inspect whether the seams were done properly instead. That was quite good money, and again I made friends with people I would never have normally met. They accepted me to a certain degree, though they had quite a bit of dirty language, which I didn't understand.

During my time at that nylon factory, the priest at the parish church said to me, 'Renate, you look miserable: carve us a figure.' So I did. And then one day in the nylon factory, the manager called me into the office, and in the office was a strange man who said: 'I believe you are the artist who carved the figure in the church next door. Would you be prepared to work for us? We are a church furnishing firm, and we are very short of carvers.' So I said, 'I have no bench. I have no wood.' He said, 'We will supply the bench. We will supply the wood.' So I worked for the best part of a year for this church furnishing firm, but it became a bit precarious because wood was difficult to get hold of, and I realised I must make myself independent.

I looked for a residential job, and found one in a girls' public school, as Matron, with the outlook to teach art as well. And I loved it. The headmistress was a beautiful woman, a far-sighted woman. I taught art and German, and I flourished there.

Anyway, I don't know what started it, but in 1959, after a year at the school, I got this inner nagging, something saying, 'Renate, you must find out if you are meant to be a Sister.' I do *not* know where this idea came from, but it came during a concert in Llandudno. I was a member of a Society who had arranged a cycle of concerts, and it was a marvellous evening, and I suddenly thought, 'You must be a Sister.' – Crazy! Now, I have not really thought about this before, but I think these high moments in my life have always been connected with music, or with art, or with a tremendous event in nature like a sunset, or the sea. They link up unconsciously inside me with what I call God.

One day I was reading the gospel of Mark with my sixth formers, and the immediacy of that language, in relation to Jesus, suddenly assumed a deeply significant implication for my own life. So I said to myself then, 'All right God, I will find out about it.' I knew Sisters from the Anglican community at Chester, and I booked to stay with them, and I thought, 'If I meet a Sister who looks reasonable, then I will talk about this nagging of mine.' But I didn't meet a Sister who looked reasonable, so I didn't talk about this nagging of mine! I waited another whole year, and then in bed one morning, I said, 'All right God, I say yes to you.' And I remember the utter relief of that decision. It was as if a terrific weight had been lifted off me. I know now that it had to do with honesty, personal honesty to myself and to God. But I had been fighting it for a long time. Ignoring it.

I always related easily to other people, but I was certainly in England hesitant to commit myself to a partner relationship. I think inwardly I was still too wounded to enter into something which would be demanding. I had many deeply loving relationships with both men and women, but I think I probably needed to receive more than I was prepared to give in return, and I never had a love which hoped to be fulfilled in marriage. And if I would have married, I would have preferred to have been without children. That sounds dreadful, but I think marriage for me would have been a deep companionship rather than being parents.

I was very fond of one man, he was older than me. They always had to be older! But he moved away and eventually we lost contact. And then the nagging to be a Sister took over, and in the end, after practically four years of struggling to ignore it, I gave in to God.

The last night of term before I entered community, I went to my sixth formers and said, 'You won't see me next term because I'm going into a convent.' And the reply was, '*You?* Into a convent? But you are so *normal!*' I dressed very smartly before, you know, I loved dressing. I don't mean this proudly, but I've very good taste. I usually made my own summer dresses, bought material because there was a wider choice, and it was cheaper. I didn't have a very elaborate wardrobe, but what I had was very good, and I don't think my sixth formers could imagine me in a habit.

I knew very little about this life. When I went to Chester, I looked at the Sisters, how they dressed. I had no idea that the dress had some significance, as far as outward appearance was concerned. And I remember very well indeed, I saw a Sister who had a white veil over her head, and the others had black, and I thought perhaps when they washed the white veil, they put the black on. I had no idea that she was a Novice. I also remember fellow guests saying, 'When they have been in a year, then they are allowed to wear socks.' Now, one Sister, she never wore socks, winter and summer, and she had been in for donkeys' years. So I realised from the talk of the guests that there is some peculiarity about being a Sister, something which is watched by others, which is fascinating. I wasn't fascinated. I was scared.

When I realised I had to make up my mind, I thought well, I'll find out about it all through a book. And I went to the religious bookshop, SPCK, and bought a book. I remember very well indeed thinking, if I have to do this thing, I will never want my friends to see me in this *ridiculous* outfit, so I will go into a community where I can't get out – an enclosed community! And I put crosses next to the enclosed communities, but I never contacted them, I don't know why. I can still see this page with some marks against enclosed communities, because I was clothes-conscious, and I didn't want to look like a black Sister!

Nothing attracted me to the life. I simply felt *compelled*. To some this wouldn't make sense at all, and I would always say that the calling does not make sense. I wrote to my parents: I asked one of the Sisters at Chester, 'Do you really think I am meant to become a Sister?' And she said 'That is for you to decide. In front of God.'

So I was thrown back onto myself, and I will always remain grateful for that. Because nobody can answer that question for you. And I believe that the Christian faith is not the faith of a book or dogma: it is the acceptance of a personal invitation. It is like someone saying to you, 'You are important to me, therefore come and join my company.' It sounds very simplistic and very primitive, but I believe that that is what it is.

When you accept an invitation, then you have to accept some kind of regulation or discipline, and for me, 'discipline' is a wonderful word because it has to do with the word 'disciple'. And the disciple is a person who follows somebody else because he or she wants to follow that somebody else – whether it is Jesus or not. So I choose whom I follow. Being a disciple is about making personal decisions about one's own application of values. And that to me is the essence of Christianity. I think quite a few of the rules and regulations which have grown up around it could easily be dismantled.

When people ask me about my faith, I am first of all a human being, a female human being, then I'm European, and only then am I a Christian. I believe my humanity is the largest basis of my ability to relate. My Europeanness is a limitation of culture and geography. My Christianity is another limitation. But if you take the creed seriously, 'I believe in God the Father, creator of all there is, seen and unseen,' and if I believe that all life around me has something to do with a being I call 'Father', then every human being is to an extent a brother or sister. So Christianity is about relationships; about healing, enrichment, fun, about being unthreatened. But if you take the creed to mean, 'Unless you believe like this you are not saved', then it becomes exclusive.

I've many times been called a heretic because I believe this, but I love to be a heretic. I believe Jesus had great difficulties: he was a Jew, through and through, and he loved his Jewish nation, yet he stepped over his social barriers. He was an artisan, and not a farmer, which was important then. He talked with Samaritans; he accepted prostitutes and tax collectors. And none of it came easy, but he did it! So he is tremendously attractive for me.

I was very much afraid that becoming a nun would narrow my life, and it was tied up in my mind with the dress of the Sisters. When I went to the house in Chester for the first time, the morning I left I had put on my lipstick, and the Sisters kissed me goodbye. And I remember with great shame that a bit of lipstick was on the white collar of one of the Sisters, and I thought, ooh, I shouldn't have done that. And I realised when I eventually came to the house here, in Malvern, that the Sisters recognised this struggle in me. Years later I said to the Sister with my lipstick on her collar, I said, 'Do you remember that morning?' She said, 'I do indeed. You looked very attractive, but I knew you were in trouble.'

I entered the community in 1963, and at that time the Novitiate was a strict time. One did not ask many questions and one had to learn to walk, even though one came in as a person who believed that she could run. So during my Novitiate, I certainly felt the restrictions of this life, and inwardly I asked God many a time: 'Well, you must know what you are doing, and help me to trust you, because to me this is ridiculous.'

During my Novitiate there was hardly any contact between Novices and Sisters on a social basis. We didn't talk with each other. We Novices knew very little about one another. We had official walks, official classes, but no debate or discussion, and it was very limited. I found it very unattractive. It seemed like nursery to me.

But I stayed because I thought, 'There must be something else to this.' I also perceived that beyond the seeming narrowness was a warmth of acceptance, a wholeness of life. During my Novitiate I was sent to the Retreat House in Chester. And there one had the same kind of prayer schedule as the Sisters, and it was altogether more relaxed in that the group was smaller, and seculars were coming in and out of the house. And I began to think, yes, there is something in it. I also was asked to visit a youth club every week, and there I began to realise something of what it meant to be a Sister, because people talked on a far deeper confidential level with me than they would have done if I had been a secular. The contact was far more immediate. And throughout my community life this has been enlarged and deepened.

Taking first vows was like having a bucket of cold water thrown over me. It was a day I longed for, I wanted to publicly declare my conviction that God meant me to be a Sister, but it was still a shock. I remember very vividly I was kneeling, and you know what the service is like, question, answer, question, answer. Well, the Reverend Mother stood beside me, and the priest turned to her and charged her that she would have to give account for me before the Almighty at the Day of Judgment. I queried this part of the service, because I thought, 'Well, she can't do that, I have to do that myself.'

But when I got to life vows I remember the strangeness, and the wonder, of our life stood up before me like two sides of a coin. I remember thinking, 'There is still time to get out,' and also, 'Well, I don't understand this, but I say *yes*.' I accepted it: it was beyond being worked out.

And with those vows my real self became far bigger. The ego, the 'I must have this, I must have that,' had to take second place to simplicity; simplicity of food, simplicity of dress, simplicity of very few personal possessions. And with it came a certain unclutteredness, both in my outer life and in my inner life. I found it very difficult to start with. But the material becomes a very small aspect of it all. The vow of poverty is also: I do not belong to any human being. I am the sister of anybody who is prepared to accept me as one.

However, I am completely certain that the perfectly legitimate desire of every human being to have a partner could be a negative aspect of the vow of poverty. And there is definitely a relationship between poverty and celibacy. Celibacy implies a freedom to be unattached, therefore available.

Even the qualifications I worked for are very secondary in my life now, because I am valued for the humanness I have, and coming from a society where success and qualifications and proving oneself is of such great importance, makes it difficult at first. However, Jesus said that unless you deny yourself, you cannot find yourself (I don't quote directly), and I know what He means. All that hinders the fullness of life must decrease, so that what I can become may increase.

Our poverty is not abject poverty, as you say, but how I live is up to me. Yes, I am provided for, I don't have to go hungry, I have a roof over my head, and – the most tremendous richness – I will be loved until I die by my fellow Sisters. I won't be pushed somewhere and made to feel that I am no longer useful. But our poverty is a simple, generous and responsible life. It is not the poverty I have witnessed in Africa. That kind of poverty is deprivation and it diminishes people. Our poverty is gratitude, and it enriches our life.

Time has enlarged our community's warm heart. When I first entered, we were made aware that in a group situation the singling out of certain people, because you preferred them, was not the way to do things. Now we dare to relate deeply. We hug each other, we kiss each other, and when we come home we are always warm in our welcoming. And onlookers, from the Guest House, always say, 'You really love each other, don't you?' And we do. But for a long time our trouble was that we didn't love ourselves, and I think that is still part of a great many Christian people's troubles. Because if you are afraid of yourself, or if you feel you have to hide something from yourself, you can't possibly approach another person in freedom.

My family reacted unfavourably when I entered. My father was distressed, I think, by his then only daughter going into a convent. But I wrote to my parents, and my father answered the letter by quoting from the New Testament: 'He, God, who has begun a good work in you, will also finish it.' And I thought, what a big father, he made no argument. He never saw me in a habit. I was for four weeks at the convent, and he died. But he accepted that he had trained me to become a free human being, and therefore he respected my decision and wouldn't query it.

My mother was upset because she thought that I would be 'locked in', as she put it, and would never see her again. Also, she thought I would not be sufficiently looked after. One of my brothers found it very difficult too. But after the initial adjustment, all of them grew to accept it. They realised very quickly that I hadn't lost my sense of humour, that I could be just as stupid and ridiculous, that I could still walk and run and jump about, and get up a mountain and that kind of thing. They realised nothing has been killed in me. And as a community, we have never, never rejected our families. We have always stressed the importance of family life.

However, although I am close to my family, and I visit them, there came a time when I decided to stay in England. I hated and resented Germany for years, but I began to accept and even love Germany again when I travelled there as a Novice, in my black habit. My parents were dead, and I went to see my brothers. I travelled by train from Berlin to Heidelberg, which is a long journey. An Indian waiter came round with a trolley, and the two of us felt outsiders, he through race, and I through dress. We realised it, and we sat and talked, and he said, 'Oh, Germany is beautiful, isn't it?' And I remember, I was ever so grateful that he said that. I remember this long train journey was the beginning of a walk back to Germany. I am now a British citizen, because I like to be able to be politically involved in the country I live in. But I am still German: I will always be.

In this community we lead what is wonderfully called 'the mixed life'. Sometimes we look at ourselves and say, 'It is indeed very mixed,' for there is a mixture of joys and tensions, of giving to, and receiving from, one another, and the mutual acceptance that that brings. We have a daily Eucharist, and we say five Offices. We have forty-five minutes' prayer time and a quarter of an hour's intercession time each day, and we are meant to read for half an hour each day too. Now, when I say it like that, time-wise it sounds very rigid, but we simply make sure that we set time for all that aside. That adds up to about three or four hours of in-active work a day.

That is one side of our life. The other is our involvement with the local community; with the blind and deaf, with the local open prison, with schools and colleges, and with the many people who come to us for help or direction, as well as those who come to stay in the Guest House for quiet refreshment. In the community we have trained nurses, trained teachers. But being qualified doesn't mean that you will teach or nurse again, because community life comes first. Your *raison d'être* is to stand before God as a Sister on behalf of the world.

Having said that, we do an amazing amount of work outside. In Anglican terminology, we are not an enclosed community. We are just attempting a balance in our life. The balance of stillness and involvement. And because being a Christian is about accept-ance, that can mean pushing against the limitations of injustice. Therefore, I would call us – Sisters – the irritants in society. I think that when society is without irritants, it becomes very bland and lifeless. I would never call us parasites, because we work. I know that people say, 'What good do you do?' and I know I go on and on about relating, but our society is a society of broken relationships, and Sisters are beginning to be thought of seriously as relaters or reconcilers, and accepted as that. I have only once experienced hostility, from a young man who shouted at me in the street, 'Why don't they shoot you bastard Christians?' and that's the only time ever. I have been ignored, I have been looked down upon, but often the opposite is true, and people approach me because of my outward appearance.

Men sometimes find it hard to approach us because they think they will meet frustrated spinsters, but instead they meet people who are very happy in their company. But then Jesus broke down some of those barriers of prejudice. He treated women amazingly. When Mary Magdalene sat at his feet, that was the place for the favourite male disciple. No other Rabbi would have done that. He went as far as he could, and I believe that he did it quite consciously, because he realised that men and women are of equal value.

But sadly, there has been a lot of inequality and insensitivity in the Church, and I don't think it has very much meaning for many people nowadays. All the attempts, like Faith In The City, to make the Church 'relevant' are important, but I don't like that term because the Church has never been irrelevant, because the Church is people. And I think with more and more housing estates growing up that people are rootless, so that the Church for them is very often presented through people who visit them. And part of our work as Sisters is to visit people and lay the ghost of people's expectations about the Church. Often I've had to visit people, and at first I don't like it at all because it feels like being a salesperson! Often I am greeted with, 'You know we're not churchgoers,' and I will say, 'That's all right, I don't mind.' There is still the idea that Christianity has to do with going to church, but Christianity is predominantly to do with daring to establish relationships with others.

And that, for me, is what prayer is all about: the establishing of a relationship with God in order that I can establish ones with others. I don't pray specifically for things or people, because I don't use words very much. I usually start with words, because they help me to become inwardly still, but that's all. I believe in this mystery we call Trinity – the Father, Son and Holy Spirit – and I believe I am a trinity too, in my body, my intellect, and my heart. When I pray I adopt a physical position which is usually sitting, sometimes lying, but always with a straight spine, and very relaxed. I put my hands together. My left hand represents my heart, and my right hand my intellect, and I join them. My outward appearance is relaxed, but shows something of my inner desire to become whole. Then I start breathing, and I breathe from my diaphragm. I often breathe in and out the name of Jesus, or I use the word love. And I do this for half an hour, forty minutes, and maybe finish with a sequence of movement.

Sometimes I lie flat on the floor when I am praying. Usually I start by standing in front of my icon, or the crucifix. I know that the suffering of Christ is the biggest question mark ever and I never attempt to answer it. All I know is it is not the end. I know Christ leapt into the darkness of faith and dared to believe that arms would catch him: and because the arms caught him he is alive, so therefore I live, I stand, I breathe.

I believe that prayer is predominantly gratitude. I realised that with that bunch of yellow tulips. I realised I had to look for the good in all situations. Prayer is also the time when I can shout to God, I can tell Him off. It stops me becoming bitter.

I don't look upon this life as a place of misery – not a bit of it – but there is another life which is beyond time and space, where the rightness and wholeness that we glimpse here from time to time, will be. I have seen terrible deaths, but about death itself I believe I am meant to prepare myself for it with trust. I also believe that death is not a sudden stepping from life into something else, but it is a gradual growing into newness, and this gradual growing I call paradise. The creed says that Jesus descended into hell, and that is it for me, except that it is not a place of punishment: it is being confronted with love, and making a final choice either for good or not.

Do you know, I love stones. I have a glass bowl full of stones that come from all different places, and I love to handle a stone, and realise the wonder of everything. Usually these stones are picked from the seaside, and they are very real to me, because I am a stone. Those stones have been thrown for millions and millions of years backwards and forwards, held in the waves of the sea, rubbing against one another, and being shaped, marvellously shaped, through that. And now and again the stones have a hole in them, and there at the bottom of the hole you will see the glimmer of a geode, a crystal.

One of my Sisters, when I spoke to her like this, said to me, 'Yes, and then one is rubbed to sand.' And I said, 'No, no, no! We are not, because we are thrown into the water, causing ripples of hope, and there we are held in the wave of God's love.' But some people do feel rubbed to sand, not just shaped beautifully, because life is hard. And sometimes stones are not very interesting, sometimes they look very dull, or they have cracks. Well, that's me too. But inside me, God can see that crystal. I believe that.

MARGARET WALSH

Hope Community, Heath Town, Wolverhampton
(A branch of the Institute of the Sisters of The Infant Jesus)
ROMAN CATHOLIC: APOSTOLIC

Age: 45
Nationality: Irish
Age at entry to community: 18
Number of years in community: 27
Previous employment: None
Dress: Ordinary

Margaret Walsh lives in a flat on a large council estate in Heath Town, Wolverhampton. You can see most of the estate – nine tower blocks, some twenty-two storeys high, and a number of smaller flats – from her windows. Margaret describes the estate as 'a dumping place for people who cannot be housed elsewhere'. Over eighty per cent of Heath Town's population, which is largely composed of teenage single parents, is on Unemployment Benefit or Income Support, and most of it is in rent arrears. An increasing number of tenants are from hospitals or residential homes which, under government policy, have been required to return people to 'care in the community'.

Margaret, her cheery fellow Sisters Coleman and Elizabeth ('Just call me Queen – that'll do'), and a fluctuating number of religious and lay people share the flat in Heath Town. When I first went there I had a quick drink with Queen Elizabeth, a chat with Margaret, and lunch on my lap with a Liverpudlian monk and a number of men and women who kept appearing with requests or queries. 'It's an open house,' Margaret pointed out, somewhat unnecessarily. 'Sure, we get all sorts here. You should see us at Christmas.'

The flat is open every day, and every weekday evening (except for Saturdays and Mondays) for activities as varied as French lessons, shared prayer, and bring-along videos evenings. Every time I went to visit Margaret somebody else would offer to be interviewed in her place: 'Ah Margaret! You don't want to be asking her about herself if you're wanting the truth. Now I could tell you a few stories about her, oh yes!'

The offer was tempting, but I interviewed only Margaret. She spoke with an Irish lilt I could happily listen to for hours, and her voice was quiet, though whether through shyness or composure I could never quite decide. She is an enigmatic woman, very still, rather droll, and slightly melancholy.

Margaret Walsh

All those close to me live in West Cork in Ireland; they're all people of the earth, all farmers. I would say close to the earth, close to one another, and close to their God. They continue to be an extended Irish family, and because I was born into that I suppose it is from that culture I am who I am, even though there are other experiences since which have continued to shape my identity, and change it a bit maybe. But most of who I am is rooted in that family and in that place and in that culture.

My father died in 1977. Both my parents came from large farming families, and they lived near to one another when they were children. We're very inter-connected and inter-related as a family. Even now, my family are all married to local people, and they all live within a fifty mile radius of one another – at the very most.

There are eight of us. I've five brothers, two sisters, all now married with families of their own, and I come somewhere in the middle. Because we lived out in the country when we were young, we were very dependent on one another for the games we played, and for companionship. We were two and a half miles away from the school, and we walked to that, and most of the way we were on our own – just with brothers and sisters. So there was always that feeling of being very responsible for one another, which continues today. I could always be certain that if I was in any kind of crisis, that the family would automatically be at my side, wanting to bail me out, or whatever: there's a great sense of responsibility towards one another.

That kind of responsibility extended outside the family too. There's a great sense of neighbourliness, even though most of the neighbours are relatives! Our most immediate neighbours worked for my father, or worked for other local farmers, although in a strange kind of way my father wasn't class-conscious, really. In Ireland, farmers are a class on their own, anyway. My father would always emphasise the importance of the neighbour. Whenever we went anywhere, our first, well, it was almost a duty, when we got back, was to go and visit the neighbours. So from a very young age, the neighbour has always been very important.

Ah, now sure we were a religious family, my God yes. We're Irish! I cannot remember when I was taught to make the sign of the cross, and I can see why, because my mother to this day, when there's a little one, a baby, she will trace the sign of the cross on the child, and she will have done that with all of us. We certainly prayed together as a family every night, and went to church together every Sunday. It was just the norm within the family, and certainly the Sabbath churchgoing continues to be the norm. I'm not so sure that this generation's as committed as the older generation was, but having said that, church bells still peal in Ireland at twelve o'clock for the Angelus, and also at six o'clock on television.

In some ways Ireland's hardly changed in my lifetime, you know. I was recently in the home of a former Lord Mayor of Cork, and the Angelus bell rang: well, we were having a conversation, but he just stopped mid-sentence, and quite spontaneously said the Hail Marys and we all answered. Then when I was home visiting my mother in hospital last week, every night the person in charge of the ward would kneel and say the rosary on the corridor, and all the people in the wards would be sitting there with their rosary beads and praying. It's true, you know, and that was only last week. I was quite surprised, I thought that was only something that went on when I was young, but it's still happening.

So my earliest faith memories are of prayers, but also of a loving father who cared for us: yes, that's for sure. He was also someone who was distant, and who was in charge, and who really had control of the situation. I remember I was terrified of thunder storms: unfortunately, the electricity wasn't very good or efficient in those days – I'm talking about the early fifties in West Cork, mind – so even as soon as the distant rumbles began, you could expect all the lights to go out. And I always used to think that the thunder was God's anger, ah sure. It was quite frightening for a child.

When the thunder came, the tradition was to kneel and pray. Well, you needed light to do that, so of course you would get the blessed candle – not just any old candle, it had to be one that had already been blessed. This would be lit, and we would pray to God, and if the candle went out, I thought it was a mark of His displeasure. Added to that was an almighty scare that many of us had when I was about ten, that the world was going to end in three days. And this became so credible, it was even printed in some of the newspapers, and everyone was talking about it. I was petrified. I really firmly believed that the world was going to end, and so did others: in fact, it was so firmly believed in by the people that the priest had to talk about it from the altar, telling them what a lot of nonsense it was, and that it wasn't going to happen.

I think all of those sorts of things were associated with my fear that if I wasn't good, then God would punish me, so I loved and feared Him at the same time. Not Jesus, though. At that time I couldn't really cope with Jesus, I didn't have much confidence in Him, really. It might have had something to do with the gallery of pictures on the kitchen wall, which depicted a very weak and effeminate Jesus: you know, He wasn't strong. Also, He ends up being crucified, doesn't He? I mean, if He couldn't look after himself, and He's supposed to be God – well, I just didn't have much confidence in Jesus, that's all. And as for the Holy Spirit! The Holy Spirit was a total unknown. I had the notion that the Spirit was somebody you went to when you were in trouble, or when you wanted guidance of some sort, and I abandoned the Spirit also. You see I wasn't a very good student – mainly because I didn't do any homework – and so when the Spirit didn't present me with the right answers to exam questions, despite the fact that I had prayed really very hard beforehand, I thought the Spirit wasn't worth the trouble, either.

So it took me a long time to meet Jesus, or to have any kind of a personal relationship with God. But all the same, one of my earliest memories of the nearness of God was through my grandmother. Sure, there was the rosary, and mass, but I some-times stayed with my grandmother, and I remember she longed for death. She was in fact ninety-five when she died, but her husband died thirty-something years before, and she just wanted to be with him, and with her friends. She used to say, 'Oh, it's lonely, it gets more lonely here.' And when she'd get ill, and then she'd get better, and she'd say: 'Oh, why doesn't the Lord take me?' and she used to describe it as 'going home'. So from a very young age, I had the idea of death as being released into another state of life, and that has remained with me.

My grandmother also used to talk to God, and I remember overhearing her one day, and from then on I began to realise that I could talk to God too. That's one of the earliest memories I have of the possibility of a personal relationship with God, and I must have been six or seven then. I suppose that's when everything started, really.

I was educated at a little country school; one room and four classes, a big fire which kept us warm, and bottles of cocoa which my mother made for us, and which we put by the fire. It was a very caring school, and there was an advantage to being in one room, which was that you could tune in to any level, you weren't stuck to a particular class. It was relaxed, and I have very positive memories of that school.

My secondary education was very different. I cut out, literally; I just did not settle at all, ever. Because it was a big convent school, a lot was assumed: like that most people in the classes would have been through the junior part of the secondary school, and would approach the subjects in a particular way. Well, those of us who came from the little country schools had a different beginning, and we were left behind, basically. So I have very few positive memories of that school. In fact, I hated it, I counted the days until I was out of it, and I got by with the minimum – passed, like, just about. Spent a lot of my time reading and doing my own thing; doing what I had to do to avoid trouble, planning ways of getting the homework from somebody who had done it. I would have had that sussed before going in to lessons: in fact, that would have been my main homework activity. I never, ever enjoyed any of it.

However, I did have lots of friends at school. I was the class clown, I reckon. At least, that's how I would describe someone like me in a classroom today – someone who was just an almighty nuisance. I was often at the back of the class, or else right up at the front so that I wouldn't distract others. I was terrible: whatever mischief was going, I was in it – and initiating it.

I don't think my parents had much idea of how terrible I was. They weren't educated in the academic sense, so my mother would see me reading a book and assume that it had something to do with whatever subject I was supposed to be studying – she wouldn't even ask, I mean, we were absolutely trusted. I'm quite embarrassed really at how we abused that trust – or I did. Also, we got television when I was maybe fifteen or sixteen, and all the programmes I watched were 'educational', or so I told them.

So I wasn't someone to be trusted. Yet when my poor exam results came, they just said, 'Oh well, you've done your best – that's okay,' which was terrible really, because I hadn't. Anyway, more important to my mother than any further education was that we should be good housekeepers and good parents. She sent me, and my sisters ahead of me, to a domestic science school, a school of housecraft, when we'd finished in the secondary school. That was for one year, and we did cooking, sewing, dairy and poultry: we were taught how to lay the table, and our manners too, that was all taught. All to make us good housekeepers, good wives.

I didn't particularly want to go to that school, but at the time all I could worry about was going to the same one as my sister. My chief concern was to go somewhere different from her, because she came back with all the trophies, and I thought, 'Well, anywhere's better than there,' because I could not compete with her standard of excellence. So I got a list of places that I could go to instead, and I thought, okay, wherever my finger stops, I'm going there.

Well, my finger stopped at a school called Drishane, and I thought, 'That sounds nice.' It wasn't too far from home, which kept my parents happy, and it was in the countryside, so I went there and I had a wonderful year. Best year of my life. I loved it. There was no academic pressure and the Sisters were wonderful – great women. We also met all kinds of interesting people, people who had come back from missions and that, and sure I felt at home in the place in about a fortnight. I just thought: there is something here for me. And they're the Sisters I joined.

*

199

The idea of being a nun had been with me since I was about four or five, even though we didn't have any Sisters in our family. In fact, there are no nuns in my family at all, so I'd never actually met one, except at a distance. There were Sisters at my secondary school, and my experience of them was very negative on the whole: I could not relate to them at all, no *way* was there any meeting place. Nuns were a phenomenon quite beyond me. So what I saw and experienced of religious life when I was a child had nothing to do with this 'something' that was calling me to a life of commitment.

Anyway, this 'something' went on calling me all through my childhood and adolescence, and as the years went on I tried to forget it, and couldn't. Eventually, I began to realise it was something I had to do in order to be at peace with myself, and when I went to Drishane, everything just slotted into place. I just thought, 'This is it, this is it,' although I had no idea how to go about joining a religious community. I didn't know anything much about the Sisters there, and I didn't tell anyone how I felt, either. I was so naïve that I thought the Sisters would be delighted to receive me if I just turned up: I almost just arrived at the door and said, 'I've come.'

Nowadays we do all sorts of things to help people discern whether or not they're called to the religious life, and we're talking about years sometimes. Yet I didn't even ask questions about it. It was just a very simple faith and trust in the God who was calling me to it, and I was prepared for anything. In some senses, I was prepared for whatever it took – but I was absolutely confident that if this was what God wanted me to do, He would sort it out. There was no need for me to worry at all.

My family worried, however. They had great difficulty with it, because I suddenly announced this, and went. In fact, it wasn't just my family, but the whole neighbourhood. They still talk about it. When I was back in Ireland only last week I met somebody who said that one of my friends, when she heard about me entering, was so shocked that she got on her bicycle and cycled I don't know how many miles away to tell everybody. Nobody could believe it, it was so out of character. We had a reunion last year of my secondary school class, and much of the time was spent in general laughing about the shock it all was. Some I hadn't met since leaving school, and they still wanted to say to me: 'Ah my God, now why did you do it? Are you still there?' Because I was a terror – or so they tell me – but then they exaggerated the stories that night, of all that I used to do, and I thought then, 'Please God, don't let any of these people ever write a book or I am ruined for life!'

Mind you, I had shown no sign whatsoever of being particularly religious, and I suppose my family certainly had a very traditional understanding of the good holy nun, and I just didn't fit this. But because they had such respect for what I wanted to do with my life, they didn't challenge me on it: they just thought, 'Perhaps one day we'll understand.' They'd come and see me in the convent, and we'd look at one another, and they didn't know what they were looking at really, or who I was any more. I think they thought that I must be somebody very different from who they thought I was. It was very hard for them. And I think in some sense I was an embarrassment. I'd come home and people would say: 'What do we call you now? Sister?' I'd say: 'Call me what you always call me – my friends do.' And as the years went on, people began to realise that I hadn't changed very much at all.

I entered the convent at a very good time. Everything was just beginning to change after Vatican II, thank God. The community's an international one, very big, with about fifteen hundred of us worldwide, and the convent was the normal institutional type of convent, in the most beautiful setting. It was used for the film *The House of Brede*, in fact.

In my particular group of Postulants there were four. I'm the only one that has survived – survival of the fittest by supernatural selection! The others left and married. We are an endangered species, you know! I never considered leaving, because all the questions about getting married and all that I'd have to give up in this way of life, they'd been going on from a very early age, the opportunities, the chances. I love children – oh gosh, I do – and before I entered, not having my own was something I had to come to terms with, sure. And it's been around all the time. But I made a commitment, which I've kept. It doesn't mean to say it's easy, because it isn't. And the whole thing of human relationships; you know, like any other normal human being, I want that, and am trying to find it through a celibate way of life.

However, as the years have gone on, it's become much easier, because I'm beginning to appreciate more and more the importance of, and the need for, deep friendships, in order to bring about fulfilment. But in the earlier years I would have been an awful lot more unsure, and wondering if I'd done the right thing. I mean there's just no way this life is 'normal,' no way. Over the years, I have been attracted, of course, but you make your choice, you renew your commitment, and you find new ways to handle it all the time, which is quite challenging. You learn.

It's like the vows. You don't just make them, and that's it, like. You have to remake and remake, in order to remain faithful, depending on your circumstances. I find myself over the years being called into a deeper and deeper commitment – and again, it's choice: you're always free to say, 'Well, tough, I've had enough of this,' even though the day I set off from home, my intention was to do this for life. This was it, like.

I really can't say exactly why I felt that way. I suppose at the very core of it all was the relationship with God, which over the years has become more and more exclusive. I just knew that I would find no rest, except in Him. I had plenty of other relationships, but nothing else satisfied me. That is one side of it – the satisfaction and peace that it gave me.

The other side was what I would call nowadays the 'Kingdom of God'. I think the Kingdom is something that's around us and within us now, and it's something that we have to uncover and discover. I don't see it as something particular that has to be worked for. I'm putting it very badly, but suffice it to say that you can talk about justice, you can talk about caring, you can talk about all sorts of ministries, but the Kingdom itself is something very exciting, very mysterious – and yet something very tangible. It's an adventure, an exploration, and for me, coming to Heath Town was part of that exploration. The time I have spent here has been the most fulfilling time of all my religious life.

Our congregation was very much a teaching and a missionary one, and in fact, it was founded for the Sisters to be available wherever we were needed in Christendom – and of course, that was amongst the poor. Right from the beginning, our founder, who was French, wanted people to help him to provide something for the neglected, and he simply asked some men and women whether they would help him. A couple of years later he said: 'Do you want to live in community? Maybe we could have a meal together occasionally.' So it all started like that, and for two hundred years we had no vows or cloister or anything. He wanted us to be totally free and not to get caught into the Church structure. So now, in Heath Town, we're going back to all that at last.

The trouble was that once the Church got in on it all, that was it. The Church insisted that we become cloistered, so that when the Sisters wanted to go to Spain because there was a need there, the then bishop said, 'I want you recognised by Rome first.' Then all the trappings were added, and we became as institutionalised as any good Sisters and nuns would have been in those days. So thank God for Vatican II, which said, 'Get *back* to where you came from.' That's why we're selling places now, like Drishane, and why for the last twenty years we've moved out of many of our traditional communities; it's in order to respond to that call again, and go back to our origins. Being somewhere like Heath Town is nothing new: we were doing it three hundred years ago.

Before I came to Heath Town I taught for nine years. I was head of Religious Education in a comprehensive school in Crewe, and I loved it. I loved the young people and I loved the teaching itself. I miss it still. We had good fun in the classroom. We had a great headmaster, who's still there, God bless him, and he allowed us the freedom to do what we liked as teachers, to scrap RE exams if we liked, and to be creative and take the kids away to places. So we had a ball a lot of the time.

So the experience of teaching RE was a positive one, and the kids used to give good vibes about it, too. They probably didn't dislike it, as many kids do, because I wouldn't set exams. In fact, there's an Irish word that comes into my head when I think about their attitude: 'meas.' Back home my mother would say, 'They didn't have a whole lot of meas on it.' In other words, they didn't have to take it seriously because they could just enjoy it.

Leaving teaching was almost as traumatic as leaving home. As I said, I loved it, but all the time I was doing it there was this deeper call, to do something a bit more radical and a bit more among people who I thought might need me more. I did live in community when I was teaching, but it was still 'the big house across from the church' type of set-up, with a nice garden. All very safe.

For quite a long time I'd been a member of the local justice and peace group, and we spent a lot of our meetings discussing the third world and related issues, and what we could do about them. We often prepared evenings when we tried to help others understand what was going on, and we did fundraising and stuff. But as time went on, I began to ask, within the group: 'What about Britain? What about the inner cities here? Can't we do something about here as well?' It was becoming clear to me that the situation in the inner cities was far from good, and that more and more people were being pushed to the margins of society. And that view fitted in naturally with my own views about being a Sister of the Infant Jesus: I am meant to be alongside people who are in the margins of society.

I was also becoming more and more aware, as my relationship with Jesus Christ was deepening, of how He walked with the outcasts of his society, and I just felt that I'd never meet Him until I also walked in the same kind of place. I knew it would be easier for me to understand the word of God by moving into a concrete situation of poverty. It was time to move on.

The question was: 'Where to?' That was in the autumn of 1984, and to cut a long story short, I arrived in Wolverhampton with the blessing of my Institute, to where a community had already been set up. And there I was given the freedom to explore my questions, and to find what I was looking for.

I wandered around these estates, and the surrounding area, and tried to become as informed as I could be about Wolverhampton town. I went around asking people: 'Where are the poor?' Honest to God! Where are the poor in Wolverhampton?! I was looking for the poor in Wolverhampton?! I just didn't see, and I began by thinking, 'Well, I'll find the poor in the dole queue.' I was unemployed myself, so I drew the dole in order to queue up with the others, – while at the same time going back to my three course meal in the evening, and perhaps getting myself to the unemployment office by car, and maybe, on occasion, calling into the travel agency to book a flight home. It was so ludicrous. I knew it wasn't very real. Mind you, I certainly had good fun filling out the forms, because you have to answer all sorts of questions about your dependants, and I ended up describing myself as belonging to a charitable institute.

Soon after being on the dole I took a job as a teacher. Some of the local schools really needed staff, so I felt I had to take a job, really. However, it was only part-time, and one day, a priest came looking for somebody to help in his parish – which is actually this parish – and on the way to the presbytery, we passed by the flats on the estate, and I thought: 'That's it: the poor are behind the concrete.'

Father, of course, wanted me to do chaplaincy work in a hospital and the school. But I couldn't see or think of anything else. All I knew was, behind those walls, I am going to find what I am looking for. I thought of maybe doing a census on the estate, simply as a way of knocking on people's doors, and Father agreed. Very shortly afterwards, three of us began to move about this estate, just knocking on doors. Sometimes, and seldom, people answered them. We realised after a while that people were frightened to open the door to strangers, and some people, especially those from outside the estate, thought we were crazy, and unaware of the dangers of being here. Even within the estate, I remember this woman showing me the knife that she had up her sleeve at all times, but I can't say we were frightened, really, because we weren't.

The census was an excuse. It was an excuse to knock on people's doors and say. 'We're from St Patrick's parish, and we wondered if anybody here needed a call from the church?' It was a useful tool to have, a means of access to people. Soon, when people did open their doors, many of them just wanted to talk, and we soon heard stories of loneliness, of being forgotten, of fear.

We knew from very early on that our response to the people was very limited unless we came to live here permanently. Going round the estate confirmed me in my realisation that I was not aware of what was really going on in these people's lives – what was going on in my own, even – and that I needed to be here. So somehow when we came in here, we came in knowing that we had a lot to learn, and that the people here would teach us. We acknowledged that our coming here wasn't anything but our own need. All right, we were a listening ear, with a love for people, I hope, but otherwise our commitment was just to belong here, and to be as civic-minded as possible.

Soon we got involved in all sorts of local organisations that were improving quality of life on the estate, because we were committed to doing so, but also, once we became tenants, because we had a right and a duty to do that. We certainly didn't want to be separate from the problems. Even so, we really could not identify with most of the people here, because our backgrounds are so different. You know, we're all teachers by profession. And the other huge difference between us and the people who live here is that we're here by choice and we don't have to remain here. We can go when we want, and that makes all the difference to how you perceive life and your future and your hopes and your expectations. It makes all the difference.

Thank God we realised at an early stage that we could not identify with the people, and that it's a bit phoney to pretend we're all the same, because we're not. No matter how hard we try to be the same, we're different. Therefore, instead of 'identification', I'd be a lot happier to use the word 'solidarity'. We can be in solidarity with people here, because we're suffering from the same noise of the builders outside; if there's a blues party at night, we're awake the same as anybody else is; if the laundry or other facilities get broken down, then we can all talk about the same thing, because we're experiencing the same environment.

Being here has turned my life upside-down, because I came here very much a product of the culture, some of which holds us in bondage, really. I came in to Heath Town as a professional, as somebody with a status in society. I came in with a whole cultural bias towards thinking: you work hard in order to *get there*. Also, because it's important to me that I'm efficient and competent, I felt that I couldn't get by unless I had, say, the modern technology to produce results. So when I came here I realised that I was poorer in some ways than many of those that I live alongside now, because none of those things are important here. And it made me think: what's life about? It forced me to ask the most fundamental questions.

Take my vows, for example. They're quite unnatural, really, all of them. Take poverty, like: at the level of not actually owning anything – that's just not natural. I would like to be in ownership, and in more control of my environment, for example, but poverty is also about the spiritual dimension of detachment. Well, on a good day I believe that!

I think, though, in a situation like this, you have very little to distract you from what you're doing, and that's good. Like if I hadn't become a Sister, I would very likely be in some family circumstances in West Cork, where everything would be very secure, very familiar. Instead of that, I'm here, with no security in terms of family, in terms of possessions, in terms of culture, I'm an alien, and at one level that can be very threatening to one's identity: you know, who am I now?

The positive side of being here is that it is very challenging to find those values in life which are eternal. It's all this 'discovery' that I talked about earlier: it's the reverse side of the sacrifice. There's a tremendous realisation that as life goes on there is a Kingdom here on earth, and you can find it in the most extraordinary way. Like the time when you are most destitute and alien is the time when you are actually most liberated, because it frees you to explore all kinds of other things, explore values that you've taken for granted. You're challenged into saying: 'Is success important? Is money important, really? Is it absolutely essential to have an intimate relationship with one person in order to be fully human?'

Since coming here I've learnt so much about myself. I know my own pain, now. I know my own poverty, like I've never known it before. I also know my own darkness, because somehow or other, when you listen to people with the compassion of Christ, you take on a lot of pain. It unleashes your own darkness, and it's then that you begin to see how poor you are, and how much in need you are. And for me, that need is met in prayer, in my relationship with God through other people. And all the time, there has to be a focus on hope here, otherwise you can become just as frustrated, just as hopeless, as powerless, as many others here on the estate. When that happens, instead of actually being part of any movement to improve the quality of life here, you're just down in the mire with everybody else. We have to watch that here. Constantly.

We're called the Hope Community. It's a good name, because it reflects something that is going on here. There is lots of hope here; in the people, in their amazing resilience, in the way their lives challenge the whole socio-political, economic system and its limitations.

There's also a lot of hope in the people who have so much compassion for one another. It's tremendous. All right, there's a lot of isolation and loneliness here, that's for sure; but for those who have remained here there's a great focus on community, on the needs of other people out there, the needs of your neighbours. So rather than focusing on the individual, which I think this society has done over the last several years, here you can find the fruits of togetherness.

I've found love, joy, peace and patience here unlike I've found them anywhere else: the fact that many of the people here will do without tomorrow, in order to share what they have for today. You know, people can teach each other such a lot through their deprivations, about where we as a society are going wrong, if you like, about why we're in social decline. Society certainly isn't working if it pushes people into places like this. It has left them; left them forgotten on the margins. Any society that has that to answer for isn't worth . . . Well, put it like this: it needs to do something drastic to bring a meaning back into the lives of many people.

I acknowledge that there's a lot that's good about our society. Obviously, I am grateful to society for my education; I am grateful for my professional skills; I am grateful to democracy for my freedom, for many aspects of this culture which we should hold on to. But there are many aspects of it that are no good, like the tremendous emphasis on competition and consumerism and efficiency, and the individual, success, status – and it's in a place like this that you meet them head-on.

It's not only broader society that makes me angry, either: the Church makes me angry, too. I am really critical of the models of social structure that we see in the Church because they are institutional, hierarchical, traditional, male-dominated, and we should have outgrown all that.

When I talk about the hierarchical Church I am talking about the power resting with the clergy. That is why I am totally committed to the grass roots, to the gifts and priesthood of the laity, and creating opportunities for the ordinary person to be more involved in the Church at all kinds of levels. This is why I haven't got a great passion for, say, fighting the cause for the ordination of women. I am far more concerned about the empowerment of the laity, and I sometimes think that issues like the ordination of women and Church unity somewhat distract from it. Power to the people is critical.

I do love the Church, though. I love the eucharist in its many forms, the whole concept of us as a eucharistic community. When you take Jesus Christ as your inspiration, how He lived His life for others, and gathered His followers around the table at the Last Supper, then living Christianity makes a lot of sense. But when you come in to a situation like the one here at Heath Town, you have to make new models of Christian worship with the people here, because they are people who have been crushed by the Church system. They are alienated from church, from the liturgy, from its ritual, its language, its everything. It often reflects the larger system that crushes them, that refuses to take them seriously.

So what we do here is gather people together. We ask them to lead, ask them to make decisions about our language, our ritual, our liturgy. We ask them to create something that makes sense to them. We ask them what they want us to preach and teach, what scriptures we're going to use in discussions etcetera. It is *they* who make the decisions, and that is so powerful a message, it's wonderful. The Church can learn so much from people who, unlike myself, are not conditioned into Church norms and practice. People like me can find it hard to abandon such things after years of inculturation, whereas people here are much freer – oh, ever so much freer – to explore new models. As I say, the Church has a lot to learn from them.

Shall I tell you what I've been thinking as I've been talking about all this? I've been thinking: 'What in God's name am I doing sitting here in front of a tape recorder?' It's so hard to explain what something, what God, means to you, and yet as the years have gone on I've become far more tuned in to the God who is in everything – people, circumstances, things that happen.

I suppose when I was younger I was looking for the miracles and the spectacular, but much as I tried to do that I just found God in the ordinary, really. God's been there all the time, even when I didn't notice Him. Certainly unless you maintain a relationship with God all the time, regardless of whether or not you're very aware of Him at the time, the religious life can be a bit of a farce. As a community we share with one another where we have met God in our day. We're very committed to contemplating God in our own day-to-day reality, because unless one makes a very real, disciplined attempt to be contemplative in this life, it just doesn't work.

Mind you, the contemplative life on its own, ah my God I wouldn't survive for half a day! I'd be less called to that than my own family or friends would be called to my way of life. Oh no, I need excitement, I need people. I need all of that for who I am. I'm not called to a quiet kind of life. I really admire those people, I think they're great, but oh my God, it's not for me.

I actually have a terrific need to have people around me. I need to be alone, but always with someone else near me. I think that's partly my upbringing. I was never alone in my whole life until I came to sleep in one of our flats here. And when that happened I was in my thirties, and I thought, oh God, where is everybody? I'd go around searching for people because I couldn't sleep! I need people, and I also need to be doing active things, to be involved with God.

Reaching out beyond ourselves is very important, and I would say that work and activity in God's name is part of doing that. You were asking me earlier how far I hold myself responsible for what goes on around me, and how far I hold God responsible, and my usual response to that sort of question is 'I don't know.' There is so much that I will be wanting to know when I get to the next world because so much of it is a mystery to me. I've never had a problem saying, 'I don't know.' I'm quite agnostic myself, and I am willing to share that. I think it is important for me to keep exploring the whole concept of God.

However, I do get very angry with God sometimes. I want to know where God is in suffering, in pain. I mean, I wasn't even talking to God last week, or the week before. I had a bad time over Christmas because my mother was seriously ill, and I was furious really. You know, there she was in hospital, some old lady of eighty who'd never done a thing wrong in her life, who happens to be my mother. Why does God not just take her?

And you know, when she was ill, I couldn't pray at all, no way. I still went to Mass, though. I said, 'Here I am,' and in my heart of hearts I knew that God was in it, but I was impatient, and I wanted to understand the suffering. Then when my mother began to get better I thought I should be on my bended knees apologising and thanking God, because a great sense of relief had set in. But then a friend of mine, now her brother is dying of cancer, and he's a young man with little children. And I said to God: 'Okay, you didn't take my mother, but *now* what are you doing?' So I am afraid that there is an ongoing dispute there at the moment with God.

Having said that, there's a lot of mystery in life, and God's a great mystery. For a long time I've struggled and wrestled with many questions about the nature of God, and through those struggles I've rediscovered the meaning of that passage in scripture which says: unless you be as little children, you cannot enter the Kingdom. I certainly find that attitude in the people here, even if I find it hard myself: that despite the questions, despite their sufferings, despite everything that conspires against them, they have faith and trust in a loving God, and in the future.

The other thing is, and it surprised me at first, how much appreciation there is of us as a community here. Far more than we deserve, too. A few years ago, they had a surprise party for us in the community centre, to say thank you, like. A whole lot of people fundraised and God knows what else just to put it on. And then last Christmas, they went and bought a microwave for the community too.

They're so generous here, and we've so many good friends who support us elsewhere too; we've never been short of anything as long as we've been here, and that's not because we've got enough money to survive on, because we haven't. We've never asked anyone for anything. We've never had patronage, because our founder insisted that we didn't take on patrons. The Lord looks after us, which is just as well, because at the moment only one of us is being paid, and that's only part-time. So that's half a salary which we have for the core community – me, Coleman and Elizabeth – and the people who come and join us for a year or two, they give us fifteen pounds a week towards their accommodation if they can afford it, and because they are available for work too, they draw dole.

It must sound odd to you, because it's not a very usual kind of religious community – a group of religious and lay people living together and drawing dole in order to carry out their life and work together – but it makes such sense to me. After all, we often have people who are called to do this kind of thing for a length of time, but not necessarily for life. In no way do we try to persuade people to be Sisters or priests. We expect commitment from people while they are here, but we don't expect them to stay forever. God forbid! There wouldn't be room for the lot of us.

Yet I think what we're doing here is very important. Church is so alien to most of the people here. They are too embarrassed to go because they haven't got money for the collection; they don't feel heard; the priest and the altar – the symbols of authority – are always 'over there', and they're always 'down here'. The other thing is that most of the people who live in Heath Town are Afro-Caribbean or mixed race, and churchgoing people in Britain are predominantly white, middle-class, with enough money. It's no wonder people feel intimidated.

I think one of the saddest things is that in many places, both in Church and society, we still haven't found the means to provide channels of communication so that people can be heard, and their experience and creativity and their potential tapped so that they can bring about change. It's so difficult to give people enough confidence and self-esteem to believe and hope in the future. It's very difficult for them to believe in themselves as human beings when they think – know – that a lot of the time, whatever they say doesn't make a blind bit of difference to the way society is run, that their contribution isn't important to others.

So one of our dreams when we came here was to explore models of religious life in which all sorts of different people, both men and women, can be included in community for different lengths of time, including members who live nearby. We want to allow a common ministry between different denominations, and between the religious and the laity, to evolve in order to give Christian meaning to our lives here.

Living as we do: it may not be perfect, but I really do believe that it spreads Christ's good news, and I firmly believe that it doesn't matter what form the religious life takes, as long as it somehow provides opportunities for people to follow Christ and bring in His kingdom. I think apostolic religious life as we have known it is going to be a thing of the past, I really do. If we are not just to be a sub-culture, if we are to be relevant to today's world, then we must live in it. Our purpose is to bring people forward, to enable them to come out of the shadows.

My hope is that I can carry on doing this kind of work, and that I die doing it. I want to die in a place like this, amongst people like this, because I believe that unless we are in relationship with those in the margins, we'll be in a very alien environment in the next world, because that's who we'll find. I'm sure of that. The only other thing I'd say is that I hope to God I can be active in the next world, because I'd sure dread a future where I couldn't get up and go.

BARBARA ANNE

Community of St Mary The Virgin, Wantage, Oxfordshire
ANGLICAN: APOSTOLIC

Age: 36
Nationality: South African
Age at entry to community: 24
Number of years in community: 12
Previous employment: Theologian
Present employment: Silversmith/Sculptor/Icon painter
Dress: Habit

---

*The Community of Saint Mary the Virgin, which was founded in
1848, is the world's second oldest Anglican female religious order.
It is well-known for being a teaching order, but its founder, the
then Vicar of Wantage, also wanted help with parochial work, and
felt that an order of nuns would provide it. Over the years the
community has extended throughout Britain, and beyond it to
Africa and India. It also set up many 'women's refuges' in the
nineteenth century, and a number of nursing homes for the elderly.*

*Barbara Anne and I talked in one of the parlours of the enor-
mous Victorian gothic convent in Wantage, which she shares with
sixty-seven others. The room was furnished with the kind of green
hessian-covered chairs which can be found in old-fashioned school
staffrooms or veterinary surgeries, one or two landscape paintings,
and back copies of* Reader's Digest.

*When we first met, I found Barbara Anne surprisingly abrupt
and prickly. I wondered whether this was somehow my fault, until
she suddenly launched into dramatic self-explanation: 'There are
certain events that have shaped my life and it's important that you
know what they are. It's important that you know where I'm
coming from, Mary, so that you know what you're dealing with.
Am I making sense?' Briefly, and with some difficulty, she outlined
her history, emphasising, as if by way of warning, the parts she*

215

felt I should know before I interviewed her. She seemed uncertain of herself: 'Not sure I'm what you want.'

As we got to know one another better, the relationship blossomed into great friendship, and Barbara Anne's reticence moved over to make way for a wicked and rather anarchic sense of humour. Halfway through the interviews, she took me to see the old stable block which she has converted into a wood and metalwork studio. There she showed me a stunning abstract wood-carving of Mary Magdalene, which she had made with another Sister. It had just been sent back, to her delight, by the church who had commissioned it: 'Not quite what we had in mind.' She also showed me hundreds of beautiful stones that she picked up in the Namib desert in South Africa, on her last visit home. She gave me a streaky beige agate as a present, which I treasure.

Barbara Anne

What *kind* of family do I come from? Well, a difficult family, I think. My parents married quite late, and they were both very independent and different people: if your parents are opposite ends of poles it sets up the same sort of polarisation both in the family and in yourself. My father was unpredictable, Irish, an artist and an intellectual, and he had a very romantic streak. My mother was pragmatic, organised, self-contained, a sort of earthy, down-to-earth person. I was the only daughter in the family and I came last, there were two brothers ahead of me. My parents were in their thirties when I was born, and my mother wanted a daughter very much, so I think that made my birth special in some ways.

I was very close to my mother, all my devotion was to her, which is interesting because I take after my father. My relationship with my father was very complex, and I was acutely aware of that. I don't think I ever *loved* my father as a child. I was certainly the apple of his eye and I think that was very hard for him. You know? If you're devoted to your daughter and it's not reciprocated it's hard. Yet somehow I felt okay about not loving him the way he loved me, because I was aware, even as a small child, that I was carrying the burden of their relationship. It was focused in me, I had to absorb their pain and their need, and the situation didn't allow me to express my own. But there was a fierce independence in the middle, without which I would not have survived. Maybe it's got something to do with having been a caesarean, where you don't have that sort of primary instant experience of being with your mother; you have it afterwards. Or maybe the combination of artistic Irish intellectual and pragmatic German fused okay in me somewhere!

My mother was a very tender woman, and a very strong woman. Enormously strong – and silent. I can't remember anything she ever said; her love wasn't manifested in that way. The experience of her love was physical, it was a sort of *suffering* love. It was very strong, very mature, a total experience for a child. I found it hard to go to school and I never really separated from her psychologically until she died.

My mother was someone who had a very strong sense of God. Her brother had become a monk, she was educated in a convent. She sent me to a convent school, my brothers to monasteries. I heard after she died that she had been engaged to someone who had just left a community, but they hadn't actually got married, and I think there was something in her which was fascinated by God and the call that someone else might have, whereas my father couldn't be doing with that sort of thing.

My father was a sort of self-styled engineer. He was always very careful to let us explore our talents, our individual gifts. He was marvellous, he made all our toys for us. Huge trains that moved around the garden. Fishponds. Once, he carved a wonderful throne, with the queenly throne for me in the middle, and my two brothers as kings on either side. He put his creative energy into that, it was his way of showing his affection. There was also a very funny side to him which made him liveable with. I think there was a lot in him that was unresolved and wounded, and because of that, he would take flight into play. I was an acutely sensitive child, and I could sense the element of projection in there somewhere, so I distanced myself from it.

He had had a horrific war experience, he was captured at Tobruk. He was on one of the death marches and actually fell, but was picked up by one of the other people on the march and carried – they normally left people to die – and I think that must have had an effect on his personality. I'm referring to that because he had no ambition at all, he was one of these people who was very gifted in several ways but never actualised anything. And with hindsight I wonder whether after the war he could only think of living in terms of *being*. I say that because in a sense he didn't care what he did. I can see the same pattern repeated in my older brother too, whose only desire is to live, and to some extent in religious life I can see that in myself as well. There's a choice to *live* primarily, and the actualisation of one's gifts is extra, not really part of the priority.

I would not call my father an institutionalised religious person, and I'm pleased about that. The only time I ever remember him in a church was when he lit a cigarette in the sermon because he didn't approve of it! He just did not conform; I think he was impatient with so much that was religiously trite. I mean, he'd been through the war, he'd come out with shrapnel wounds in his head. How do you then take hold of the kind of facile churchy stuff?

I've understood him much more as I've grown older, because I'm like him. I have had to learn self-knowledge and how to hold together the areas of myself – the intellectual, the artist, the mystic – that he had in himself as well, and it's not easy to live with. My mother was a foil to him, a balance I suppose. They were opposites, and I think my mother demanded a great deal of integrity from my father, which isn't necessarily what she always got. In the sense of her *containing* those things in her which he couldn't contain himself, there was a bond, but I think the tensions pulled them apart.

I was always introvert when I was small. I read a lot, but we grew up in a beach culture, in Port Elizabeth. The entertainment side of life in a coastal, surfing place like that is the beach. We used to go mountain climbing when we were older, but as children you lived on the beach. You went surfing, you bought a sweet melon, and spent the day on the beach.

I had friends. I would bond quite strongly in friendships, but my brothers said that as a child I could always take care of myself. They still say it to me. It's not self-sufficiency, it's more a sense of knowing who one is, and that one is alone, and I think I always had it. I remember going to the cinema with them once and they decided to hitch-hike home. I must have been about seven and I refused to hitch-hike, so they left me in the centre of the city. But I got home, and it was about six miles away. It never worried me to walk alone anywhere, because I always felt at home in the world, and I'm sure it's got something to do with the fact that I was so loved as a child. Having been so deeply loved by both my parents is something which has stood me in good stead through other things that have come later, though if I'm really honest I remember my early childhood as a tremendous mixture of pain and a time that I feel enormous gratitude for. But because both my parents died when I was so young, I've had to look very carefully and objectively at this whole area. I've had to ask myself what was real about my childhood, and what was my own psychological compensation for death?

I had a very sacramental upbringing. I went to mass during the week and on Sundays. I made my first confession when I was seven years old, my first retreat when I was about ten, and I can remember as a small child breaking a Good Friday fast with macaroni! So it was knit into everything, part of the texture of life. God wasn't separate.

I think as far as I was concerned God was an emotional thing. My father was somehow part of the darkness in God, and my mother was the maternal God, and I think that my feeling responses to them ran into my feeling responses to God. My father made it possible for me to explore the inexplicable, to be comfortable later on with the kind of things that can't be easily accommodated in an image of God.

Having said all that, my experience of God was also independent of both my parents from a very early age, and I remember distinctly a moment when I felt the need to alone with God as a child. I went into silence – I just wouldn't speak – and I cut my mother out of the experience, which was a huge thing for me to do having bonded so closely to her, and it was very painful for her. I can remember clearly her bewilderment that I wanted her out of the way, and she couldn't make me break my silence. It's ridiculous really when I think about it! It wasn't at all like running away though, I did that for real when I was six years old. It was my father. He'd been mending the plumbing and said, 'Don't turn the outside tap on', so I turned it on – I mean, children do that, don't they – and the result was catastrophic because he got completely showered. Oh my father. We had some fun. In between the horrors.

My father died when I was ten. He had a heart attack. It was very sudden, he just dropped like a tree and was gone. He was fifty-four, quite young, but he had lived hard and through a great deal, so it's not totally surprising.

As I said, I didn't love my father in the way he loved me. I had reserve. And I didn't experience any sense of loss of my father, or grief even. My concern was for my mother in the midst of it, and I think it was my first conscious experience of being absolutely amazed at what a sort of complex mystery love is. I can remember being brought home from school, my dad had just dropped dead in the house, and seeing my mother across the kitchen was the first time we'd seen each other since this had happened, and I looked at her, and her face told me everything. She was in a state of shock and grief and it had been traumatic and was a tragedy for her, and I remember thinking, how do you get hold of it? There were these tensions between them, tensions between him and me, and yet the love was there, and love embraces these tensions. I don't think those words were in my mind then, but I think the words later were: 'Love can actually encompass that dark side. Love can actually hold what seems unable to he held.'

It was a moment when I had to revise all my assumptions. I had to realise something of the bigness of my mother – that she had a very difficult husband, a very gifted, complex person, and he'd taken a lot from her; and yet when he died there was a strange sense of freedom in the midst of it. There was a lot of insecurity in the sense that the family unit had been shaken, and my mother was clearly under enormous stress in trying to deal with my brothers' grief. But she was also freer, and I felt her discovering her independence. I can remember her going out and doing things she hadn't done before.

You asked me how she coped. Well, she coped by herself. She contained her feelings because that was the kind of person she was, but it was a tremendously stressful period. She had two adolescent boys and a daughter of ten, and it left her with too much to handle, I think, and six months later she died. She wouldn't accept any support, she was an intensely private person, and I think in those six months she held it all inside herself. She contracted cancer. I don't know where it started but it was total. She was young. Forty-eight . . .

Stop. Please.
Thank you. No, I'm okay.

*

When she died it was catastrophic. The world just collapsed. I would say that all the classic experiences of grief were true of me, I was just shattered. I went through all the sorts of things one goes through; searching for the person, dreaming about them, trying to find some sort of physical aspect that was left so that you could say, 'This was part of her.' All those things were part of grieving for her, but certainly not part of grieving for my father. My mother was my world, the total rock; my father was a sort of dark part of the world. He wasn't a child's person. If I'd grown up I think I could have formed a very good relationship with him, but it's hypothetical. As a child his death didn't affect me traumatically, it affected the family traumatically, and that's different. Anyway, what is grief? It's an absence of the physical, isn't it, and how somebody deals with grief and loss is very personal; some of it one can share, some of it one can never share. You've got to find your own symbols and your own way of expressing your feelings, and I couldn't talk about that, so it had to be done by myself, in private.

I had a lot coming at me from what other people were saying was God's role in this, and I felt a tremendous sense of detachment from it, rejected a lot of what was being said. I think because in those days you just didn't have things like broken homes in the set-up I grew up in, I was unusual in my class. There was a tremendous distance between myself and my peer group, and there was no way I could relate to it any more, our experience was completely different. But there was no way that I blamed God. The kind of thing that teachers would say was, 'Why did God allow this to happen to you?' or 'Why did God take Barbara Anne's parents?' and I would be indignant at this. I was quite clear God didn't do it.

However, I think the experience of a child's bereavement is the experience of rejection. You think you've been rejected. That's the ambivalent element that comes into love: 'I'm deeply loved but they've left me.' In that sense the child feels that it was the parents' decision, not God's. I felt later on, as I came to understand death more, that there was probably on both my parents' parts some unconscious decision to die, and I had far more difficulty in coming to terms with that than I had in coming to terms with

God. I do think that when people die naturally there is some sort of unconscious, if not decision, then certainly acquiescence, and one can't ever hold it against another person if they unconsciously relinquish responsibility for those who are still dependent on them.

Nevertheless, I had huge feelings of anger. I felt angry with my mother. A tremendous ambivalence arose in me about what the meaning of her enormous love really was, and that could have been a point of intolerable pain if I hadn't actually had the sense of her after her death. Quite soon after her death I had a sense of guardianship, and as I grew older it became quite logical. If somebody is such a good mother and loves very deeply, it must be very hard to let go, so the transition to death for her must have carried some commitment to ongoing guardianship. I would quite often find myself in situations where I felt, 'I am not alone, it's all right.' Certainly at key points in my life I've experienced it very clearly indeed; not just in a vague way, but very tangibly. Death is not the great divider that one sometimes feels it is.

God was at the centre of all this. I never questioned God's being with me, in me, round me or for me until much later, just as I never blamed God in any sense, or held God responsible. I was at peace with myself and at peace with God. There was that slight ambivalence because my parents 'left' me, but in those areas where my experience of God was independent I could stand back and say, 'I don't know, and I'd rather reserve my judgment.' It's a mature reaction, but you do suddenly get shot into maturity.

When both your parents die you lose your home as well, and then there's a total experience of finding yourself absolutely alone, standing on your own two feet, with nobody else to refer to. It projects you into maturity instantly on several levels, while on other levels you just stay where you were when it happened. It takes time to bring those two things together. I can remember taking on the world like a little adult at the age of ten, and arguing with the world on its own terms. And as it wasn't possible for me and my brothers to stay together, one no longer thought of oneself as part of a family, one suddenly thought of oneself as oneself; you know, the sudden realisation that 'I am I'. You're suddenly grappling with things that perhaps most people only grapple with in their thirties, and you're doing it with the only resources you've got.

So although there was a slight ambivalence with God, I could handle it. It didn't destroy anything. In fact, I think it brought me much closer to God, because two things were happening simultaneously. On the one hand, my identity had been profoundly threatened and attacked; on the other hand, it was getting stronger and stronger. It was an experience of both terrific inner fragility and tremendous strength. It was like suddenly standing on the edge of an abyss and looking down. That sense of the abyss being very close has never quite left me. It's always there for people who have lost parents young. Suddenly you're on the edge of a cliff; it's an infinite drop, and you're standing there. I have since fallen into the abyss, which was crucial. It needed to happen.

My mother's sister and brother-in-law didn't have any children, and they offered to give us a roof over our heads. My brothers didn't remain there very long. I did, but I was very detached from the situation. We all became wards of court, so our board, lodging and physical needs were paid every month from the estate left by our parents. I think that if your board and lodging is being paid every month there is a sense in which no moral claim can be made on you by someone who's in loco parentis, and I certainly guarded that jealously. It's a psychological thing. I had nothing in common with my relations and I would never have called that my home. It wasn't possible. There's so much involved in the process of grieving and loss of your own home you can't just have a big transference, it doesn't work. So I led my own life, though I have since come to realise, through talking to some of my family, just how completely out of their depth they were with an orphan, which has greatly increased my compassion and understanding for them.

I quickly became aware that in order to make my way in South Africa I was going to have to be educated, because there's no social welfare system there, you have to be able to support yourself. The school I was at was small; in South Africa we'd call it a private school – which meant that it was independent of government funding. It was very homely, very feminine. There was a lot of creativity there, and political engagement, which was rare in South Africa. It was a school which tried very hard to cater for the whole person, not just to give them an education, but actually to bring them out and develop them, and I loved it, I took to that richness. But the emotional experience that was so big inside myself was far more important for me than what was coming at me in a classroom, and it was a painful time. The Sisters made mistakes in dealing with a child who was grieving for its parents, but they did far more good for me than made mistakes, and without them I'm not sure how I would have handled the huge internal transitions that I had to make. They took special care of me, and as I moved into my teens and went into the secondary school, my relationships with them grew and deepened rather than with my peer group.

The Sisters who ran the school were Dominicans, and Dominicans are involved in the anti-apartheid struggle to the hilt, so I was politically engaged from quite young. As a child, before my parents died, I experienced black African women as mother figures. They carried you, and you rolled along on this wonderful broad black back. I always felt their presence as good, and I loved that. It was only later on that I realised what a horrendous political situation I'd been born into, without knowing anything else. Politics and apartheid wasn't really part of our home consciousness.

However, I had a tremendous amount of anger about the whole political situation, and I became a sort of leftist radical. In South Africa we had a movement called Christian Life groups, and I was president of our local one when I was twelve. We spoke out very freely against apartheid, in school, within the conference structures of the Christian Life groups, and in political meetings in the town. We also organised meetings with people of other races on an equal level, which was almost impossible then, because in order to meet with our black counterparts we had to break the law. Sometimes we would go into their townships, which was illegal for us: otherwise, we would arrange to meet in a white area, which was illegal for them. It was all very risky, but it was rich as well, because to relate when there are such costs involved is important. In fact, apart from the nuns, most of the friendships I had at that time were with black people, though there were some from the Indian township as well.

My uncle and aunt couldn't handle it at all. They couldn't handle me anyway, so this was absolutely the end! I suppose they would have been described as English-speaking merchants, and they were the South African version of English nationalists, not in the sense that they bore a sort of fascist hatred for black people like the Afrikaner nationalists do, but in the sense that black people were never equals and they were never free. It was always with a very distinct master-servant structure built into the relationship, and they did it with the kind of integrity that they felt they had. So because of my political choices I was alienated from my extended family right from my early teens.

There were one or two teenage attractions at this time too – mostly white. I was often attracted to black boys, but to have explored that could have resulted in death. Not mine, theirs. Very few white people were killed – though they were questioned. In fact, the place in Port Elizabeth where the police used to question people was ironically called the Life Insurance Building, and people used to jump from the windows there – or be pushed; how does one know? After all, the Special Branch in South Africa was a kind of police force of which possibly the KGB was the only equivalent. They're not very bright. They function on emotional hatred and a sense of survival for their own race, so in one sense to be questioned by them is nothing, because intellectually they can't hold their own at all, they're very dim. But emotionally and psychologically, they know exactly how to manipulate you in order to bring you to the end of your resources: they're taught how to do it. I was always afraid that it would happen to me. In fact, by the time I left school I had a file in the Special Branch office. I was being watched by the police, I had been questioned, and my teachers were being questioned about me too.

So you can see that relationships with black boys were something that I would never have allowed to happen, it was just not worth it. And the relationships with the few white chaps that formed anything steady I found very unsatisfying because I had been through so much, and they were still young teenage boys, so it was all very shallow.

I think some things need to go to the grave with one, but possibly the most important thing that happened to me as a teenager was when I fell in love with somebody much older. That was a huge, very deep, mutual experience of being in love, and it was that experience which definitively brought me to my vocation. In a sense, everything that had been emotionally held up until that point was no longer held. It was like an explosion, an evolutionary leap for me, psychologically, emotionally and in terms of my personality, and God was very much at the middle of that.

I was just carried along on something which I knew was stretching my whole being, not just my feelings. I was being intellectually opened up, artistically opened up. It was necessary, it had to happen sometime. And I suppose it was all a mixture of development and projection – projection in the sense that I recognised in the other person huge areas of myself, but I couldn't separate it out. It was a very intense experience of joy and pain; of both the capacity to form a bond with another human being and experience the deep need for autonomy, which in the end is what I chose.

I experienced God intensely in the middle of love; at the same time I experienced a threat to my autonomy and a sense of being magnetically drawn towards the total giving of myself to God. It was definitive because although I experienced God in love, celibacy represented freedom, space to breathe, wholeness of self, autonomy of being. The other represented something deeply rich, that was infinitely valuable and always treasured, but not the ultimate for me. On the way to the ultimate, but not the ultimate.

So that experience of being in love was an intense experience of God and the nature of celibacy. What was involved in choosing a celibate way of life? That was the question at the very heart of that relationship. How did one find God both in another person, and yet in a commitment to something that was bigger than the relationship? Although the autonomy was too strong to go on relinquishing itself in the end, it was an involvement that went on until I was about nineteen. This person then went to another country and married somebody else, which was right. I'm sure it was right. It was very painful, but the whole relationship involved a life-death choice right the way through it. The demise of the relationship and its falling away was the first thing to make me question the strength of my own identity and the capacity to endure any more pain. 'How much more pain can I actually live with?' became a key question for me at that time. And although it was a vital experience, it wasn't something to commit myself to for life.

A religious of another generation would say, 'You had a sense of being a celibate, you had a sense of being called,' but I don't know if I could use that language. It's just that when you've had that huge existential experience of being alone in the world, reality changes. It's like breakdown. False things crumble and you're left in the ruins, alone with the Alone.

How I ever got through my final exams at school I simply do not know. It was a miracle. I got to a threshold of pain where I felt, 'I can't stand another minute of this.' Psychologically, I couldn't handle any more pain without exploding somewhere, and there was nowhere to explode, which I think indicated where one grief extended into another. Statistically, the suicide tendency for people who've lost their parents in their childhood is very high, and in a sense there's a natural psychological pattern there: you want to die too. And I came up against that, for the first time. At that age I couldn't distinguish between what was past grief and what was present grief, I just didn't have those kinds of skills or the ability to stand back, but it was a very profound experience, because afterwards it was like being given my life back, like the phoenix, like being reborn.

I went to university with a sense of a new life, with a tremendous sense of potential and joy opening up, and in my first year it was liberating. There were good friendships, parties and good times, and I got a lot out of my system. I just played – and enjoyed it. They were a tremendous five years, one degree followed by another, because I changed. I wanted to explore theology so I had to start again and read it from scratch. I think I probably did theology and stayed on at university because there was a need to hold on to my sense of call to the religious life, which I'd felt since I was a small child, and also the need to go on exploring other things.

However, I did discover a religious community while I was at university, and I loved it very much. It was a small community, different from anything else I've come across. Foolishly, I asked to enter their novitiate while I was still in my final year at university, and I did leave university for a bit, but the community felt that I should go back into the world and learn more about it. It was a very valuable experience to have done that and learnt more about the kind of religious life I felt was right for me, because I discovered that it definitely wasn't the active, or apostolic, life I was after; it was the contemplative life, which primarily involves just *being*. Nevertheless, it was extremely painful being asked to leave that community, because at the time I thought it was the right one. And it was so quick, very badly handled. I was told within a week, and then I was gone.

That experience brought me head-on with God – in a collision. For the first time in my life I wanted to have it out with God, and that brought me to the brink of a nervous breakdown. That experience awoke all kinds of grief that I had experienced before. I didn't have a breakdown, but I lost all sense of who I was, and who God was. By this time I'd left university, and I had a teaching job. I managed to keep it, but my inner world was like a post-nuclear war area. There was nothing left standing. Any preconceived ideas I'd had of God had gone. God had meant the world to me ever since I could remember, and it felt then as though God was rejecting me. I just could not come to terms with it.

After a while I resigned the teaching job, and got a job in a computer section of a firm, which for me was soft, because it didn't involve any relating or human dynamics, which was exactly what I needed while I allowed something to rise from the ashes. Yet the call to enter a community was enormously strong all through that time for some extraordinary reason which I can't understand. Instead of dying with everything else, it lived somehow.

I decided I wasn't going to enter a community until I'd made a journey for myself – a symbolic journey. So I decided to travel. I made some money, and with it I got on a plane, went to Europe, and travelled completely alone – I just put on my rucksack and went. I blew all my money, travelled until I ran out. I didn't care. I enjoyed it, had a fling, let my hair down, it was important. But I *had* to enter a community. I just knew that whether I lived or died, that was where my feet should take me. So I came back to South Africa, got off the plane and entered the Novitiate of this community, Community of Saint Mary the Virgin, on the same day. The plane was late and they thought I'd changed my mind.

I think from the beginning the South African community experienced me as someone who had lost my sense of identity. They were introduced to me by the Bishop of Pretoria who had been a tutor at my university, and they really had no idea of the full extent of what I'd been through. I think I was probably a handful, but who wouldn't be after all that? So it wasn't perfect – how could it be? – but because they are very warm, big people, it was all right. The group thing was very strong out there, and your own needs were always sacrificed for the needs of the group. That was a very strong experience for me – that the community came first. For the first time, my commitment was to them and not to my own needs.

But I still had an enormous amount that I needed to address in order to mature, as a person, and in God, and in the religious life. I couldn't do it within that situation because the enabling help was not there. So to me, being in South Africa in community was a desert experience. It was just me alone with my rubbish, you know? And it was either find God or die.

But I loved the people in the community, I had an enormous amount which needed to get earthed in God, and I knew much more clearly what I was looking for in terms of the kind of religious life I wanted. CSMV is an apostolic order, but with a strong contemplative side, and it was the nearest I could get to a contemplative order in South Africa. There aren't contemplative communities to speak of in South Africa; it's a violent society, and they don't flourish in that sort of violence. Anyway, I'm not sure, looking back on it, that a strictly enclosed community would have been right for me.

Something about the flexibility of CSMV was right for me. Having gone through so much personal trauma, I was left with huge questions about the value of practical apostolic engagement on its own, and CSMV was a good mixture of both. Also, as a young white radical, it was clear to me that really radical black people didn't want what they would call 'leftist whities' fighting their battles for them in the political system. That contributed to my sense of opting on the whole for the being rather than the doing. To pray through something was more meaningful for me that an active lobbying: what I had to give was not activity, not some kind of social work within a religious framework. If it were, then I'd go and do social work. The whole political situation raised huge questions for me about the quality of life – anybody's life – and for me there was a link between how I would live the contemplative life, and the people on behalf of whom I would live it: the actual living out of the contemplative life was a sort of living intercession which took everything. It took the whole of me.

Being a contemplative is like removing oneself to the fringe of something, and by being on the fringe one has a particular relationship to the centre. By becoming a fringe member of society I feel I'm engaging very deeply with the centre of what's happening. In my consciousness, in my prayer, I am in tune very differently with the centre than I would be if I were outside rushing around and doing a job, because the quality of my consciousness has altered. I am *centred*, and I think there's a particular ability to hold the pain and struggle of others when one is centred.

It's terribly difficult to talk about this whole area, because words don't cover it easily, and it's here that there's a clash of spiritual cultures even among people who are religious. Basically, it's a different way of engaging in the issues that are around us. The contemplative tends to take the thing within themselves and hold it there and pray within. The apostolic will go out and, say, raise money to do something about it. Which is not to say the contemplative doesn't do a little bit of the other, or vice versa, but primarily, the interior place from which you engage is different.

I hope I'm making sense, because this is important. For me, every action following consecration was an action on behalf of creation. I wouldn't have thought of it in 'churchy' terms at all; in fact, in many ways I came into community because I wanted to distance myself from churchiness. Prayer for me is more a quality of attentiveness. I've always had a very strong need to be able to work with complete attentiveness, and within that kind of concentration to seek to be in tune with God on behalf of others – not in a facile way, but in a relationship. The prayer relationship is an inner awareness of another that I love; it's a changing, living thing like any relationship, and I think the essential understanding of prayer is not as something I *do*, but something that *happens*, and I am not at all clear about its boundaries. To say 'Life without prayer' is to say life without any God-consciousness, and is it really possible to live without the consciousness of God?

You know, there's a whole area where I think we theologians are way behind. Our concepts of reality and the world are still very bound up with outmoded ideas, yet people like nuclear physicists are pushing back horizons, opening doors, which mystics have sensed intuitively for centuries. And the possibilities of such concepts! What they can offer for one's understanding of God and life and oneself and prayer! I mean, who *is* God? One can only look in that direction. And for me, it's where my gaze is directed rather than what I'm looking at.

Enclosure . . . Oh heavens, where shall I start? With the suggestion that I'm being escapist? Well, this way of life is not the only way of life that needs to separate itself in order to be what it is. A community's need for enclosure is the same as a family's need for enclosure. I would say to someone who feels that enclosure or boundary is a threat to them that if they walked into the home of a married couple, would they feel the same way? If they couldn't go into the bedroom, would they accuse the married couple of escaping or imprisoning themselves because they needed space to explore something else? You know, it's not a problem for me: why is it a problem for anyone else?

On the most basic level you just need space to be together. If a group of people is going to have a group experience, they need a particular environment in which to do that. The fruits of that experience can then go back into society. In order to be attentive one needs an atmosphere of concentratedness, and I'm not going to get that on the tube. I'm not going to get it in frenzied activity anywhere. The role of silence, and corporate silence, is crucial if one is going to try to live a life of prayer, and if we were to scrap enclosure tomorrow, and everybody who came to visit us could just go anywhere they liked, then what we would have to give them in terms of *stabilitas* and the way of living would be completely eroded. And although I believe that there are many ways of living the religious life, and religious life is more than just community, living in community humanises you. You're like pebbles in a barrel being turned, constantly coming up against each other, learning self-knowledge, becoming more fully human.

By 'becoming fully human' I mean allowing the truth of my being to emerge without defences. Allowing my humanity to be laid bare in order to embrace joy and pain, because that is where Christ and I meet, and that is where compassion and love for others are born. I see the vows as one threefold vow, and the day that I was elected to life vows I had a distinct visual image of a horizon with a clear path opening up in front of me. The fact that the door was closed behind me was a very liberating experience. I could not go back. You know, you either take a vow or you don't: you diminish the value of the vow if you enter it thinking, 'If this doesn't work, I'll leave.'

I feel incredibly strongly about my vow. In terms of my womanhood the vow of poverty means a barrenness which is fruitful. In terms of my lack of possessions for myself I'm free and I'm light. I'm simply a Sister among Sisters. I'm not rooting for myself, not on the ladder of competition. I don't have to carve out something for my ego. I can't use my earnings from the studio to go and buy myself a tape recorder, it's as basic as that. I can't even look after my own body in the way I might like to. And I think the fact that we share things in common is poverty, of a particular kind. I don't have my own theology books, for example. On the other hand, I do have my own bed. I might be asked to move out of it tomorrow and go and sleep somewhere else, but that's different.

I'm free, and I don't feel emotionally deprived. I'm an earthy woman! The flesh is very important for me. At profession my flesh was consecrated, and for me, that is the key to the whole thing. It was my *humanity* that was consecrated. What I've *renounced* is using my body in certain games – okay, good games, but I've renounced them. I've renounced using my body sexually in a narrow sense of engagement in society. But I have not renounced my body – I am my body – and I have not renounced my sexuality, no way! And if I can't see the beauty of my own body, how can I see the beauty of somebody else's?

However, if you talk about celibacy as chastity, and people do confuse the two, then it begs the question: are you saying, that physical love is unchaste? I would see marriage as a chaste relationship. I think calling celibacy 'chastity' belongs to a certain way of thinking about sex as impure, and I can't see that as so. For me, the experience of God is also in the flesh, and for two people to express love can also be an experience of God. However, celibacy for me has increasingly meant that transcendence of the physical, sexual expression of a union. But I mean, being a woman one always loves with the whole of oneself, and I can't split off my sexuality from my loving. I've forgone the sexual expression which goes towards a particular moment for two people, said no to a particular direction with a particular end, and I think it was a conscious sacrifice as I was twenty-eight at the time. We're all sexual beings and there are times when one longs for physical intimacy with another human being, but I know I would never have been satisfied by marriage.

Obedience was definitely the most horrific aspect of religious life. I find it very hard to talk in terms of obedience to God because I think it's very hard to know the will of God. One can only say, 'I *think* I know something of,' or, 'I believe and have faith in.' To say, 'This *is* the will of God' does not ring any truth to me.

The other aspect is deeply personal. If you've relied on your own insight and intuition from the age of ten, it's very hard to relinquish that. I went through unspeakable hell at the thought of having to actually put my life in the hands of the community for ever. I found it deeply threatening and compensated for it by trying to be utterly, blindly obedient. And the first year after I was professed, I just cracked. Since then, it's taken me a lot to get to the point where I can say, 'I don't believe in this linear, hierarchical obedience and I have to say that.' I believe that obedience is mutual and that we all hold the mind of Christ in community. *Together* we discern.

But I *need* disciplined structure. I *need* limits and choices put to me, so that I don't just dissipate myself. And if I weren't in this life I would impose those disciplines on myself. So when I cracked up, it brought me to the point of having to lay my cards on the table: 'I am a contemplative, this is my true nature, and if you put me in certain situations it is going to go against my deepest inclinations. I feel called to follow the spring to its source, and I need solitude for that.' Something like that's quite hard to say in religious life when the understanding of obedience has had to change in the community.

But at that point Mother Allyne was thinking creatively about our work anyway, and the two things came together. She sent me off to the Polytechnic to do a very short crash course in silversmithing, and I've built up the studio since then. Incidentally, I love that brooch you're wearing; where did it come from? Can I have a look at how it's made? I guess this bit must have been beaten down first and then the fishes and the weeds made separately and soldered on afterwards. It's lovely.

Oh, I must take you up to the studio. I've built it up myself, really, shelves and stuff from old bits and pieces. Shall we go over now? Would you like to? Okay, great.

I would never want to be too closely identified with the Church. I would rather want to be identified with the world, of which the Church is a part. I don't actually believe salvation is in the Church. I believe salvation is in the world, and I see religious life as intrinsic to the world. But there are so many people out there who are so humble, so saintly, so good, who are not wrapped up in any sort of ecclesiastical structure at all, and *that's* where it is. I think of so many black people – suffering people – whose quality of being leaves one speechless.

But yes, because of the way of life I've chosen I've had lots of criticism levelled at me when I've been engaged with groups of people outside, and I've had it levelled at me from within my own family sometimes. I think my way of life can be a terrific threat to somebody who is caught up (and this is not a value judgment) in the need to compete, the need to earn money. It's a materialistic society, you've got to live, and if your whole being is going in that direction you can sometimes feel that somebody who opts for a completely different set of values, in which the material is almost irrelevant, is making a judgment on what you've opted for, and it's not so.

However, some people just have a problem with the whole idea of nuns and they need to abuse it. I have to ask myself why the way of dealing with it is abuse and attack. I have experienced being intensely verbally abused myself, actually by a priest. The most horrific things were thrown at me by this person, who obviously had enormous problems and a terrific sense of sexual inadequacy. But I think that a lot of men today are feeling increasingly sexually inadequate, and threatened by women's potency and freedom. However you feel about it, the pill has drastically altered the expectations of women. As a consequence, some men are suddenly feeling terribly threatened. But if a man who reacts abusively to a Sister is feeling in some sense castrated by her choice, then it's the crisis underneath in *him*.

And abuse in the streets happens increasingly. I've known Sisters who've been spat at. Mocked. For the Sister, the question is: how does she affirm that person? I get *wildly* angry about it, not so much at the hypocrisy, but there's something so cowardly about it, it's such a coward's way. The anger in me is frustration at the misconception, the projection: I wonder whether it's got something to do with the kind of pornography that exploits the archetype of the nun. Is it because we represent some sort of caring aspect? Or care mixed with innocence? Is it some kind of image of the woman that feels inaccessible to the man? You know, it's somehow not available and therefore has to be brought there by force – raped. They seem to have to project the image of the ideal woman onto a Virgin Mary archetype because they can't handle real women.

The sexist language of the Church gets up my nose, but I ignore it. Sometimes I feel a transient sense of frustration, or it will irritate me, but when one's in the middle of liturgy, something else is happening on a non-verbal level, which is much more important – for me anyway. However, I feel very strongly about the feminine in the godhead. Jung's idea of the Virgin Mary being the fourth corner, to balance out the Trinity and make a quaternity, renewed the feminine. Society is so dominated by the masculine principle. Even to talk about the feminine principle is to get it into your mind rather than to *feel* you are a woman. But Woman is part of God, and God is earthed in Christ, and Christ was born from a woman's womb. I mean, that's tremendous, it's wonderful, though I have to say I feel very anti the cult of the Virgin Mary.

So I certainly wouldn't want to put a gender limit on my feelings about God, or even about Christ, because I relate very deeply to the feminine aspects of Christ as well as the masculine, and I think that the Church needs women who are able to be as fully functioning within the Church as men. I certainly don't think sex and gender should be determining factors in terms of ministry, and I sense a crisis in the priesthood, which is reflected in the kind of arguments men use to say that women should not be ordained. I feel strongly about it because the arguments say much more about the inadequate understanding of the priesthood than about the ordination, or lack of ordination, of women. So I think it's the priesthood that's in question rather than whether women should or shouldn't be ordained.

Tradition is important, but tradition is not God. And if some men are so deeply threatened by the possibility of women priests that they fall apart or become schismatic, then tradition's only important from a negative point of view, because one's having to cope with the consequences of people who can't move beyond it. And I think the argument that the ordination of women is going to prevent the reunification of the Roman Catholic and Anglican Churches is a fatuous one because the Roman Catholic Church is already split down the middle on the issue. The Roman Catholic Church is stuffed *full* of apostolic Sisters who are frustrated because they are not recognised and valued by the Roman Catholic Church, even though they've contributed phenomenally to its involvement in the world since the eighteenth century.

So. If the Church has evolved to a point when tradition is no longer helpful when expressed in a particular way, then it's a question of life: and is one going to calcify at a particular point or is one going to grow beyond it? I think we should *always* be questioning tradition and structure because they themselves are not life – they're meant to *hold* life. If they're no longer doing so, if life is bursting out of them, they need to go. And this is also true of the religious life. It has to change and grow all the time otherwise it dies and those within it cannot live fully.

Living fully is so important, you know. My own commitment to be fully alive is very deep now, and it has altered my attitude towards many things, particularly towards my own death. I cannot live less than fully because I only have one life. I'm not afraid of the unknown on the other side, and I don't have any sense that my self will disappear when I die, but I think if someone who's been immensely close to you has died, you do have some sense of what has happened. You have some sharing in it somewhere, some part of yourself is almost carried over.

When our own Sisters die we always lay them out. We wash and robe the Sister in her habit, and say the last prayers over her. There's a tremendous sense of straddling two worlds because she's still warm, she's still there, and yet she's gone. Laying out one of my Sisters has been one of the most powerful experiences I've ever had. The dying journey is such a journey. Our dying is part of our living, and the kind of death someone dies is often so in tune with the way they've lived.

So although I have a natural question about the way I might die, my experience of God is of the uniqueness of myself, and I would hope that when I die, I will become more truly who I am, rather than just be lost somewhere in an amorphous consciousness. On a very simple level I long to be with the one who's loved me for so long, and that I've loved. That's going to be good.

I sound so sure? I *am* sure. I am! It isn't always easy. I mean, I've experienced death of God, when God's just died, God's gone. But that 'gone' is so pregnant with his absence that He's got to be there! It's a kind of blessed black darkness, not a vacuum. Rather like the call. For me there was no sense of 'call' in the sense of God calling me. I was just walking blind because my feet took me that way. Do you see? I mean, I just *know* God loves me. I've always known it, but I can't explain why. Maybe it's my need that creates the sense of being loved by God: maybe I need to know God loves me. I don't know. All I do know is that when I enter a place of deep solitude with God, I'm happiest, I'm most at peace.

MARION EVA

Order of the Holy Paraclete, Whitby, West Yorkshire
ANGLICAN: APOSTOLIC

Age: 65
Nationality: English
Age at entry to community: 44
Number of years in community: 21
Previous employment: Consultant anaesthetist
Present employment: Deacon/Member of General Synod/
Doctor in hospice for terminally sick children
Dress: Habit

The order of the Holy Paraclete was founded in Whitby in 1914,
as a teaching order, and for some years many of the local residents
thought that the Sisters were German spies in disguise. The com-
munity is based at a Sneaton Castle, and before I went to visit
Marion Eva I worked myself into a state of excitement at the
prospect of staying there: aware that it was the legacy of a socially
ambitious Victorian, I nevertheless indulged myself in dreams of
ramparts, bats and a drawbridge.

My dreams were shattered. Marion Eva was living and working
at a purpose-built children's hospice just outside Wetherby, that
looked to all intents and purposes like a Little Chef. Inside, how-
ever, all similarity ended. The hospice was beautifully designed
and incredibly peaceful. It was built in a semi-circle around a large
garden, with careful attention to the varying needs of those who
used it: there were low windows and furniture for the children on
the ground floor, and an upstairs 'retreat' for parents. Separated
by a long corridor were living quarters for the resident Sisters, and
a chapel which was shared by everyone.

Marion Eva and I talked in the Sisters' capacious sitting room,
which had clearly been furnished to lend peace to the heart and
the eye: the carpet, sofa and walls were all in quiet pastel colours,
and there was little unnecessary decoration. Marion Eva, rather

like the room, was calm and unfussy. She spoke in a very steady monotone, stopping every so often to emphasise words and ideas not with variation of speed or register, but with pauses; rather like a long-distance walker pacing herself according to distance and taking in the view on the way. She was kindly, firm and sensible, with a strong face, and an old-fashioned authority shot through her manner like veins through marble.

Marion Eva

I come from a very happy and united family. My parents are now dead, though they both lived to a good age. I have one brother, who's nearly two years younger than I am, and I shall be sixty-six this year.

My father left school at the age of twelve, and became an engineer. He served in the first world war, and when he came out of the Forces he thought he'd like to be in the country, and had an idea of living in the south, rearing poultry. And like so many ex-servicemen of that time and generation, it went in the depression, so he went back into his own world of engineering and salesmanship, where he was very successful.

Because he'd not had many opportunities, he was very keen that my brother and I should have the ones he'd missed: not for any money-making or social reasons, but because he valued the world of education and knowledge which had never been his. He was a very great reader, he had a great zest for life, and because he wanted us to have a good Christian education he sent my brother and myself to good schools, and paid for us to have a higher education.

Our mother put herself through grammar school and university on scholarships before the first world war. She came from a family which valued education: we had a Methodist grandmother, who lived and died with us when we were small children, and who read to us when we were small; I still remember it. She was also very keen that we said our prayers, worshipped. She was very firm – she broke the ruler on my brother's knuckles teaching him table manners one time – but she was a very loving old lady too.

I look back on my childhood as a secure and happy time. It was certainly a time of difficulty for my parents, with the early 1930s and the depression, but that didn't percolate through to us children, and we always had a lot of fun. Christmas was always a tremendous family festival, and picnics and family outings and holidays, all that sort of thing.

We grew up in Leeds, in West Yorkshire – not a stone's throw from here – and we were at school and university there too. I don't remember my early days at school, really. My mother always tells me that I was frightened of so many children about, I'd never seen quite so many all at once, but my chief recollection of being at school is the fun of reading and learning to write stories. I loved writing stories. I hadn't a vast number of friends, one or two close ones, and an amicable relationship with the rest, I think. I'm still in touch with my school friends from that far back, though.

My parents were very regular churchgoers. My father had been brought up an Anglican, but Mother was a better member of her church, which was the Methodist church, so we were brought up Methodist. Both my parents were in the choir. Mother was a Sunday School teacher, and Dad was one of the stewards. I think they were disciplined rather than strict. My father was a good Victorian, and believed in discipline, but there was nothing repressive about him.

Our house was certainly a house of firm faith. We said grace before meals. We didn't have family prayers, but were encouraged to say our own; certainly religion and Christianity was part of the atmosphere. It was also, I suppose by today's standards, slightly old-fashioned in its Sabbatarianism. We didn't cook on Sundays, we didn't take a Sunday paper, and the clocks were wound on Saturdays.

I remember those things very clearly. And it's funny, I think some of the things that irk a child become endearing later on. When I was first old enough to go to school on my own, my father would say, 'Now watch how you go, and mind the traffic.' And as I grew up, and was working in the hospital and so on, he would still say, 'Now watch how you go, and mind the traffic,' and as a teenager I found it almost insulting. But when he was eighty-five and dying in hospital, and I took my mother to see him, and he said, 'Watch how you go, and mind the traffic,' it was very endearing.

I can't remember that God was ever talked about at home. I know we were taught to say our prayers, and I remember being small enough to say my prayers to my mother or my grandmother. I know we had bible stories read to us, and we were taught to sing hymns out of the old Methodist school hymn book. I think

I probably saw God best in the terms of the old children's hymn, 'There's a friend for little children above the bright blue sky;' somebody who lived above the bright blue sky, and loved little children and looked after everybody – a benevolent, loving God. God was never a God who punished, so hell didn't figure in all this. Heaven did, but I can't remember that it was ever talked about. God and religion were just there: they were part of life. I don't remember either of my grandfathers, they both died before I was born, but I always imagined that God would have been much like them had I known them.

When I got into the sixth form at school I began to study organic chemistry, and then faith was very different, because there ceased to be any room for God in a scientific world. Life was expressed in one of our textbooks as one of the properties of the nitrogenous compounds of carbon, which is perfectly true, I suppose, and to a teenager that took away any of the possibilities for a God.

Intellectually, I couldn't accept the tenet of Christianity, but on the other hand, having grown up with a personal God, I didn't want to lose Him. It was a time of great perplexity, which lasted for some years; sometimes wavering slightly to the side of faith, more often wavering to the side of intellectual honesty, which couldn't accept faith.

Then the war came when I was fourteen, and for a while my brother and I were evacuated to different places. I went to Lincoln, my brother to Ripon, but in fact, Lincoln had more damage than ever Leeds did, they made steel in Lincoln. Leeds was a potential target because it had heavy engineering, and they always said that it was never bombed simply because nobody could find it, there was so much fog and smoke above it! And in pre-war days, there may have been truth in that.

From fairly early on, I wanted to do medicine. I'm not sure why: I think people go into medicine with varying expectations. I went into it with the idea of service, and at the time I thought of medicine, I'd thought of missionary work, or something similar, which vision speedily left me because of my ideas of Christianity. But it's a fascinating subject that engages the whole person, intellectually and personally, and I found it very attractive.

After sixth form I went on to Leeds University, and I had a marvellous time there. I enjoyed the medicine, and I had a great social life. I used to go Youth Hostelling in the vacations, and my brother and I used to go to the Edinburgh Festival together every year. It was tremendous fun, and all these things were affordable then, you see. It was a very, very different world.

I didn't have close boyfriends at that time, though I had by the time I qualified at twenty-three. There were boys in medical school, and boys in hospital when we were resident, but most of us weren't married. We had tremendous parties on Saturday nights, hospital dances and all the rest of it, but on the whole I think people tended to pair off a bit later than they do now. The other difference nowadays is that people tend to live together and all sorts of things, which in our day one did not do. So there was no one desperately important until a bit later. But then you see, medicine was rather all-absorbing. I was keen, and I started fairly early on to specialise in anaesthesia, which was not an over-crowded speciality at the time. It was a time when anaesthetics was developing tremendously rapidly, it was a time when intensive care became possible, when anaesthetics had developed enough to make cardiac surgery possible, and so on. So it was an exciting time for me.

When I qualified, I worked at Jimmy's – St James' Hospital, Leeds. In those days, before the Abortion Act, we took all the illegal abortions, and that meant that three months after every Bank Holiday we had an epidemic which overflowed a part of the acute beds, and we did see some pretty squalid medicine from those situations. This led me seriously to think, and to ponder why I thought that these things were wrong; not morally wrong, but just degrading, and degraded, and squalid. The sort of things which in a world of goodness and beauty and caring *should* not be and *would* not be. I began to wonder by what standards I was judging them and by what criteria, and it eventually brought me back to my faith. I had to make a leap of faith to accept Christianity, but it was the only logical and right step in the face of what to me was degrading and ugly.

Also, when I was a student at Leeds, I'd met an Anglican

monastic order, the Community of the Resurrection, who had a house in Leeds. I'd got to know them through the Student Christian movement, so I became an Anglican and was confirmed. I started to say my prayers again, and practise my religion. To start with, it was rather a duty – literally. I can remember saying the Lord's Prayer before going to the confirmation service, because I felt it was my duty to pray. But after a while, it became very much more personal. God was no longer the friend for little children above the bright blue sky: He was more of a person.

I also had a greater sense of *sin*, which was not a sense that one had broken any laws or knocked off a certain number of the Ten Commandments, but a sense that one was doing things which were grieving or insulting to God. And with a deeper sense of sin came a deeper sense of God's forgiveness.

I've never really thought of all this before, you know, I don't go in for biography, but while the childhood God was present in outings and holidays and Christmas, or when we went walking in the Lake District or cycling in Scotland or something – He was not necessarily present in Jimmy's. Not for a long time. Now God is with the whole of life, and it was through prayer and worship that one got in touch Him, with the author of rightness and fitness.

I went on climbing the medical ladder. I became a consultant when I was thirty-one. I had also, by then, become a Companion of Mirfield – a sort of member of the community's extended lay family – which was very important to me. I began to go on retreats, which was part of the Companions' Rule, you had to go on a retreat every year. The first retreat I ever went on, nobody had told me they were silent. They all told me it was a good thing to do, but nobody mentioned you were silent. I arrived late on the first night, came down all bright and chirpy in the morning and speedily learnt to be quiet. It was all rather overwhelming, but I knew I'd be coming back. I think it was through all that that I eventually got the idea of testing my vocation to the religious life.

After I'd qualified, there were two folk I went out with for a time, but we decided that it wasn't going to be a good thing. I was very comfortable on my own after that. I wouldn't have been unduly bothered if I'd stayed single. I had a very good social life, and I was involved in a lot of things that were going on around me. I joined the Soroptomist club: it's like Rotary, only it's women. It's concerned with social concerns in the locality, and it also had the aim of advancing the status of women. In no sense is it feminist: I think the feminists would regard the Soroptomists as rather fuddy-duddy and unrevolutionary. But I made a lot of friends through it, and travelled all over the world with it. I'd been proposed for the regional Presidency, and people were interested in grooming me for national office. So I had a very happy professional and social life, and I think if it'd been right for me with either of my friends I should have been very happy. But marriage wasn't an overwhelming interest, put it that way.

I should have liked to have had children, though. I think that's one of the greatest denials of a single life. I think it's a very *necessary* denial, because I think all children need a father as well as a mother, and I wouldn't have wanted children on my own — either for their sake or mine. But I think it's a loss. I like children.

I hadn't really thought about the religious life until I got involved with the things from Mirfield, as I said. It came on me as a shock. When I was at one of the summer schools – at Wantage, incidentally – we went to visit the enclosed Convent of the Incarnation at Fairacres. You don't see much of the community from the visitors' part of the chapel, but from where I was kneeling you could just get the odd glimpse, and the realisation that this was what I should be doing just hit me. Just like that. It hit me. It hit me like a sledgehammer: with that sort of force, and with not a very welcome force! And I thought that if it was left alone it would go away, you know, and it didn't. It would not go away, and it was obvious that it had to be investigated.

It's very hard to explain, but it's like if you're struggling with an experiment, or an idea, and you can't get the solution, and then you suddenly see it: it jumps at you, it's there, it's obvious, it's in front of you. It was like that. And I didn't want to know. Anyway, at the time, it wasn't altogether practical. Both my parents were still alive, and I had a certain degree of responsibility for them. But a few years later my father died and my mother –

we'd had a housekeeper since I was five years old – my mother was comfortably settled with her. And so that was it. I was able to go.

In retrospect, although it was a sledgehammer call, I don't think the Lord wastes effort on those who don't need it. Probably things had been working underneath for a considerable period, and without a sledgehammer I wouldn't have moved. Now I think about it, I remember going on retreat years before, and seeing the Sisters there in choir and thinking: yes, perhaps I should have done this. But I was then on the way to a medical career and thought, oh well, I'm a doctor, so that's that. And I suppose one could have described me as a career woman, with all the social contacts and interests that go with that, so it needed the sledgehammer to move me.

Because it had really hit me at Fairacres, which is an enclosed community, I assumed that that was where I should be going. But when I consulted someone about it, he felt I ought to visit other communities. He suggested Wantage, because they had medical work overseas, but a Whitby Sister who I knew was highly indignant at the suggestion, and said that I ought to visit Whitby. So I visited Whitby, which was nearer. I told Mother Anne that I had been attracted to Fairacres, and her comment was, "Oh no, dear, you're far too talkative," so Whitby it was. Whitby did at that time do a lot of medical work in Ghana, so there was still the possibility of medical work for me.

However, although joining the community meant leaving medicine, medicine wasn't the most important thing. I didn't think I should be losing anything very important by leaving it. Medicine was only the way of life, so my leaving it was simply leaving one way of life for another way of life. And anyway, it didn't only involve giving up medicine. Family and friends were far more important to me, and leaving them was hard.

I was forty-four when I entered, which is late. It's about as late as we would accept. Obviously people vary and there are exceptions like there are in everything else, but as people grow that much older they get more set in their ways, and they haven't the energy to change their domestic habits and their way of life. It demands a certain degree of strength to cope with the emotional changes as well.

I felt nervous, though not in a practical sense. I mean, the logistics of getting there were quite simple: put in your resignation; commute your life insurance; sell your house; sell your car; sell your furniture and so on. That was simple. Make sure you go with whatever's on the clothes list. It's like going to boarding school, isn't it? It's easy. You get the right things and turn up with a suitcase. But I certainly felt nervous about going into a way of life that I didn't know, with people I didn't know, and I remember on one of my first visits sitting next to the Novice Mistress at table, praying: 'Oh God, please don't let me be sick,' because I felt sick with nervousness. I often do.

The worst part was leaving my family and friends. My mother was distressed, initially – she obviously thought she would be losing me – and I think quite a number of my friends were too. I remember some of my colleagues at the hospital gave me a leaving party. They gave me a nice watch, which I wear: one of them took great trouble to find out from a local convent what sort of watches nuns wore! And the chap who presented it made a speech saying it was tragic and a waste. But he meant it nicely. He wasn't trying to undermine me.

In fact, I thought at the time I entered the community that the medicine would be used, which subsequently it wasn't: the community gave up medical work in Ghana during my Novitiate. And I think the fact that I couldn't use my medical training made me think more deeply about the nature of the religious life, about being available to God for whatever *His* purposes might be. It isn't about what *we* bring in terms of talents or education or possessions – but what God can do in and through us if we follow in the steps that He's leading.

I think the things which I found more difficult, far more difficult, were things like living with my Sisters, who are super people, but whom I'd never met before. Having lived alone for a long time, that was very difficult. We were quite a polyglot lot, and at the time that I was a Novice, the Novices had less contact with the professed Sisters than they do now. It's changed since, of course.

I suppose having – this is going to sound a bit pious – but having tried to live a Christian life, and trust in God for a number of years, I felt that if this is what God wants, well, okay. That went for every aspect of the religious life for me, including the vows. After all, I was prepared for them when I went into the community. All Christians are called to chastity, whether it's within marriage or outside of marriage. In the religious life we're vowed to *celibacy*, and that's the distinction I would make. Likewise, all Christians are meant to obediently follow the will of God. And before I entered the religious life I lived comfortably, but I used to tithe, and I believed in stewardship – a sense of responsibility for the things of the earth – so poverty here was just an extension of that.

When I was first professed, I had a term working at the diocesan Retreat House, in York, which is a place where people in the diocese, particularly the clergy, come for a break and some quiet. After that, the community didn't know quite what to do with me as a Novice. The order had been founded as a teaching order, something which I obviously wasn't particularly fitted for, so they sent me to study for a diploma in Theology at London University. I later continued to the degree in Theology and that kept me amused for a bit. I was a form mistress for a couple of terms at the end of my Novitiate, but I think it confirmed everybody in their belief that I was not cut out to be a teacher. I liked the girls, but I didn't like the school. School organisation – it was foreign to me.

After a term at the Retreat House, I was sent to Hull University as Assistant Chaplain. This was 1973, when students were shaggy and hairy and noisy, and I really thought that the Superior must have had a rush of blood or something, because I couldn't imagine myself in that environment at all. They had a chaplaincy house with a basement, and the basement had a large kitchen where coffee was served after the Eucharist on Sunday mornings, and we had parties down there too, you could make as much noise as you liked without disturbing anybody. And the first Sunday morning, going down those stairs into a seething mass of noise and long hair, I wondered what on earth had hit me. But they were *lovely*, I had one of the happiest times of my life in that chaplaincy.

Then, shortly after I went to Hull, the Sister who had preceded me at the chaplaincy, and who had been on General Synod, was sent to Africa. I was sent to General Synod in her place, and this was a bit of a turning point, because I continued on General Synod for nearly fifteen years. I speedily discovered about ACCM (the Advisory Council for the Church's Ministry, the committee which selects people for training to the ordained ministry), and about the ordination of women. It was then decided by the community that I should go to ACCM to become an accredited lay worker. An accredited lay worker is someone who is selected by ACCM for non-ordained ministry within the church, and it means you can work wherever you happen to be – you're not just confined to your own diocese. Well, until then I hadn't known there were such things, but I went ahead with it. It was okay by me.

Having moved into the Church of England from one of the Free Churches and through the influence of the Anglo-Catholic wing – as often happens, I became fairly extreme in my views. I was therefore quite sure that the ordination of women was wrong. I was quite sure that the priesthood should be male, because Christ was male, and all the usual arguments. I changed my mind fairly soon after that, not because of my own experience, but because through Synod and its debates I heard the arguments thoroughly aired by both sides. I met a number of women who felt pulled to the priesthood, who were obviously sincere people, whose vocation I had to respect, and whose ministry I couldn't but respect. They convinced me that ordination for women was right.

Working at Hull opened my eyes very considerably too. It was a new world, and a new generation. I hadn't had anything to do with students since I was a Senior Registrar and we had medical students in the hospital. It was a very, very different world, and they were all way out in their clothes and their way of life, but I think they regarded me as being just as way out. I was known as the Heaven's Angel of Hull, because I rode a moped. Oh, there was a super chap who was the Vice-President of the Students' Union, and he used to say to me, looking at my habit: 'Marion, you mustn't go to a fancy dress party *every* day!'

I've never minded the habit, however. On the whole I'm in favour of it, because it marks you for what you are and where you belong. And it does just occasionally have practical results. Very frequently I've been stopped by people, and I was someone who was safe to stop because I was in a habit. So I think if you are marked, it's a form of service, it has its uses. You can hide behind your profession or your identity or you can be yourself within it. I'm a nun and I'm me: I can't separate the two, and I don't particularly want to. But I think a lot of people perceive nuns as being without sexuality because they're vowed to celibacy. And that's what they see when they see a habit. So either they regard nuns with awe and reverence or else they react in the way of jokes and innuendoes or whatever to get over it. Nuns are vowed to celibacy, but that doesn't mean to say they're completely asexual. I'm not. Doesn't mean I go around thinking about it, or every handsome man I meet, but I'm aware. I'm not asexual, just celibate. Quite different.

General Synod was a little bewildering to me at first. It meets three times a year, for about three or four days at a time. It meets in the autumn, before Lent, and in the summer. Some of the summer sessions are residential at York, and the others are at Church House, Westminster.

I've never been one who found high finance fascinating – and a lot of Synod is taken up with finance and routine legal stuff, although a good deal of what goes on there is very interesting. One of the fascinating things about Synod, whatever you're debating, is that there are always people there who do know a good deal about the subject being debated – whether it's the death penalty, or the storage of ancient documents, or the transfer of industry, or whatever.

I think Synod is probably rather middle class, just as I think the Church tends to be middle class. Being a member does also demand that one is able to be present, which means that either you have got to be able to get time off work, or you've got to have some degree of leisure to be there, or be able to take holiday to be there, and that obviously limits the sort of people who can become members. So I'm not sure how representative Synod really is of the folk in the pew. I suspect that some representatives of Synod are as remote from their constituents as MPs are from theirs. Sometimes when I was there I used to think, 'What's this got to do with my boys and girls back in Hull, who don't know much about how the Church works? And what has some of our legislation to do with some of our ordinary citizens, who haven't a clue how it works either?' It is undoubtedly rather remote.

After about six years I was invited by the Archbishop of Canterbury to be on the panel of Chairmen. You get a letter from the Archbishop of Canterbury inviting you to stand, and they tend to invite people who don't seem afraid to speak on their feet and seem comfortable, and who also don't feel that it's important to share their thoughts on every subject with the General Synod.

Robert Runcie became Archbishop when I was on the panel, and I saw a lot of him. He was a person for whom I conceived a very great respect. He was the first person to address me as 'Sister Chairman,' which I thought was rather nice. He had a nice sense of humour, and one felt that he had a good grasp of all that he was doing. He was also a man of prayer and a man of faith – and I felt we had a good Archbishop.

When I was in Synod, I tended to speak on medical/ethical subjects; abortion, euthanasia, *in vitro* fertilisation. They're subjects that are always coming up, and as one's ideas keep on moving to some extent, I don't have a static formed opinion on any of them, although euthanasia is one which I feel strongly against. Abortion is one which, in most circumstances, I would feel against – but I've moved in the area of gross handicap. With abortion in the case of rape, I think one has to take each case on its merit. But I think if you're talking in general terms about the right of a woman to have an abortion at any time, then I would say no, because you're not considering solely the life of the woman; you're considering the life of the child and the life of the father, and I think these have to be taken into consideration.

I have the same problem with this question of *in vitro* fertilisation of virgins. Lord Mackay, I gather, rules that this is a right which cannot be taken away, and yet the consultative document on *in vitro* fertilisation says that one must consider the need of a child for a father as well as a mother. I don't think it is the right of any woman to be pregnant or not to be pregnant, because we have responsibilities as well as rights.

I am also totally against gay couples with children. Not because I wish to penalise people who are gay: I don't. I have very good friends who are gay. But again, we're not considering solely the rights of the gay person: we are considering the relationships which the young person, or the baby, being adopted, will meet when he or she is growing up. And I have seen some very great problems for children being brought up by two people of the same sex. So I would be totally against it. Though I'm a bit like the Gilbert and Sullivan character who said, 'Well, hardly ever.'

Euthanasia's a bit different. My reasons for being against it are Christian and medical, and my medical reasons are relational. If I were going in to see an elderly patient, I wouldn't like to feel that they might think I was coming as the Lord High Executioner. I would like them to feel that I was coming to look after them. And if they asked me, I know I would refuse, if only for the sake of any others who might think that I would do it to them! Also, I don't believe in the taking of innocent life, and nor do I think that most old people who are secure and comfortable really wish their life to be taken. I think we have a responsibility to see that their lives are secure and comfortable, and I think that's part of what the hospice movement is about. Now I know this puts great strains on society, and I don't know how our global village is going to cope with all its problems, but that belief is the one by which I live. And in Synod, these were the things I spoke about most often.

During my time on Synod, I also became very interested in ministry, because after a while I was put on the council of ACCM, and I began to experience some of the problems of selecting people to train for the priesthood. One selects people as part of a team, looking at the person's sense of vocation, his knowledge of God, his prayer life, his relationships with other people – because after all, he's not going to be a priest in isolation, he's going to be a priest in relationship with other people, men and women. One looks at the activity of his mind, and whether he's got the capacity to spread the gospel, because you're not selecting ready-made priests, you're selecting people who have the potential to fulfil what it is that God's asking. All these things are looked at by the team, and if there is any disagreement, then the selectors each write their views to the diocesan bishop, and he has the final say.

I suppose the system could be regarded as unfair in some ways, but with vocation one's looking at what people call 'the scandal of particularity' – that God should choose some people and not others. I think all of us who have any sense of vocation to anything suffer from a sense of why on earth me? And vice versa: you can look at your fellows and think: good God, why did he choose such-and-such?

There's a chap at Mirfield, a certain elderly father, and he once told me years ago that he looked round the refectory and thought, 'Good God, there isn't a man here I'd have known if I hadn't joined the community. And what's more, there isn't a man here who I'd have *wanted* to know.' Lovely isn't it! But it's true. Not all priests are likeable, not all religious are likeable: you must have found that. In fact, some of them you wonder if they're even good at their job. But nonetheless, for some reason God's laid his hand on them. And anyway, what is a good priest or nun, or a lousy priest or nun? We don't really know: nobody but nobody is perfect.

I certainly think we should see a completion, a completeness, of the priesthood, however, if women were ordained. I've met women priests from the US, and I think ordained women would bring themselves, bring the feminine, to the priesthood. God is neither male nor female, but God is both the creator and the accepter. God accepts what is done to Him. This balance is traditionally seen as the relationship of male and female, the active and the passive, the powerful and the vulnerable, and without women the balance is not there.

I am a deacon myself, something the community has made possible, and it is very important to me now. Although I haven't been licensed in a particular parish, because I've retired from active ministry, the diocese has given me a permission to officiate, which means that I can officiate at certain services anywhere in the diocese without anyone getting permission from the bishop first. But being ordained is not only about what you can do, it's about what you are given, and I've been amazed at how this gift of ordination has increased my sense of vocation and calling, increased my sense of service of God and my fellows. Yet my primary call was to the religious life, never to the priesthood, and I don't feel called to be a priest myself.

There are three ranks of Holy Orders within the Church of England – bishops, priests and deacons. Deacons, because they are not priests, cannot perform all the ceremonies that priests can. All bishops are priests, but only those priests who become bishops can perform ordinations, for example. So deacons, the lowest of the ranks if you like, can't perform blessings, absolutions or celebrate Holy Communion: they can perform marriages, funerals and various other services. I'm told that many people like to have women take funerals or weddings, which women deacons do. I think most of the women who are deacons would go forward to priesthood if they could, and I really don't see why women shouldn't be bishops, like Bishop Penny in New Zealand and Bishop Barbara in America. We should be able to see the complete range of ministry in the Church.

I'm no longer on the panel of chairmen on Synod. I've been working here, at this hospice, for two years now. The paediatricians and oncologists in the Leeds and Bradford area were aware of the need for a place like this. They knew of Helen House in Oxford, and they wanted somewhere like that to give respite care to many of their families. They had a lot of people who were in need of a place like this, for as you may be aware, this part of Yorkshire is very densely populated. However, they also knew that Helen House was founded by a religious community, and they decided that they too wanted a religious community involved to give the place continuity and stability. They asked the vicar of Boston Spa to find a religious community, because they didn't know where to look for one, he came and spoke to us, and that was how we became involved.

We were involved right from the beginning in the founding of the hospice, but we don't own it. It is run by a management committee, and the then Prioress and Sister Betty, whom you've met, were on the committee when it launched the appeal for funding. The hospice opened about three years ago, and four

Sisters now work on the care team. There are also nurses, nursery nurses, physiotherapists, teachers, social workers. They do the day to day looking after the children, and we sort of muck in where we're needed.

We can take in, at a time, nine sick children. We also work with the entire family, so that the parents, grandparents, and the well brothers and sisters may come in as well – and often do. Two thirds of our children have some sort of genetic disorder, like muscular dystrophy, and about a third have a malignant disease like cancer or leukaemia. They're not all terminally ill in the sense that they're going to die 'now,' but they're all children who are going to die. But with some of the genetic things they're often well on in their teens before they die, and they become increasingly helpless. Often, genetic disorders affect more than one child in the family, and when that's the case the parents never have a break, and they too need care, which is why they come here.

Other children of course, die quickly. Some families prefer the children to die here, some at home. If they want them to die here, then we have all the facilities: occasionally, if they've died in hospital, they're brought here after they've died. We have what we call the 'little room,' which is just like a bedroom, and they can be dressed and laid in their bed, with their toys or whatever around them. The room is cool too, so they can stay there while the family decides how it wants the funeral to happen.

A lot of the people who work here are practising Christians; others are not. Some of our families are Christian, some are ortho-dox Jews, some Muslims, some Hindu, some are nothing. It doesn't matter. They're all well looked after by our Anglican and Roman Catholic chaplains. He's *delightful* with children, the Roman Catholic one.

For me, of course, it was a different branch of medicine from what I had worked in, and I hadn't done any medical work for some time. But as all our children come in already diagnosed, we do the sort of work which basically you would do in general practice. And you know, it has revealed a tremendous need. We have over three hundred families with sick children who come here now; another hundred families who are bereaved, who come back. And this is just in three years. Thankfully, there's another hospice like this opening in Manchester this summer.

The day to day financing of it is not easy. We're entirely and completely dependent on the thousands and thousands of good folk who give us money, which has its advantages and its disadvantages. Certainly we need the income, because we get so many people here. We get children from North Wales, the other side of the Pennines, all round this area of course, Hull and Humberside, Middlesbrough, Teesside, Tyneside, even up from Scotland.

It would be very nice to get funding from the NHS, but the problem with the NHS is that it was founded on a totally false premise; the premise that health care was financially containable, when in fact, the sky's the limit. The NHS could use all the money that the government could put into it, but it was founded before the great explosion of intensive care, thoracic surgery, just at the beginning of the antibiotic era.

I've been qualified medically for forty years now. Many of our children here wouldn't have survived birth or infancy before: now they all live far longer than they would ever have lived at the time I qualified, and one hopes, when you look at what is possible with genetic mapping, that in the foreseeable future some of these diseases will no longer exist. I remember girls at school dying of diphtheria – you never see it now. We've moved on. And this is what I mean when I talk about the making of creation, the bringing in of the new kingdom. Not everybody sees it like that, I suppose, but if you see the life of faith and the life of the world as a whole, you see God at work in it all.

This work opens your eyes. It opens your mind, and your prayers, and your soul. And naturally it makes you ponder the nature of belief. Obviously there is great grief in this work, particularly for some of the young teenagers just on the edge of life, dying of something like cancer or leukaemia, knowing what is happening, and being very gallant and very thoughtful of other people at the same time. Obviously there is anger too. Great anger, great impotence, great frustration, great weariness for the families. Anger is part of grief, a stage in grief. Anger is often the thing that gives the drive which makes things possible; it depends how it's used.

It's the same with frustration and impotence. We are helpless in the face of death, and people are bound to rail against God. It wouldn't be rational and sensible if they didn't from time to time. 'Is there a God? And if there is, what is He, and what is He doing?' That's not a question that one argues about, it's a sign that someone needs to talk out their grief and their pain. There are also people who come to a faith through all this, because through it all they find care and love and a knowledge of the God that gives care and love. But the shock of finding one's child ill or dying is – it's the sort of thing people in a sense don't get over, it's always there.

There was an American rabbi whose little boy died, and he said that he knew himself to be a far better man and a far better rabbi because of the death of his little Aaron, but that he'd give it all up if he could have Aaron back. And I think all parents would feel that. But when you see parents dancing with a handicapped child in their arms, and the fun and the joy which they have together, and the whole family have together, it's great. It is happy.

Doing this work has also raised all sorts of questions in my mind about the nature of creation, and the tremendous freedom which we are given by God. God has put all this here, He's put us here, and He's given us the capacity to work with Him. So the way I see it, we are all working together in medicine and art and science to make creation as God would have it be. Although it often seems, thinking of some of the awful catastrophes we've got at the moment, with Bangladesh and the earthquakes on the Horn of Africa, and the Kurds – it often seems that as we solve one problem we make a bigger one.

I pray about it all, of course, and although other people might see it differently, I think prayer is two-fold. On the one hand, we are bound to hold others in the presence of God in our prayer: on the other hand, we have our own relationship with God in prayer. In a sense, all of us here are impotent. The children here are going to die. Our families are helpless in the face of that. Nothing they can do to stop it, nothing we can do to stop it, and yet we're still seeking to share the love and care of God, and to bring in His kingdom, to glorify Him, through it all. And it's only if we keep close to God in prayer that we can do that.

It was brought home to me very much six years ago, because I very nearly died myself. I ruptured my oesophagus, and then I went into liver failure. When I recovered consciousness, I knew that the probability was that I was going to die – both conditions carry a very high mortality. I don't think I was particularly frightened by the possibility, but I was perplexed. I didn't want to die; I enjoy life. On the other hand, I could see that it didn't unduly matter if I did die. But I was perplexed in that I didn't know how or what I ought to pray. I didn't feel that if I had a condition from which other people died, why God should particularly heal me. I couldn't really see that I could ask Him to heal me, nor could I really see that I could ask Him for His will to be done, because I didn't really know what His will was. And it's a cop-out just to say piously, 'Your will be done' if you don't want God's will to be done, or don't know what that will is. All I could see was that I should pray that He was glorified – whether I lived, or whether I died. I had to leave it to God.

Now this kind of attitude raises tremendous problems when one's faced with the almost overwhelming individual pain of our families, or the catastrophic pain of some of the natural catastrophes of the world. But it's what I firmly believe. There's no glory in suffering itself. The only glory of God, as I see it – and it isn't like a great sunburst – is in self-giving love, and the suffering of self-giving love. The glory of God, in other words, is in the cross. The cross was self-giving, and Christ went knowingly and willingly to his death.

So glory isn't seen just in suffering *per se* without love. The sort of glory that one saw in the holocaust was in those Jews who in the middle of it all could forgive; and the glory of the concentration camps was seen in that priest who went to his death instead of a fellow man. The glory of God in some of the situations of starvation is seen in those who will give up their rights for others in love and in care.

I agree that there is no glory in lack of human dignity; there is no glory in suffering without love. On the other hand, there is no glory in success without love. That is power without glory. It's self-seeking. It's cruel. Not glorious at all.

I don't know what I'd have been like if I hadn't been brought up a Christian, but I think that people who have great faith can hand themselves over to God, and die peacefully. I think people who don't believe there is a God can also do the same, though there are times when it is difficult, particularly for people who have to leave families, children, responsibilities.

In a sense, one can't ever approach death easily, but for those who do believe there's something after death, 'What are we going on to?' is quite a thought. I believe in an after-life. I believe in a personal after-life, simply because I don't believe that love and God cease at the moment of death. And I believe it's personal, at the very least, because God has made himself known to us in the person of Jesus Christ. I believe it is something which is eternal, but in what form I do not know. The only thing I can say is that when I die I look forward to meeting folk I've known, and one or two that I've never known. I always think it would be super to meet St Luke, the man who wrote that lovely gospel: I always think what a lovely man he must have been, who could write that.

It's a simple way of looking at it, perhaps, but as time goes on, I find that things do become more and more simple. You said that I strike you as a pragmatic person. I'm not quite sure – the onlooker sees most of the game – but I think perhaps I'm a bit *simple*, I see things in a simple way. As life goes on, things get stripped away so that God takes over, and as we get older, or get sick – perhaps what Teilhard de Chardin means by our 'diminutions' – Christ grows in us.

At the moment we're seeing terrible tragedies, terrible evil – as we always have. It was one of the things that brought me to a faith. But we're also seeing marvellous acts of goodness and sacrifice and love. And I think that's what the religious life has come to be about for me. Things become more bright and more stark. The things which seem evil and the things which hurt become far more painful as time goes on, but the things which are good shine with an ever greater goodness.

But then I've just been lucky. I've had a lovely life.

BRIGITTA

Christa Prema Seva Ashram, Pune, India
(Member of Community of St Mary The Virgin, Wantage,
Oxfordshire)
ANGLICAN: APOSTOLIC

Age: 76
Nationality: German
Age at entry to community: 29
Number of years in community: 47
Previous employment: Apprentice horse trainer/Teacher
Dress: Sari/Punjabi suit (Indian shirt and trousers)

---

*Brigitta lives on an ashram in Pune, India, which she shares with
a number of Roman Catholics and Hindus. She has been there for
fourteen years, and she is one of a number of Sisters from various
communities who have been led by a mixture of desire and circum-
stance to lead their religious lives overseas. When I first came across
Brigitta she was meditating in the lotus position on the verandah
outside her room, slim, straight-backed and elegant. My first
thought was, 'I hope I look as good when I'm seventy-six.' Brigitta
was barefoot, and wearing, as she usually does, not the full habit
of her community back in England, but a cool Punjabi suit – loose
cotton shirt and trousers – and her long white hair was tied back.*

*The ashram (a word which means 'shared work') is 'a place
of serious spiritual quest, with life and worship centred around
Christianity, but drawing on ideas and practices of other religious
traditions, particularly Hinduism.' The day begins at 4am with
meditation and ends at 9pm after a group discussion. In between
there is a demanding, but informal, timetable of meals, yoga practice, discussions and prayer. The community does not earn any
money but is supported by the orders who comprise it, and visitors
are asked to pay for their keep.*

*I stayed at the ashram for six weeks, eating on the floor with
community members and visitors, sleeping on the roof in the*

terrible heat. There were no fans: even in a climate where the temperature rises to 45°C they are considered an unnecessary luxury by the community. There is also practically no furniture.

I interviewed Brigitta in her room in a small wooden hut. There we talked daily for a week, in peace except for the constant shrieking of tropical birds, and interruptions from one of the ashram dogs, who loved Brigitta dearly. We sat on a straw mat on her wooden bed; she, cross-legged or hugging one knee, I rather shamefully, on a cushion. The dog lay panting beneath us.

Brigitta is renowned for her erudition and commanding presence, but I remember her for her quiet kindness and her sensitivity. She is matter-of-fact, amusing, entirely unsentimental, and she responded to my questions with immense humility.

During my time in Pune, Brigitta taught me much, from Indian table manners to the Hindi names of venomous snakes. She also persuaded me to try her personal form of relaxation – hanging upside down from two ropes which were suspended, of all places, from the ceiling in the ashram library. When I left the ashram she gave me one of her saris. 'It is an Indian custom,' she said simply, 'a mark of friendship and respect.'

Brigitta

I was born in East Germany. Both my parents came from the upper middle class, so they were comfortably off, not exactly wealthy but comfortably off. My father was from Silesia, and my mother was English. They were married in 1906 and my brother was born in 1908, which was the year they came to live in England. They liked England, and intended to stay there, but my father was an equerry in the Imperial Court, and when the first world war came he had to return to Germany to serve. I was born in 1916, during the war, and at that time we lived in Berlin, though our estates were all in Silesia. Presumably we did not suffer from starvation as many did, because food came from the estates. As far as I know, I was quite adequately fed as a baby.

Both my parents' families were deeply devout, especially my father's family, who were Lutherans. My father himself was an agnostic, my mother was a person who, as my father said, had 'a high-church tendency much deplored by the family.' She had a definite relationship with God that she imparted to me by the prayer she taught me; it came through quite obviously. But we never went to church, or had prayers before meals, or family prayers, which at the time was still fairly common, certainly in Germany.

My mother died when I was twelve so my father was the only stable element in my life and that only occasional. I think I loved him but it was never a very close relationship. Being in the war, he came into my life only occasionally before I was three and I didn't see much point in him. He was tolerated, shall I say, by me. I was very close to my mother, and when she died I missed her terribly. Of course, when one is in one's teens an elder brother is of immense importance so he and I were close, too, though we hardly ever lived together. Recently I spent three weeks with my brother and we decided it was the longest we'd ever been together since we were children.

One thing which would sound very odd now is that we travelled constantly and I didn't go to school, so I had virtually no friends.

I had a much beloved and very young nanny, a Swiss woman, who brought me up from the age of three until I was seven, and she was really the only companionship I had. We lived in Majorca for a time and I was sent to a kindergarten there to meet children, and I remember one friend at my father's home in Germany, but as she was the only one, it's no wonder. For three years we had a house in England and there also I had a friend, but otherwise no childhood friends at all. Provided I was with my parents it didn't matter, I was used to accepting what came. However, I wouldn't wish my childhood on to other people; there was too much instability, constant packing and travelling, which my parents loved and I took in my stride. It's not very good for a child having to grow up without other children, and when I did eventually go to boarding school, which was a very unfortunate time in my life soon after my mother's death, I just couldn't relate to anyone.

I never talked about my mother's death or my feelings. There was no support, and I was just driven into myself. My father came to visit me once in the year, my brother came at Christmas, but otherwise I just had to cope with it myself. When I went to school I survived because some of the eldest girls took pity on me, but I think it was eighteen months before I made a friend. Then things took their shape, but those eighteen months really were hell, terribly painful. School was a tremendous shock, and I was by two years the youngest so I had no contemporaries to relate to.

Anyway, I don't think it did permanent damage, but for many years I was too self-sufficient and unable to relate at all at a deep level. I remember making a definite decision while I was at school: emotions were too painful and I wouldn't have any. I think I more or less repressed the ability to love, because I felt let down by the one person that I loved particularly and I couldn't cope. Obviously those were childish reactions which eventually had to be overcome, but that didn't happen for long, long years. I learnt never to be open, and I didn't trust anybody – especially aunts, of whom I had many. I just felt nobody understood.

I'm not sure how my father felt because I saw him so seldom, only in the summer holidays. I think he was embarrassed. He wrote very regularly, and I know he loved me, but he didn't know what to do with me as an adolescent. He found a good school for me and that was that. I was badly neglected as far as clothes and things went. Nobody was actually responsible for me, so I was a bit of a waif and I just did what I could – stole when I needed to, lied regularly, because keeping out of trouble was very important. I remember stealing somebody's shoes, because I needed shoes. Of course it would have been only too simple to go to the headmistress and say, 'I need some shoes,' but I . . . I couldn't.

After school I had a year in France in a boarding school, which I thoroughly enjoyed. Then my father asked me whether I wished to live in England or Germany and without hesitation I chose England. Germany I *loathed*. It was associated with the loss of the earlier home in England and with school which I disliked. I was not attracted by the marches and 'Heil Hitlers' of National Socialism, about which so many of my contemporaries were enthusiastic, so I chose England. As I was passionately interested in horses I said that I would make horses my career, and that lasted until the war. What I really loved was doing physical work, mucking out the horses, grooming them, but I was also being trained to teach riding and take children hunting and that kind of thing. I was occasionally in a hunter trial, but I was never a very good horsewoman.

My aunts had found me family friends in Warwickshire, and I was with them on and off for about three years. I didn't meet anybody of any great interest there – I led a very simple country life – but I found it completely satisfying and it healed an awful lot of wounds, though my sense of faith throughout this time was absolutely nil. God was very real, but churchgoing, which had been compulsory in school, had been a new and unpleasant experience. It was a total bore, dull, singing things I didn't know, sermons I didn't understand, a total waste of time. But God remained real. Certainly I had no experience of God and I don't think I had any superstition about it either. I'd simply continued to pray what my mother had taught me, preserving it. My mother'd lived by it and she was my model.

Other people at this point were quite unimportant. I had no close friends. I think I felt I was too unattractive for a social life.

I was always convinced I was terribly unattractive – fat, lanky hair – and I was convinced of it for a very long time. I spent some time with a relation in London, who had a daughter my age. The daughter had a very full social life, but I think that they all regarded me as unused to the ways of society and rather a lump and I wasn't invited out much. I went to occasional dances and found them terribly dull. This was at the time when you had one partner and danced the entire evening with that partner. And one had adolescent crushes and that kind of thing, but I had one or two unpleasant experiences, so I wasn't especially out for relationships with men. There was a kick in it and the feeling that one was grown up but not more than that. I was totally unused to English society because of having been at school in Germany, and I suppose I had a distaste for that kind of social life. It just felt so artificial, and probably was. So there were no men of importance at all; this seems to have been suppressed in me too. Looking back, I had a strong feeling of inferiority, which was probably encouraged by the way in which other people reacted to me.

Just before the war broke out I was staying with friends. They had two small boys whom they wanted to get out of a danger area, so they asked me to take them to Shropshire where their grandmother lived. I was with them for about a year, until Dunkirk. But during the Dunkirk crisis, enemy aliens were not allowed within a certain number of miles of the sea, and I, being an enemy alien, had to leave in a hurry, within forty-eight hours, and I had nowhere to go. I was totally alone and really couldn't see any future at all, until somebody, a woman with a habit of helping girls on their own, came to the rescue. She found me a job in a small school, and then a place to live – a vicarage near Ludlow where the vicar's wife needed help in the garden. The vicar's wife was a bit mad, but apart from that it was quite reasonable.

Then Lancing College was evacuated into that region and the Modern Language master was quartered in the vicarage. After a few months he decided to do war work using his languages and I was offered his job. So I spent the rest of the war teaching modern languages at Lancing which was tremendously lucky, and for the first time I felt completely accepted: there was no case of, 'She's

German, she's German,' which of course one met otherwise. I didn't meet any great hatred but it didn't exactly help one's peace of mind or sense of acceptance to be an enemy alien. And I denied it, anyway. I denied I was German to myself. I wasn't even aware that I had a strong German accent, and if I was told that I had, I denied that too. I convinced myself that I was as English as anyone else: it was just unfortunate that I had a German name.

However, I worried about my family. The secret service was coming after me and that was very unpleasant. My brother was in the Foreign Office in Berlin, my father was in a neutral country (Switzerland), and I was in England. They tried to persuade me that it was my moral duty to act as a go-between between the German Foreign Office and England. I said no. Once or twice they tried again, and then they left me alone, more or less. It was very frightening, but also there was the sense of, *was* it really my duty? It wasn't easy.

Yet apart from periods of great insecurity the war was actually a very happy period, because I made good friends at that time. No close friends, because I just hadn't got the experience it takes of how to be a close friend, and I remember being a bit worried by the fact that I didn't love anybody, other than my brother and my father who were far away: I felt there must be something a bit wrong with me if I didn't love anybody. I was aware of that, and it's really why I officially joined the Anglican Church.

When I was about seventeen I'd made a decision to go to church on my own. I seemed to have found a need for it, or a purpose in it, provided it wasn't compulsory. Then at Lancing I had my first encounter with educated people whom I respected, who were convinced Christians, and the kind of worship that was practised there was something that was absolutely new to me. It was marvellous. So I think a vocation began to grow slowly out of this. I began to make sense of God and worship.

I should also mention that during the war I belonged to something called the Anglo-German Christian Fellowship in Wartime, which met once a year in a house in Leicestershire where a German refugee community was staying; that was a very broadening experience. Here I made my first *real* friend, a German woman a bit older than myself – a Jewish refugee – who was organising this fellowship. That was a breakthrough for me, very gradual, but nevertheless a breakthrough because I felt accepted as I was without the need for pretence.

At the meetings I became aware, for the first time, of the ecumenical movement, and from that came the conviction that I must *do* something. I felt that God was calling me, but to what? There seemed to be two choices. One was to join the Quaker organisation and train for relief work in Germany; the other was to join a religious community. Very different. I felt a definite call to the second and a great distaste for the first.

Why? Well, I had such distaste for Germany, I just didn't want to be associated with it; very likely, I was afraid of what I might see or be asked to do. From accounts of people who'd been there, it was terrible. Also, I'd developed a taste for study and intelligent conversation, and I thought it would be the end of that for a long time. I often wonder if it was actually cowardice: the fact that it's remained pretty vivid may point to it. But the reasons why one's joined a community are always partly self-seeking. They're bound to be. So it was undoubtedly a search for security; that I think loomed very large. The war was ending, the job I had would also end within a year or two because the men would be returning, and they wouldn't go on employing women much longer.

I never thought of going to university or studying to be a teacher. I thought that at thirty I was too old for university and I felt that joining a community was something acceptable that one could do. Of course, it's very difficult to know what's a call and what isn't. What I do know is that it's done me an immense amount of good, though other alternatives might have done the same.

Although it might seem so now, nobody then thought that joining a community was very extraordinary. The friends I had came from Anglo-Catholic backgrounds themselves and thought this was quite a normal thing to do. My father, as far as I knew, was still alive, but he was in Germany, so I'd lost contact, and he never knew. He'd have been horrified of course, and I think by the time I wrote he was already dead. He'd been living with his brother in the family home in Silesia and when it became obvious that the Russians were coming, everybody fled. There was no petrol, so they fled on horse sledges and apparently he just jumped out; the general feeling was that he didn't want to be a burden on the others. He perhaps felt that he was dying. Anyway, one cousin of mine rode back on a horse and made enquiries, and yes, an old gentleman had been found dead, and here was his watch. So . . .

But I mean that was just war. Everybody was losing people all round.

Absolutely nothing attracted me to the religious life: I *loathed* the idea. I just felt this was what God was asking of me. I would say there was an idea of reparation for what had been done during the war, the sense that I'd had it jolly good and so many people had suffered so terribly, so this was some kind of reparation I could make for what my country had done. It seems a curious theology to me now, but I should think at the time it was pretty prevalent. The war was *so* awful. And although I'd been very sheltered physically, I'd been through a lot. But I certainly felt it as a calling, yes, and I can pin it down exactly.

I had never been confirmed in the Anglican Church and I decided that as I intended to stay in England I ought to be. The chaplain from Lancing took me down to Hereford where there was a confirmation, and I was told I would have to wear a veil, which I thought was a most *odd* thing: I disliked the idea, though it was a minor matter. And then suddenly came this conviction, some sort of inner voice saying, 'I want you to wear a veil always,' and this came through quite clearly. And I couldn't think of anything except that this *must* be a call to be a Sister. At the time, I didn't even *know* there were such things in the Anglican Church: I'd never met an Anglican Sister in my life. I was horrified, of course, because this sort of thing didn't happen in my life, in my world, but it could hardly have been invented. And then soon after this I had a strange experience.

I always had trouble finding somewhere to spend the holidays, and one Christmas I was staying with a family in Somerset. On Christmas Eve the daughter of the house said, 'Come and help me arrange the crib,' and she said, 'they're very beautiful figures – they were made at Wantage.' So I said, 'What's Wantage?', and she explained to me about the religious community at Wantage.

This was about three weeks after I first had the idea that I should join a community. Which is strange, isn't it. I've found in my life that things build up like that, totally out of the blue. I personally think it was a call.

I wrote to the Mother General, who then invited me to come and be seen, and I must say when I went (it was December) it was the coldest place. It wasn't the present convent, it was a very ugly, stone cottage, a horrible house. It really was terrible. It was bitterly cold and the bath was in the coal-hole, which was a bit surprising: I suppose it was convenient because you could then heat the bath with the coal that was stored there – but that was my induction to convent life. Chilly. Dirty. And then these hordes of sisters trailing all over the corridors and cloisters, mostly limp-ing, with iron calipers on their legs. I suppose I'm exaggerating, but there were vast numbers, and they were so black. But if God wanted me, that was where I had to be, cost what it may. Though the Novice Mistress was rather offputting. She asked me what I'd been doing before the war. I said, 'Oh, training young horses and riding.' She said, 'Ah well, here you can learn to train *yourself*,' which was fairly stark.

That was December, and I joined in September the next year, 1945. One goes with great trepidation obviously, but to my great surprise after a few weeks I found I was happy. There was defi-nitely a sense of home, which I'd had for only three years in my life. It's virtually unimaginable for most people not to have walls in which you know you're going to stay. Nowadays of course there's a bit more moving around, but to have absolutely nowhere for more than six months ... looking back I can see what a tremendous loss this must have been.

But don't forget, when I joined there was no need to relate to anybody, it wasn't encouraged. The Novitiate rules were such that one should never talk about anything important to anybody except the Novice Mistress. You could talk about the weather, of course, and books I suppose, trivial things. But you could never talk about yourself. Mind you, one found out a great deal about one's fellow Novices just by the very fact that it wasn't allowed. But I never talked about anything I *should* have talked about, which was most unfortunate. And I had the naïve idea that once you joined a religious community they'd know all about you without you saying anything; I didn't realise that something was expected of me as well. So I think that if the right questions had been asked I could, slowly and painfully, have got out of my isolation.

As it was, I wasn't touched, not really. I came to realise during the Novitiate that I didn't really want to know myself, and that clearly indicates the inner conviction that what one would know wouldn't be very nice. So I definitely took steps to avoid any growth in self-knowledge, and that was a pity. I should have had much more help than I did, but really the help we got from Confessors was minimal, and Sisters had absolutely no training in anybody as complicated as myself, so I went on playing the part. I had no difficulty about the discipline. Wearing a habit was marvellous; I'd left the past behind, finished with. I was a new person. So it was very unreal, and unfortunately I was regarded as a model Novice and a model Sister because I did as I was told, accepted things, didn't grumble – and that lasted a very long time.

Two years after I was professed as a Sister, I was told I should study, and unfortunately they did not send me to Oxford university as they might have done. It would have been very good for me if I'd actually joined in college life, but the community didn't do things like that, which was all part of the Victorian background. 'We don't do this kind of thing. We use the training Sisters have and otherwise we don't send them to study.' But they wanted to use me as Headmistress of St Mary's School in Wantage, and I had to be qualified to do that. They invited me to study Modern Languages. I didn't want to. I wanted to study theology, so instead I took the Lambeth Diploma of Theology by correspondence, and became Headmistress.

I was Headmistress from 1957 to 1964 and it was a very, very good experience. But of course these things don't last. When the time came for the Mother General to retire she thought I might be a likely successor, which was a pretty big thing to swallow. It meant that I would have to leave St Mary's School in order to have the interim months at the convent in order to be known more intimately by the community.

A kind of depression sank on me which I found difficult to

account for. Physical troubles as well. I didn't loathe the idea of being Mother but there was a kind of fog of fear hanging over me. I didn't break down until the actual day I left the school, and then I was totally overwhelmed, which was difficult to account for. Why should I be so distraught? After all, I was going on to possible promotion. But all that meant absolutely nothing: I was leaving the sphere where I was *somebody*, where I was very much needed, wanted, loved.

During that period I had also made a very close friend of one of the junior Sisters, and this was definitely emotional – not in the sense that I felt I couldn't do without her, but emotions were very much in it. I realise now that this was a great blessing, the gradual realisation that I *had* emotions that needed expressing, but when I left the school I realised that I was much more involved than she was, and it led to one or two very painful experiences and eventually a complete break. It's not so now, but it was very painful at the time. It was also very necessary in the sense that I went through the whole gamut of emotions.

In the community, though one kissed and embraced, it meant little. Of course one had love for certain Sisters, but emotional involvement was very much frowned on. Sisters could be sent away from the community because of it. Of course it isn't easy to be both totally open and totally disciplined, it's a razor edge and one's going to fall one side or the other. And the falls are good. I think now there's no longer this terrible disapproval of a friendship, but I remember being told in my Novitiate: 'Friendships are not on. We do not have friends.' Therefore there was a feeling of guilt when one had a friend, which hindered development, certainly in my case.

So. I had a very difficult time. I was Novice Mistress as well, which didn't help. The Novices had no use for me at all. They'd just lost their beloved Novice Mistress to another post, and they didn't in the least want me, they resented a change. There was absolutely nobody I could talk to, and then, at the election, fortunately for the community and for me, I was not elected as Mother. I was made Assistant General instead.

Eventually my health gave way. Too much tension. Nothing specific, but I had an awful lot of stress symptoms. Then, a few months before my health finally broke down I was making a private retreat at Burnham Abbey, one of the Anglican enclosed communities, and I found in my bedroom a book called *Zen Catholicism* by a Benedictine monk from Ampleforth. He evidently had a deep knowledge of Indian religions and yoga, and this book just fell into my hands and was a complete eye-opener to me. This form of meditation – yoga – answered so many questions I'd been asking myself, which was merciful of God because he opened a way into the future before I ever knew there was one.

So when I got back to Wantage, I immediately got a book out of the library and started practising yoga on my own. I know it's terrible just to do it from a book, and it was a very bad book too – but this was *me*!

Then I got seriously ill, and the Sister Infirmarian said to me out of the blue that she thought I had so many stress symptoms that I ought to resign. That certainly gave me a lot to think about. I had no idea what else life could offer or what to do, so after a time of convalescence with friends it was put to me: would I like to go to Germany? I wasn't particularly anxious to go to Germany but it was at least something to do. I went and stayed with my brother for a time, and was pretty miserable and ill on and off, but it was *immensely* important, because during those six months out there I discovered I was German. I'd denied it so long that it was a rediscovery of my German roots, and I began to be actually proud of being German, to see Germany as something positive. I see now that until I discovered the German I couldn't discover myself, I had put on this English veneer and then the habit on top of that: it was impregnable!

I needed this emotional breakthrough to break down – which I did. It was very painful, and curiously in my musings I related it to the death of my mother, the similarity of being totally exposed and totally helpless. But this time of course I was able to work through it. It was the beginning of renewal.

I came back in a pretty apprehensive state to Wantage, and after only about a week I was told that I was going to our house in Oxford. In the few days I was at Wantage a man came – a Yugoslav

– and showed a film of some of the Yugoslav monasteries, which he was very enthusiastic about. But I wasn't particularly interested: I had other things to worry about.

However, when I went to Oxford I met again some of the Orthodox people I had met before I entered the community, including a Dr Zernov, a friend, and Professor of Slavonic Studies at Oxford. He wondered whether I was interested in going to Yugoslavia and living in a monastery there, and this seemed to me to be rather enticing. It meant learning the language and going into a culture where people had never met non-Orthodox before. It's a long story, but the Mother General agreed to it. I supposed she wanted to give me something that would stretch me.

I started learning Serbo-Croatian, and attending the Orthodox Church in Oxford to be familiar with the worship and festivities and the general culture. It gave me a boost, and built up my confidence, because there was the sense that I was doing something special, which at that time was quite important. When I went out for the first time it was very difficult, but a tremendous experience.

I went for four years running after that, for between one and two months a year, and I soon felt myself received there, valued, managing to talk, to make myself understood, making pilgrimages in these small buses to the monasteries and being completely accepted in a very different culture. I was also very much attracted to the long hours of worship, despite the long hours spent standing, whereas I was impatient with the Office of Readings, the prayers we say throughout the day at Wantage. They felt very stuck in the past.

So curiously the Orthodox worship, though unchanged since the fifth century, had a tremendous attraction for me. I wouldn't have joined it myself because I had the feeling that if I were to do so, I would become disillusioned by the amount of in-fighting and irregularities, but from the outside it was very endearing. The singing and sense of mystery was so marvellous, however much it was clothed in obsolete language and ritual.

During my last visit to Serbia, in 1971, I was by myself somewhere, a meadow, and I had, I suppose, 'a moment of truth,' a sense of wasting my life. A sense that I was playing at being a religious and dedicated woman, and that compared with the kind of dedication I saw in these Sisters in Yugoslavia I was a cheat, I wasn't facing anything within myself, and I wasn't working out what my own calling was meant to be. It was devastating.

When I went back to England I thought I'd better talk it over with the Mother General. She sent me to see a monk from the community at Mirfield in Yorkshire, whom I had known in the past. He talked to me for a time and then he said, 'I think you may be called to be a hermit.' Now this had *certainly* not been in my thoughts at all! He said I should be away from my own community – he was absolutely adamant about that – and find somebody who could direct me, guide me, in it. The Mother General was very open to the idea, but it had to go to the Community Council and to the Bishop: you know, you can't just hive off and be a hermit without special permission. An Anglo-Catholic priest in Wales was recommended as my Spiritual Director, and I wrote to him. He rather reluctantly said he would take me on, but I would have to realise that his views were not all that orthodox. He suggested that I did a four week retreat to see how I got on, and then we'd take it from there.

I must say, it was a *ghastly* time. I had a little cottage to myself, and I hadn't realised until then that I didn't know how to cook. I couldn't. I was asked what ingredients I needed and I hadn't the slightest idea. I could make porridge and I could cook eggs, but beyond that I did not know. It's not surprising of course: with my background, I never had to cook. I did have cooking lessons at school once, but the ingredients provided in a French boarding school are not the same things you need in a cottage in Wales, so I was always hungry and probably eating the wrong food.

It was very cold, and David's instructions were pretty demanding: keeping vigil every other night in the cold and not eating until the evening. But I managed to open up sufficiently to talk to him and perhaps if I hadn't gone through the misery I wouldn't have been able to do that. It was so miserable that after the four weeks he asked me if I really wanted to go on with it. I said yes. I felt I had to.

I think at the time I thought that being a hermit would be the next stage of my religious life. There was probably a sense that this was a higher rung on the ladder, that I was called to something rather special. At least, I'm sure that was there in the eyes of a good many Sisters. It's almost impossible to escape this sort of attitude, of course – ambition dies hard in some of us.

So I began living alone in 1973, first in a caravan in the grounds of one of our own houses in Sussex, and I joined the Sisters for lunch on Sundays. To begin with it was lovely: living in the country, a lot of physical work in the garden, going for walks and bicycle rides and that kind of thing – and of course a very stiff timetable again. Then, a year later, a Carmelite convent in Llandovery agreed to have me in a caravan in their garden. It was a great relief after that rather tough year, and it was also simply lovely country.

I had a wonderful three years there and in that time I did a tremendous amount of reading. David came to see me every two weeks or so. He himself was well into Indian and oriental spirituality rather than Western, and this was what I'd already been groping after and partially living for the past ten years or so, through Indian thought and yoga. I had learnt to meditate in the lotus posture, and I discovered the mystic, Meister Eckhart, too, and felt a deep attraction to his way of thinking. So I read, I was out of doors a great deal, and I got very fit, regained my health.

I won't say those three years were all blissful because they weren't. There was loneliness, and I did suffer from depression: only twice, but severely. Both times were when David asked me to join his place for a short time, but because I was a hermit I had to stay outside and was not allowed to join other people. Being alone when there were other people about created a sense of being excluded which I suppose stirred up the intense loneliness of adolescence and being left out of things. Fortunately it didn't last long, but I'm glad I've known what depression is.

I never felt I ought to be doing something more tangible because I'd discovered meditation in the Indian sense and I knew that that was a work in itself which was perhaps of greater importance to the world today than anything else I could possibly do with my mind. It was the sense of getting beneath the active mind. I'd discovered that when one gets out of the way then God takes over, and I began to see that that was really what I was called for.

I saw that this could be a service to the world even without actually seeing any results.

In what sense? Well, in the sense that one becomes a kind of channel, or transmitter, to which others could tune in. Putting oneself at God's disposal can make one a channel. Eckhart speaks of God 'coming to birth in the soul:' many Christian mystics have said, 'Become what you are.' And Indian spirituality says that God and Man are neither identical nor separate. I felt that compared with all that, our Office and our liturgy at Wantage was so banal. Prayer is a stirring in the depth of oneself, an awareness of something whose existence one has not previously suspected, and that 'something' is God. I found words in prayer distracting and irrelevant, and I had long found the recitation of the psalms a hindrance rather than a help. I stopped saying the Wantage Office when I was alone, I'd got more and more disillusioned with it.

I have a book, a German book, about the Desert Fathers, and the title in English would be *What It Costs To Be Human*. I haven't read it much recently but it was very decisive in my life. I'd say a lot of books have been decisive in my life. The author, a Benedictine nun, saw these early Desert Fathers as spelling out in their life, their tears, their fasting and so on, a new humanity. And their deprivations, their hours of prayer and so on, led to the creation of the full man, the whole man, the mature man, and that idea took a hold of me. And it was only by going deep inside to reach God as the *ground* of my being that I could be myself. It's only as I live and speak from that depth that I am able to be used.

But I don't think those ideas were in my mind at the time. I thought a bit in terms of something more permanent than a caravan, some place where others could come together in the search for God: an ashram's not so different. But the community was definitely not interested. They were dead against having somebody on the loose like myself; they were suspicious of me, wary, whereas I was perfectly happy doing what I was doing.

I felt no need to justify what I was doing, and still don't, because I suppose in the end we shan't be asked how much good we have done to others. Maybe you could point to a great many people you've done good to in your life, but in the end the question is,

'How much have *you* learnt to love? What have you made of the life I've given to *you*? Have you developed this talent and increased it?' And unless one's done that, then however many patients one's looked after, or children one's taught, if you haven't become someone *yourself*, it's worthless. Not *entirely* worthless: I mean, I wasn't a hopeless headmistress. But I wasn't changed. I went on with my selfish ambitious attitude.

So when I was reading about the Desert Fathers, I felt this was really what our religious teaching had been all about, but not our religious *living*. When it came to life very different values were in fact lived out, and that was a great shock. Sisters were not living according to the values they'd been taught. They were just as petty, just as critical as anybody else. There were exceptions of course, but by and large not many of us are called to be heroes.

Our community has always done work which takes us out a lot. We've always worked with drug addicts and alcoholics, and from the beginning, the community provided a refuge for women in moral danger – a 'penitentiary,' as it was called in the nineteenth century. In my time, our work consisted of supervising girls who had been picked up in army camps and led a pretty rough life. A very down-to-earth training it was too.

Nevertheless, there is a trend in people who join a community nowadays to want less activity and more withdrawal, to pray on behalf of others. This makes complete sense if you think how many people never give God a thought. They have no time for the spiritual side, especially nowadays when there's so much pressure: people are totally absorbed in work, or money-making, or running a family plus a job. There is no time for more than a brief glance at God, so we pray on behalf of those people.

Having said that, my own feeling (though most of my Sisters would disagree with me) is that we should not have life vows within the religious life. I think it would be very much better to have annual renewable vows and not keep people just because they have vowed themselves to be somewhere. There is still this terrible sense of guilt about religious vows, though I don't know how guilty I would feel if I ever felt I had to break them. We were brought up to believe it was the ultimate betrayal of God if one left the community, which now seems complete nonsense! It did great damage. All this business of, 'I've come to stay for life:' well, how do you know? If after ten, twenty years, the conviction goes, it would be a mistake to stay longer – which is *not* to say it would be a mistake to come. I admire tremendously some of the people I know who've left, some in their fifties and sixties who just felt they were not being themselves, and they must go. And at that age, without a proper training, without a pension or a family, that takes tremendous courage and integrity.

And of course, living in a large community of women can be very trying. The unwritten customs can drive you up the wall. Things like 'recreation.' Even in the past, 'recreation' was hated by almost everybody. One sat in ranks on hard chairs, having left one's needlework on the chair previously – one *must* do needlework, one can't just sit. And then the Superior would read a little bit of the paper, as much as was thought necessary for Sisters to hear. There was a whole paper out to read, but only one or two papers for eighty – mind you, this is going back a bit now – and then a book would be read. But the book must not offend anybody. *You* try and find a decent book that doesn't offend anybody! Impossible! One's left with stories about animals and children. Oh, *what* we went through, listening to stories about animals and children! Of course, even then they weren't always safe and it was very obvious when someone had jumped a bit.

It was all very Victorian and I suppose it went back to a time when individuals could not read, but it wasn't recreation, it wasn't interchange. And that was certainly so in my early years in community – that one avoided confrontation when there was an opportunity for proper discussion. It was very frustrating.

You wanted to ask me about India, and about prayer, didn't you? Well, the two are very connected.

After I'd spent some years as a hermit, the Mother General changed. The new person simply couldn't understand what I was doing, and wanted some way to get me back in circulation. She didn't really know how, and then the ashram idea came up and that to them was a great relief. It was something they could send me away to.

The idea was to come to India for six months, but just before

I left, the Mother General actually suggested I might want to stay longer, and I didn't want to commit myself because as far as I was concerned I had not finished being a hermit. As soon as I got to India I constantly got rather curt letters saying, 'Have you made up your mind yet?' Eventually I decided this was the right place for me, and I decided to stay on, but I didn't want to be rushed into it, and that's how it was. I'd thought it was meant to be a short visit to see what was going on but the community obviously felt differently. And at the time I was *bitterly* resentful of that – furious – because I didn't want to be treated like a *thing*. It was hurtful.

By this time I'd ceased accepting everything. I think obedience means something very different at different stages of one's community life and it was different for me then. I think for a Novice it is probably important to know there are certain things expected, which one just does without argument. I remember being told once: 'If you're told or asked to do something, and it isn't against your conscience, do it: it won't do any harm.' This stood me in good stead at the time, but as one becomes more mature, obedience is written into you. One shouldn't force oneself to do things which are right against the grain, and I certainly felt that the lack of consultation with me was wrong. We don't make any big decision now without full consultation with the person concerned, but the attitude when I was a Novice was, 'Whatever Mother says is right,' so you abdicated all responsibility, and that kept people as permanent children.

So I came to India with some reluctance. But as I say, it changed many things for me. I was able to develop the ideas I'd begun to explore while in the caravan in Wales. I'd begun to explore a different attitude to prayer.

Most people understand prayer to be words. I understand prayer to be a state of mind in which one allows God to be God and doesn't constantly interrupt saying, 'Here I am.' When I pray I don't try to impose my will. In fact as far as possible, as I enter more deeply into prayer, I leave myself, my ego and my will out, and become aware of God's activity: so in that way one can say that prayer is the activity of God *within* one. And the technique of praying, for me, is to gradually let go one's tight hold on what one's concerned with at the time, and become open to anything that God is doing, and possibly calling one to.

Prayer is certainly not *thinking* about God. Thinking about God is still one's ego thinking. You and I are talking about this now, but I wouldn't usually put prayer into words. I'd meditate. I would do what I did with you all in meditation class the other day – use a technique to let the inner voice become totally quiet. As soon as that happens, as soon as one really lets go, then prayer *is*. And one's probably aware of it – even if only afterwards – aware that this was prayer, God at work.

I never try to visualise God. I tried to in the past, but I found it limiting, because God is both within everything – in a stone as much as in me – and outside everything. You used to be taught meditation by reading a gospel passage, and then visualising the people, the sky, the fishing nets, that kind of thing. And no doubt that can be helpful, it's been many people's way in. But I wouldn't visualise God. If at all, I'd use an icon or a cross or a light as a focus.

I don't talk to God either. I chat. 'I'd just rather this didn't happen Lord, if it's all the same to you' – this kind of thing. One Sister here is constantly talking to Him in that tone. She says things like, 'Oh, where did I leave so-and-so?' If she stopped worrying about it, she'd remember. Anyway, what *is* the point of asking or telling Him things in words because He knows more than I do. Long, long ago, when I was in the Novitiate, I couldn't understand why people made intercessory prayers, it was totally beyond my understanding. Any God worth praying to already knows so why do I have to tell Him? It was a *major* problem. And all this *fuss* about intercessions – I think we kept up a chain of intercessions all day at the time – struck me as totally superfluous and theologically inadequate, but clearly I was in a minority of one there.

What I've always found very difficult to take is people who come and spend half an hour with us and say, 'Sister, pray for me.' I usually say yes, say an immediate prayer, and forget about it. What else can one do? So many come that one can't possibly know their names or their faces. But I can't say, 'No, I have no intention of praying for you;' it would be unkind, and I wouldn't have any desire to enter into a theological argument about it. So we do quite often pray when people have asked us to, but *what* that kind of prayer does I haven't the slightest idea.

But there's such spiritual hunger. I think many people have a hunger which they long to fulfil but don't know where or how. Many years ago, before the second world war, I read a book by an English woman called *Darkness Over Germany*. She had been asked to find out what was there to Hitler that attracted people so much. What was it? She interviewed a lot of people – children, parents, leaders – and some of the Nazi leaders said to her, 'We think it's the religious hunger which has not been satisfied and which leads people to desire these mass demonstrations.' Which was very interesting coming from that source. The Nazis had a flair for organising thousands of people into marching together, shouting 'Sieg Heil!' and waving this great display of swastikas and black, white and red flags. This kind of thing was fulfilling a deep kind of psychological need. Now if that happened then, in the 1920s and '30s, the need is still there now, in England as well as in Germany, and we're open to *tremendous* dangers if this need isn't fulfilled.

We *need* ritual. Jung has written some interesting things about the need for ritual to help people over the difficult times in life, and I suppose the very fact that there is really no way we can get experiential knowledge of prayer leaves something untouched in the human soul. I think one of the great dangers in church circles is to forget that the spiritual life grows just as our physical, individual life grows, and we tend to remain in spiritual kindergarten all our lives. That doesn't satisfy those who have gone on to standard two or three. We never get much higher in any case, but if we go on teaching the ABC and daren't even hope for the possibility of growth, then after a time people leave the Church or try other forms of religion which speak more to them. And if you're asking me for a solution, I think the answer is to break it down to small communities. Meet together in twenties rather than in hundreds, and make for a real sharing of the important things in life – which are not necessarily religious. What is religious anyway? I don't believe God is especially interested in religion.

So unless demands are made of us, we shan't grow in the faith much – and growing in the faith is not about sitting in church and being talked at. But again, when we are stuck with buildings like so many parish churches, lovely though some are, what can you do? I'm told that when architecture and liturgy clash, architecture always wins: people always give way to the pressures of their walls and pillars, and I imagine that while the buildings are maintained congregations will diminish. But perhaps in the future there'll be breakaway groups who want a different, more intimate type of worship.

Let me tell you a story.

A group had met for worship, and the priest was late. When he arrived, he apologised and said that while motoring to church he had met a family that had been turned out of their home. They were sheltering under a bridge, and they had neither food nor shelter. The congregation decided there and then they could not carry on with the Lord's supper if this family was homeless. Some of them went off to bring in these people, to give them a meal, others went to the authorities, and generally they made the people feel comfortable. Then they continued with the mass.

Now this is Christianity in *action*, and if Christianity is something which just goes on in church then we have *totally* failed to understand Christ. Christ came among men to *abolish* church institutions of his time, and we're keeping up the myth that the kind of church we have is just what He wanted.

That is one of the reasons why I felt so drawn to India. I guess that it answered a whole lot of problems which I found Christianity was just throwing up and not solving. I don't think I would have felt drawn to India had I not had a long preparation for it – totally unknown to me of course. The chance picking up of meditation and yoga, and practising it for more than ten years, becoming vegetarian at least four years before I came – all this was a preparation. And as far as reading was concerned, I was drawn to Indian teaching, gradually picking up what the Upanishads and the Bhagavadgita were all about.

The Vedic idea, the Upanishadic idea of God appealed to me. The Christian idea, of God being a *person* – just what does that man? Whereas the Vedic idea, the Upanishadic idea, is that God is in fact *beyond* personality. God is 'It' rather than 'He'. Also, the idea that God *includes* everything that is, and is *contained* within everything that is – that I did not find in Christianity. All right, God says, 'I'm in you,' but this doesn't go as far as saying that He is in a mosquito or the atom, and where does one draw the line? If He's in us why shouldn't He be in the mosquito and the atom? The only time I found it anywhere in Christian theology was in Eckhart, and he was condemned by the Christian Church.

I'll explain it a bit.

'God is Being from which all take their being.' This is a quotation from a Western philosopher. A Hindu would take no exception to that definition, though strictly speaking, the 'Brahman' (which might be translated as the 'Being') is by definition beyond name or form and therefore beyond even God.

The Brahman is beyond personality. Nothing is outside it, and it is within everything, as butter is within milk and fire within wood. The Brahman itself cannot be the object of man's thought: rather, it is the faculty in man which is *capable* of thought. There is a Sanskrit word – 'Advait' – which means 'not-two,' and it describes man's relationship to the Brahman. The Brahman must not be exclusively equated with anything, and this accounts for the bewildering number of gods and goddesses in Hinduism. The many gods of Hinduism are all aspects of ultimate reality. They serve to translate high philosophy into an accessible religion. Thus, the gods and goddesses represent different facets of the Real, including its dark, incomprehensible aspects.

Since the Brahman is Reality, it follows that outside it is nothing – 'Maya' – illusion. This has been misunderstood by the Western mind, which assumes that the Hindu considers the material world to be unreal. Neither man nor the created world is unreal, but their existence depends on what is absolutely Real, therefore their existence is relative. Like a man and his shadow: the shadow is real but depends upon the presence of the man.

In Hindu spirituality, to mistake the relative for the Absolute is 'ignorance,' which we might in Christianity equate with sin. To be delivered from ignorance is to achieve enlightenment or liberation, and that is the object of 'yoga,' a word which means 'union.' The enlightened man finds his own reality in union with absolute Reality.

Now, none of this is hostile to Christianity, but it is never taught or explored. Here at the ashram we get such crowds of people from the West who are looking for spiritual reality, spiritual experience of some sort, and it makes me realise the tremendous lack of such teaching in Christian churches.

So I found here a Christianity which satisfied my own desires and insights, and an openness in religious life, including an openness to one another. Here we all live together as members of the human family, regardless of all the religious or cultural habits we grew up with. There's no armour of a habit, or of customs, which certainly when I last lived in Wantage still regulated the behaviour of the Sisters to each other. Coming here made the externals, like the habit, seem unhelpful.

When I came here, I was given the Indian habits – two blue and two white, but it was ridiculous in this culture, and within three months we were told to get into some kind of Indian dress, which was a rather terrifying experience after forty years of a black habit! The Catholic Sisters in Pune were very critical of us at first: this just convinced them that we were imitation nuns, which some of them had felt all along anyway. Mind you, it's the case with some of our young Sisters too: some of them would rather go to the *stake* than give up the habit. Like I told you before, 'as long as possible and as black as possible.' Let's hope they'll become more free.

So I certainly appreciate the freedom here, and it's answered a lot of problems I've had with the religious life. I think Wantage has become more relaxed, but the setting of the buildings makes it impossible, and I found the weight of numbers living together very depressing when I was there last. You can't relate, and people do want to relate. But when you have to make special *appointments* to relate, well, that really is ridiculous. Normally, you relate during a meal; but the meals at Wantage are silent. You can relate on a walk; but few go for walks. So either you happen to meet somebody in the garden, or you make an *appointment* for it. You sit in one of those wretched parlours which I think are the last word in awfulness. And the very fact that so many still call each other Sister instead of using the God-given name, creates a distance, though that's changing slowly. So this place is a long way ahead because there are no barriers at all. We treat each other and the visitors in exactly the same way, and we try to be open and human.

One thing which we haven't touched on and which I think should be examined is, why are so many Sisters *ill*? Why do such a high proportion of Sisters have cancer and other diseases? Well, they do, and I think much more than other groups. So many Sisters of my generation got cancer and died long ago. It certainly is significant, because cancer is in many instances linked up with the emotional life, and many Sisters are emotionally unsatisfied: emotional satisfaction can be hard to find in this life. A Sister can find emotional satisfaction in her devotion to God or in her service of her fellow humans, but she must not find it in an emotional attachment to a fellow Sister. She must not find it in an emotional attachment to a man. And if she's not emotionally satisfied, if she's looking for something, she can't truly relate to others.

Because the tradition of the religious life is celibacy, poverty and obedience, it can put a strain on those who live it. If you ask the more traditional Indian teachers, like Goenkaji, they don't deny sexuality in a religious life, but they would say that for anybody wanting to live a deeply spiritual life, the heterosexual act should be infrequent because it does take a lot of energy. The seat of energy is in the sexual organs and if it is dissipated it is taken away from the spiritual quest.

So if people are to grow in the spiritual life, and not get ill, this sort of thing has to be tackled, and not just in the Novitiate but later too. Certainly in my time there was no such guidance, and yet one's sexuality comes into absolutely everything. There's no friendship without sexuality, no concern for others without it.

I think my own sexuality was repressed for a long time, so love just didn't come my way. Have I never been in love? No, I haven't, though I would have liked to have been. I think my fear of pain was so great that I repressed my emotions, I was probably emotionally and physically *incapable* of falling in love. This may have been a hindrance or setback in some respects but I don't think ultimately it has been. And as far as my maternal instincts are concerned, the religious life has catered well for them. At times

I have been so engaged in caring work for others that my mothering instinct was used, and I have found great satisfaction in that. After all, these are beautiful instincts a woman has, and great work has been done by nuns in that way.

I also think that women have a natural bent towards ministry, an ability to serve people, which men very often haven't got. I think it could make a *great* difference to have women clergy in the Church, precisely because women have a special aptitude for ministry. I certainly don't think there are any theological arguments against the ordination of women. I think many men have a psychological sense of inadequacy and they perhaps feel that women will be a tremendous threat, probably because the women who offer themselves will certainly be more mature than most male ordinands, and very likely of higher calibre. So I am in favour of the ordination of women, and I have been very much influenced by Elaine Pagel's book *The Gnostic Gospels*, showing that the Nag Hammadi finds in Egypt implied the existence of a parallel church during the early centuries of Christianity, in which the ministry was equally shared by men and women. That is surely the way to move forward.

Also I have to say that I think the type of man who's asking for ordination and actually is ordained is often pretty feeble. I don't know what the clergy selection committee does, but before I became a hermit I had a great deal to do with one of the theological colleges in Oxford, and I thought they were *weeds*. Nice enough lads, I suppose, but not the material to be leaders of the church militant. And the question must be, 'What are you *doing* in it all?' – a question one might well ask of many people. The Church should be able to swallow the ordination of women without *quite* so much fuss, but why go to church in any case? Why go to church? I think that's a deeper question.

I believe that with everything there comes a time when structures must be broken, and tradition changed. This goes for every aspect of the Church. It's the case with prayer, with liturgy, worship, ordination and it's the case with religious life. The religious life is not for the weak, and I think you'll still find some very frightened people behind the habit: people escaping sexuality, escaping perhaps having to earn their own living, and possibly escaping the loneliness of old age. We are sheltered, and our wants are provided for. Also, I suspect that many of us have not learnt to be comfortable with ourselves. You can quite happily live this life and never *think* about yourself. I spent *years* not wanting to know myself, quite effectively, and it didn't work in the end, it absolutely broke down.

However, that breakdown was God's gift to me, and I think one has to leave a lot to the inspiration and the grace of God in these things. I feel on the whole that what happens is what's meant to happen and that one learns from all situations. And of course religious life isn't perfect, but nothing is. It's hard, especially as far as relationships go, but I think one finds that everywhere. The religious life has been an opportunity for me to face the truth of myself, and it's been hard; but it's been good for me. *Very* good for me. It's given me life.

I'm not afraid of death. Like most people I fear pain, helplessness, loss of faculties, but I am confident that together with age comes the power to bear and accept, to let go and not cling. Certainly I want to enter consciously into my own death, and not so drugged that I'm unaware of it: to me it's the most interesting event of my life, and I want to be there when it happens. After all, it's the ultimate opportunity for you to face the truth of yourself.

I don't believe in re-birth or reincarnation myself – at least not in simple terms. I would rather regard it as being a myth, like purgatory. Actually, I see purgatory and re-birth as being parallel, although it's sheer speculation as the Bible gives us no information as to what happens after death. But there is a beautiful passage in one of the Upanishads, where death is described as 'reaching the further shore,' and with it comes the realisation that there is no river dividing the living from the dead, there is no journey, and no further shore, because one has been there all the time. Likewise, we do not enter into the presence of God when we die, because we have been there all the time. It is only our ignorance, our blindness, that separates us from God.

I'd like, if I may, to quote from an Upanishad:

'Concealed in the heart of all beings lies the Atman, the Spirit, the Self smaller than the smallest atom, greater than the greatest spaces. When by the grace of God man sees the glory of God, He sees It beyond the world of desire and then sorrows are left behind.'